Utah Valley
HEART *of* UTAH

Photography by **Christopher Adams**
Narrative by **Steve Densley**

A publication of Utah County

HPNbooks
A division of Lammert Incorporated
San Antonio, Texas

A storm has dusted the top of Lone Peak, providing an impressive backdrop for the Mt. Timpanogos Temple, one of three Mormon temples in Utah Valley.

First Edition

Copyright © 2015 HPNbooks

ISBN: 978-1-939300-92-8

Library of Congress Card Catalog Number: 2015952368

Utah Valley: Heart of Utah

photographer:	Christopher Adams
author:	Steve Densley
designer:	Glenda Tarazon Krouse
contributing photographer for photo section:	Mark Philbrick
contributing writer for photo section and Utah Valley partners :	Charlene Winters

HPNbooks

president:	Ron Lammert
project manager:	Bart Barica
administration:	Donna M. Mata, Melissa G. Quinn
book sales:	Dee Steidle
production:	Colin Hart, Evelyn Hart, Tim Lippard, Christopher D. Sturdevant, Tony Quinn

CONTENTS

REDX
1411 West 1250 South, Suite 300
Orem, Utah 84058
800-731-7339
www.theredx.com

Temkin International, Inc.
213 Temkin Way
Payson, Utah 84651
801-465-1300
temkininternational.com

MOUNTAINSTAR

Timpanogos Regional Hospital

Timpanogos Regional Hospital
750 West 800 North
Orem, Utah 84057
801-714-6000
www.timpanogosregionalhospital.com

MOUNTAINSTAR

Mountain View Hospital

Mountain View Hospital
1000 East 100 North
Payson, Utah 84651
801-465-7000
www.mvhpayson.com

Fillmore Spencer LLC
3301 North University Avenue
Provo, Utah 84604
801-426-8200
www.fslaw.com

Brigham Young University
Provo, Utah 84602
1-866-662-9888
www.byub.org

Power Innovations International, Inc.
a Lite-On Technology Company
1305 South 630 East, American Fork, Utah 84003
801-785-4123
www.power-innovations.com

Fishbowl Inventory
580 East Technology Avenue, C2500
Orem, Utah 84097
800-774-7085
www.fishbowlinventory.com

Kenny Seng Construction, Inc.
250 North Orem Boulevard
Orem, Utah 84057
801-226-4125
www.kennyseng.com

Ferrin Capital Advisors, Inc.
1955 West Grove Parkway, Suite 200
Pleasant Grove, Utah 84062
801-756-2220
www.ferrincapital.com

Young Living Essential Oils
3125 Executive Parkway
Lehi, Utah 84043
1-800-371-3515
www.youngliving.com

Intermountain Healthcare
1034 North 500 West
Provo, Utah
801-357-7850
www.intermountainhealthcare.org

Utah Valley University
800 West University Parkway
Orem, Utah 84058-6703
801-863-8000
www.uvu.edu

INTRODUCTION

Utah County may be the state's second-most populous county, but it is first in the hearts of the more than a half-million people who live there and are proud to call it home.

Utah County's motto: "The Heart of Utah," is a reflection of that. So is the area's natural beauty, which prompted the cartographer for the 1776 Dominguez-Escalante expedition to call it "the most beautiful and fertile site in all New Spain."

Settled in 1849 by pioneer families who weathered considerable hardship to scratch out a living, present-day Utah County has blossomed into a haven for families and flowered into a mecca for culture and outdoor recreation.

It emerged as an economic powerhouse that serves as a major hub for high tech firms and business entrepreneurs, as well as home to top-notch Brigham Young and Utah Valley universities.

At the core of Utah County's greatness is the commitment of its leaders and residents to time-honored principles, including love of God and country, civic involvement, service, friendliness, self-reliance, and individual responsibility.

While those values are not unique to Utah County, they are rooted and nurtured there like few other places. That's why my wife Jeanette and I choose to live in Utah County. That's why I enthusiastically recommend this book.

More than a collection of facts or figures, "Utah Valley, Heart of Utah" is a labor of love that gets to the core of what makes Utah County "the heart of Utah."

—Utah Governor Gary R. Herbert

✧

A shot from Tibble Fork Reservoir shows the stunning vistas toward Aspen Grove.

PHOTOGRAPH COURTESY OF MARK PHILBRICK.

Utah Lake sunset after storm.

When I came to Brigham Young University in the mid-1960s to play football, I expected my coaches would motivate me. What I had not imagined was that I would be equally inspired by the stunning Wasatch Mountains that cradled Cougar Stadium and the surrounding valley communities.

And I had no idea that I would make my permanent home in a region frequently listed among the best, most livable, and most profitable areas of the country.

Utah Valley is buttressed by spectacular glacier-carved peaks that display a patchwork of colors that transform themselves according to the season. The Wasatch Range (part of the Rockies) to the east, the Traverse Mountains to the north, and Lake Mountain to the west encircle a visual wonderland.

I am never surprised when out-of-town sports commentators say they have never seen sports played against a more beautiful backdrop. It didn't take me long to realize I was living in an outdoor paradise for mountain biking and hiking, rock climbing and mountaineering, skiing, fishing, boating with scenic vistas in tree-covered canyons. I felt as if I had found my home, and after thirty years as the Utah Valley Chamber of Commerce president, I still feel that way.

Among the advantages of living in this valley is its easy access to business and pleasure. Driving from my home in Provo, Utah, for example, I am perched near the base of these majestic mountains. I can be boarding a ski lift at the Sundance Mountain Resort owned by award-winning actor/director Robert Redford fifteen minutes later. Depending on the season, I can be golfing in the morning and skiing in the afternoon. Most people who live in the region can say the same thing.

If I head south, I can be strolling in acres of orchards in a pastoral atmosphere of farms, cattle, and horses. There are plenty of trails to ride a horse and capture a feeling of being in the

Thirty Years of Exploding Growth from My—and Your—Kind of Place

—Steve Densley

country. A few minutes travel northward to Lehi and surrounding small cities, and I am immersed in Utah's multiple centers of high technology business.

From my living room window, I can see nearby BYU, which, with 34,000 full-time students, is one of the largest private universities in the United States. Within ten minutes I can also step on the campus of Utah Valley University, on schedule to exceed BYU in student scholars, and the largest public university in the State of Utah. As major universities, they provide not only expansive educational opportunities but also stimulating sports programs, lectures, art exhibitions, plays, concerts and an energy typified by a student population that will soon top 40,000.

And with dozens of companies such as Google Network, Adobe, Vivint, Ancestry.com, and Qualtrics, Utah Valley boasts an enviable business climate that attracts employees from throughout the world.

At the same time, Utah Valley remains the largest agricultural county in Utah. For a long time the gentle joke has been that Utah Valley is happy valley. I prefer to call it Happening Valley. I welcome its vibrant, youthful population with a solid work ethic and high educational level that makes this mountain community especially attractive not only for business but also for the arts, fine dining, and a thriving retail economy. No wonder so many list Utah at or near the top when designating ideal places to live.

It is always been that way. Early tribes, explorers, hunters, trappers, Native Americans, and Mormon settlers discovered the region long before its discovery as a robust and prosperous valley with abundant financial, social, and quality of life possibilities.

Right: The Wasatch Mountain range, which frames the east side of most of Utah County, is the western edge of famous Rocky Mountains.

Opposite: Autumn foliage provides colorful accents to Mount Timpanogos. This view was taken from the top of Squaw Peak, looking west.

Ancient Lake Bonneville once covered Utah Valley, but when the lake eventually expanded its banks into southern Idaho, it receded, creating a verdant valley and leaving a freshwater body known as Utah Lake. Prehistoric cultures found fertile hunting grounds in Utah Valley as did the Fremont Indians (700-1300 A.D.), and, much later, the Utah tribes who used the area for hunting, fishing, grazing and farming.

These native inhabitants first encountered white men when Spanish monks traveled through the region in 1776. Fray Francisco Atanasio Dominguez and Fray Francisco Silvestre Vélez de Escalante led a small group into the valley while seeking a route from Santa Fe to Monterey. Escalante described it as "the most pleasant, beautiful, and fertile in all New Spain."

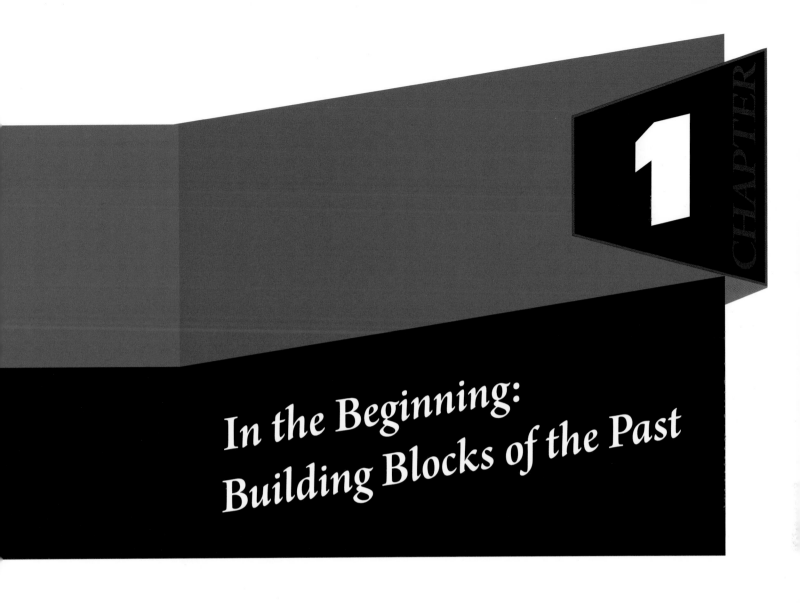

In the Beginning: Building Blocks of the Past

✧

Left: While the aspen is often cited among the most beautiful trees of autumn, there is also a stark beauty to its white and black silhouette against a Utah winter backdrop.

Above: Remarkable quaking aspens, part of a massive colony of a single quaking aspen that shares a giant underground root system.

Above: Utah Valley canyon landscapes show a beautiful mixture of sagebrush, pines, and interesting rock formations against unblemished blue skies.

Right: Moose, mule deer and other wildlife are common sights in local canyons and when winter weather is particularly harsh, they are also evident—sometimes in abundance—in local neighborhoods.

Opposite: Payson Lakes in the south end of Utah Valley.

Their visits did little to change the centuries-old lifestyle in the valley. But life among the indigenous inhabitants changed dramatically during the first three decades of the nineteenth century when fur traders and trappers capitalized on the Utes' hunting skills. They, in turn, supplied the Indians with food, guns, and other supplies.

Life, however, was not always harmonious between the Indians and the hunters. French-Canadian trapper Etienne Provost learned this firsthand along the banks of the Jordan River when he managed to escape a skirmish that took the lives of most of the

Opposite: Wildflowers in eye-catching golden hues.

Above: Mother nature showcases floral beauty in lacey, pastel lavender.

Over time the names of his colleagues slid into obscurity and were forgotten, but Provost's name remains prominent, because the Provo River—which was incorrectly identified as the battle site—was named for him. Mormons who had colonized the valley at the behest of their leader, Brigham Young, chose Provo as the name of the lively settlement emerging in the valley. And the canyon with a fork that leads toward Sundance Resort and the origins of the internationally-known Sundance Film Festival is called Provo Canyon. As of the 2012 census, 112,480 people called Provo home, and a rapid increase of population in the Provo-Orem metropolitan area means 526,810 residents live in Utah Valley.

✦

Students head to class near the Harris Fine Arts Center on the BYU campus.

PHOTOGRAPH COURTESY OF MARK PHILBRICK.

✧

Above: Every canyon in Utah Valley shows new life emerging from dead and decaying trees in their abundant forests.

Opposite: Caked earth provides a spidery, if troubling, appeal in times of drought.

Above: Star trails in Diamond Fork Canyon, which splits off from Spanish Fork Canyon.

Opposite: Indian Paintbrush in Diamond Fork Canyon.

Diamond Fork Canyon

Above: Beaver dams in Provo Canyon.

Left: The scenic south fork of Provo Canyon south.

Below: Moss-covered stones add their own brand of beauty to mountain streams.

Opposite: Aspen Grove in Provo Canyon, near the Theater in the Pines.

Provo Canyon

✧

Left: Wild roses bloom in Diamond Fork Canyon near Spanish Fork.

Below: Utah Valley's canyons abound with wild flowers.

Opposite: A maple tree leaf in Provo Canyon.

As towns and small cities sprang into being, the valley's progress was measured, in large part, from an economy gleaned from the land with farms, mills, and mining.

Geneva Steel, a mill named after a resort that once operated on the shore of nearby Utah Lake, became a major employer during World War II. Constructed from federal funds, the inland plant provided a way to manufacture steel away from the West Coast where Japanese air attacks were a continual threat. It operated as a U.S. government facility from 1944 to 1946 before being purchased by U.S. Steel.

In its prime Geneva Steel produced sixty percent of the steel used in the Western United States, prompting many ancillary businesses to be located in Central Utah and employ thousands of workers. Its survival philosophy of "zero errors" kept a plant located in an unlikely place open until November 2001. In homage to the former steel plant, Timpanogos Harley-Davidson erected a business on the site of a truck stop many truckers used during the Geneva Steel years. It was built from salvaged materials and beams as well as walls, doors, and partitions from the old plant.

The Roots of Dynamic Business, Technology—and Farming, Too

Much of the region's manufacturing was built on the shoulders of Geneva's roots, and we value the legacy of a former leading employer.

✧

Above: The Geneva Nitrogen Plant is one of the last vestiges of what was once a robust steel manufacturing mill on the shores of Utah Lake.

Left: A couple takes a walk in Vineyard, near the site of the old Geneva Steel plant.

✧

Above: Since the early 1900s Lehi Roller Mill and Elevator Company has been milling high-quality wheat to produce the best baking flour available. It serves large corporations and commercial bakeries but also offers gourmet baking mixes around the country in hundreds of retail outlets.

Acres of farmland show the country side of Utah Valley life.

Even a modest farm with its old silo is not exempt from the beauty of Utah Valley rural life.

Cash crops in Utah Valley include corn, pumpkins and alfalfa.

UTAH VALLEY HEART of UTAH

38

*Ranching continues to provide a
traditional western way of life.*

Building construction is continuous in Lehi and surrounding towns along I-15 and the Alpine Highway, a growth area often referred to as Silicon Slopes.

One can say the same thing about WordPerfect, a word processing system that at the height of its popularity in the 1980s became a dominant player in the world's word processing market. Although its use has long been eclipsed by Microsoft Windows, its success heralded the possibility of other emerging industries, and the subsequent pulse of progress has burst forth to reflect a diverse economy in software technologies, biotech companies, business corporate giants, and manufacturing.

✧

Opposite, top: Micron.

Opposite, bottom: Xactware.

Above: Oracle.

Businesses both large and small have found a climate for success in Utah Valley. The region is a mecca for entrepreneurs such as Chris Bennett of 97th Floor in Lehi, whose company develops link building infographics, social advancement and reputation management. He works with big names; Vivint, Moz, Rio Tinto, and O. C. Tanner are representative of the more than 100 companies that wait to do business with him. Or look at the success of Todd Pedersen whose Vivint was sold for $2 billion—the largest tech deal in Utah history. There is John Pestana of ObservePoint in Provo, who co-formed Omniture, which Adobe purchased for $1.8 billion. And as the largest for-profit genealogy company in the world Ancestry.com has access to more than 13 billion records and nearly 2.2 million paying subscribers. These examples are a mere token of the businesses that make Utah Valley their hub.

✧

Above: A wind farm generates electricity in Spanish Fork Canyon.

Opposite: Spanish Fork Canyon provides dependably strong winds for large groups of wind generators.

Fueling a Robust Economy

Below: A fisherman finds ideal angling at the Deer Creek diversion dams, which are used to divert water for culinary, drinking, and power generation.

Opposite page: A major source of electricity comes from the Utah Power Plant in Lindon.

UTAH POWER & LIGHT
OLMSTED
HYDRO ELECTRIC
PLANT

DEAD END
NO THRU TRAFFIC

PROVO CANYON
PARKWAY ➡

Opposite page: PacifiCorp Power located in Vineyard.

This page: Solar panels used at Camp Williams, a military base near Lehi.

A Utah Transit Authority FrontRunner commuter train.
The 750 route connects Pleasant View to Provo,
a ninety-mile north to south journey.

✧

Above: The Convention Center in downtown Provo made the city a more attractive venue for conferences, workshops and trade shows.

Left: A sunset over Utah Valley as seen from the Squaw Peak lookout.

Managing the rapid growth prompted the Utah Valley Chamber of Commerce to launch the Executive Roundtable in 2012. If offers a forum for the valley's top business leaders to help enhance the business climate and quality of life in the area. Roundtable members, composed of key executives of Utah Valley's top companies and organizations, work to promote a pro-business climate and one of the nation's top places to live and work,

There is also plenty of room for the smaller entrepreneur, typified by Mary Crafts-Homer of Culinary Crafts, whose business started by selling homemade bread from a wagon and grew to become the largest catering company in Utah and the only Utah company to have ever won the International Caterer of the Year award. Her clients have included U.S. presidents, British royalty, international figureheads, and celebrities that include Oprah Winfrey, Jay Leno, and Diane Keaton.

Powerful businesses succeed in our low-crime, well-educated, high-opportunity region. Among them are Adobe, Google Internet, Vivint, Novell, NAI, Fibernet, Semantic, Manifi, Xango, Properto, Solutions, Task and Big D Construction.

This is a minute sampling of the companies who are finding a toe-hold in Utah Valley and establishing thriving industries.

✧

Above and inset: The glass windows of Adobe corporate headquarters in Lehi reflect the landscape east side of the I-15.

According to former Utah Valley Chamber president, Val Hale, technology jobs topped 55,000 in 2013, and many more jobs—often beginning at six figures—were left unfilled, waiting for motivated employees with the specific computer and engineering skills to satisfy the job requirements. Representative of a thriving economic and cultural community is Provo, which was ranked first in Forbes' 2012 best places for business and careers survey. The next year Forbes ranked third as best place to raise a family, and with great excitement, Provo City announced in April 2013 that it would be the third metropolitan area in the United States to offer Google Fiber, made possible when Google purchased an existing city-owned fiber-optic network.

Whether the view is from Camp Williams looking east, from homes in Alpine City, or a valley look near Thanksgiving Point, all vistas share a common, magnificent panorama of the valley.

CHAPTER 3

59

✧

Above and opposite: Utah Valley features
many desirable, safe residential neighborhoods.

✦

Clockwise starting from the top:

Cherry Hill Farm is a small dairy farm in Orem and the barn has been reproduced many times on posters, pillows and signs.

Delicate, fleeting beauty of a cherry blossom.

Apricot trees are a popular fruit both for commercial farmers and home gardeners.

Often referred to as the "queen of fruits," Utah Valley typically enjoys a bountiful apricot harvest in August and September.

But this is also a diverse valley that offers urban, suburban, and rural options. Its agricultural roots go deep, and Central Utah ranks as one of the strongest agricultural counties in the State of Utah, ranking first in the production of pears, sweet and tart cherries, and apples, second in peaches, apricots and corn for grain, and third in honey, oats, barley, winter wheat, and potatoes. It also tops the state in cash receipts from crop production and third in revenue from livestock.

✧

Above: The Red Barn in Santaquin, Utah, a great spot to shop for local produce.

Left and below: Wooden fences dividing properties add to the rural scenery at the southern end of Utah County.

It may not be a place where the buffalo still roam, but one can still be "home, home on the range." Those who embrace a more bucolic life with generous doses of country charm, can find it in the valley.

Fascinating Places: Natural and Manmade

Adventurers and nature seekers can find plenty of excitement year round in the breathtaking beauty of Utah Valley. Nestled in the majestic range framing Central Utah are an abundance of canyons, gardens, flowers, lakes, rivers, caves, and waterfalls. The region boasts a profusion of parks, forests, and wilderness areas. And the bonus is that nearly every city and town in the valley is located mere minutes away from a mountain, a valley, and a chance to be absorbed in natural wonders.

Left: Provo River boasts blue ribbon fishing and brings anglers throughout the country.

PHOTOGRAPH COURTESY OF MARK PHILBRICK.

Right: Take the scenic route through Provo Canyon on Highway 189 and you will see Bridal Veil Falls, a double cataract waterfall that drops 607 feet into the Provo River. The base of the falls has a nice, shallow pool idea for little kids to splash in, and the surrounding trails provide breathtaking views.

PHOTOGRAPH COURTESY OF MARK PHILBRICK.

*Aspen and fir trees surround Payson Lakes,
which provide ample opportunities for
canoeing, fishing and swimming.*

For those who want to see the valley by car, rides through American Fork Canyon, Hobble Creek Canyon, Provo Canyon, and Nebo Loop provide visual treats any time of the year—but especially when the fall foliage reaches its peak. Slip out of your vehicle and take a short walk to other natural pleasures such as Cascade Springs, an oasis of lush vegetation, pools and cascading waterfalls in the Uinta National Forest in the Wasatch Range.

Serious hikers may prefer the rigorous 1.5-mile hike to the Timpanogos Cave National Monument where three natural limestone caverns feature an array of colorful formations. Additional access to the splendid mountain scenery is possible via campgrounds and hiking and biking trails for the outdoor enthusiast.

Above: Cascade Springs, an oasis of lush vegetation, also features cascading waterfalls and pools in the Uinta National Forest, east of American Fork Canyon. Look closely you might see otters, beaver, deer, elk, turkeys and a wide variety of birds.

Opposite: Tibble Fork Reservoir, a popular fishing spot in American Fork Canyon, north of Mount Timpanogos.

Opposite: Ice fishing on the Provo River is a popular winter sport.

PHOTOGRAPH COURTESY OF MARK PHILBRICK

Top: Utah Valley is framed by mountains and Utah Lake. A look at the lake in late winter shows ice that forms on the lake and a vista of the Wasatch to the east.

Sundance

Winter brings some of the best powdery snow on earth, and snow and ski enthusiasts can visit Sundance Resort for a day on the slopes before dining in a choice of four- and five-star restaurants (The Sundance Tree Room boasts Zagat's highest-rated restaurant in Utah). Snow enthusiasts can also find abundant powder for snowmobiling, snowshoeing, and cross country skiing in mountain landscapes so picturesque one would think they had to have been photographically manipulated. It is a bit like living in a picture postcard. A few blocks from downtown Provo finds ice skaters using the Peaks Ice Arena, which was created for the 2002 Winter Olympics.

Utah Valley offers a veritable winter wonderland against a snowy purple mountain backdrop.

✧

Left: A cluster of buildings at the base of the Sundance Mountain Resort in Provo includes restaurants and shops and blends into the surrounding scenery, a deliberate design choice from the beginning to radiate the art of untouched nature.

Above: Side view of the Tree Room Restaurant at Sundance Resort.

Below: A water feature adds beauty at Sundance Lodge.

CHAPTER 4

Inset: Skiers and snowboarders prepare for a day at Sundance.

The Sundance ski area in Provo Canyon gets its name from the Sundance Kid,
a character owner/actor Robert Redford made famous in the 1969 movie,
Butch Cassidy and the Sundance Kid.

UTAH VALLEY: HEART of UTAH

✧

Above: Provo Canyon splits between Mount Timpanogos on the north and Mount Cascade on the south. U.S. Route 189 is the main thoroughfare with Orem on its west end and Heber on its east. Not far from the opening of the canyon on the west is Bridal Veil Falls. Other attractions within the area are Vivian Park and the Heber Valley Historic Railroad.

Left: Heber Valley Historic Railroad, popularly called the "Heber Creeper," is a tourist attraction based in Heber City, Utah, and travels between Heber City and Vivian Park in Provo Canyon.

The new Provo Recreation Center offers state-of-the-art recreation opportunities for Provo residents. Included is an indoor aquatic center with slides, rock cliffs, waterfall rock walls, and rivers; a fitness mezzanine; and four basketball courts.

Seven Peaks
Waterpark

Well-known for its blue ribbon fly fishing, crystal mountain waters also make a splash for such sports as rafting kayaking, canoeing, water skiing, jet skiing, and sailing. These sports, as well as cycling, paragliding, and climbing, are enjoyed much of the year.

✧

The south end of Provo offers an amazing view of the
area's mountain range and its 260 acre park features winding
waterslides, a wave pool and lazy river, cabanas and food vendors.
The specialties range from mild to wild: the Rocky Mountain Beach
wave pool and a series of attractions called mudslide gorge,
cave-in, flash flood, rapid ravine, avalanche, tadpole pond,
adventure bay, vortex, boomerang, summit plunge,
lily pad walk, cascade falls, canyon river,
sky breaker, jagged edge, free fall,
tykes peak, hot spring and
shotgun falls.

For those who prefer to take in the visual wonders of Utah Valley by carrying a wood or an iron, about a dozen golf clubs capitalize on the beauty of the valley with lush golf greens.

✧

Opposite, top: Riverside Country Club.

Opposite, bottom and this page: Sleepy Ridge Golf Course, Orem.

✧

Above: For more than twenty years, Spanish Fork has celebrated its llama farms with the Llama Fest
at the Krishna Temple in Spanish Fork. Besides a chance to see llamas up close and personal, the event also
offers food, music, spinning, weaving, demonstrations, dance, music and competitions between the llamas and their handlers.

As if Mother Nature did not provide enough of the good life, every city demonstrates community pride with an annual celebration. Some point to their past, such as Steel Days in American Fork, a nod to its steel plant heritage, or Pleasant Grove, whose Strawberry Days began in 1921 when strawberries were a major crop in the city.

In total, twenty-six communities take pride in their hometown by throwing a party, but none does it with more vigor than Provo, which organizes twenty-five patriotic events every June and July and culminates with one of the nation's largest Fourth of July fireworks shows and concerts in LaVell Edwards Stadium. Called Stadium of Fire, it attracts crowds from all fifty states to see traditional American values unfold in a surge of patriotism and pyrotechnics. Recent stadium performers have included Carrie Underwood, the Jonas Brothers, and Blue Man Group.

Celebrations and Lifestyle

The Festival Of Colors is a Hari Krishna traditional celebration of spring.

Winter is whisked away by burning an effigy of A Winter Witch who is considered to be evil.

Traditional Krishna music and dancing are part of the celebration. At just the right moment during the burning, all of the guests in attendance throw brightly colored corn starch powder into the air to welcome in the beginning of spring. Food and dance continues throughout the day. Today, through the popularity of Facebook, the Temple is bombarded by as many as seventy thousand guests, and it takes multiple days and multiple throwing of colors to accommodate all of the participants.

Strawberry Days Rodeo

✧

This page and opposite: The Pleasant Grove Strawberry Days Rodeo began in 1921, making it the longest continually running rodeo in Utah.

✧

Left: "I Love a Parade" could be the motto of Utah Valley's towns, because their city celebrations also feature local bands, queens, dignitaries and others who form a processional down main street as part of their city days.

Below: Free summer band concerts makes good use of Utah County's many city parks.

Opposite, top: Nearly every weekend during the summer vendors, crafters, carnivals and food stands set up business in Utah County towns and cities to celebrate what make their community distinct.

Opposite, bottom: Kids ride on a train at American Fork Steel Days.

✧

Opposite: One young boy may look comical, but his headgear provides shade from Utah's penetrating summer light.

Above: City-sponsored recreation programs are abundant, such as this girl's softball league.

Golden Onion Days

✧

Known for its production of onions, since 1933 Payson has celebrated Golden Onion Days.

Features include onion-related foods as well as amusement rides, fireworks, a parade,

arts and crafts, entertainment, and a demolition derby.

For decades adjacent Salt Lake Valley provided abundant shopping and dining options as well as cultural arts for Utah Valley. For the towns strung along the mountainside like beads on a necklace, the I-15 Interstate made it a straight (if congested) shot to the city. In recent years, however, Utah Valley has provided its residents with the best opportunities for quality of life without needing to travel north, and its public transit options have made valley travel much more accessible.

✧

Porter's Place, a family-owned restaurant in Lehi, Utah, is dedicated to honoring the heritage of Mormon pioneer Orrin Porter Rockwell. It sits on Lehi's historic Main Street in a 1915 brick building and has been open for business since 1971.

America's Freedom Festival

Grand Parade

✧

Opposite: From Santaquin south to Alpine north, Utah Valley summer skies boast a profusion of pyrotechnics.

Above: Spanish Fork, Utah, is only one of Utah Valley's many towns and cities that highlight their city queens in America's Freedom Festival at Provo's Grand Parade.

Left: If you are in Utah and it is July 4, the place to be is America's Freedom Festival Grand Parade, a large parade that highlights freedom through bands, floats, giant helium balloons, and local and national performers. Approximately 300,000 spectators see a procession that follows a vision of "celebrating, teaching, honoring and strengthening the traditional values of God, family, freedom and country."

✦
Above: The Nu Skin Building on the Fourth of July also reflects the surrounding mountain landscape.

UTAH VALLEY: HEART *of* UTAH

This page and opposite, bottom: Google fiber highlights its business with human fibers at America's Freedom Festival Grand Parade.

America's Freedom Festival
Grand Parade

✧

Below: Provo's old-fashioned fire truck is an annual entry at America's Freedom Festival at Provo's grand parade.

Opposite: The Utah County Sheriff's mounted posse brings up the rear at America's Freedom Festival at Provo parade.

America's Freedom Festival
Grand Parade

A gigantic American Flag is part of the opening ceremonies at Stadium of Fire,
part of America's Freedom Festival at Provo.

America's Freedom Festival
Grand Parade

Left: Even babies and their buggies show red, white and blue patriotism at the parade for America's Freedom Festival at Provo.

Below: Children enjoying the America's Freedom Festival Parade.

America's Freedom Festival
Grand Parade

Balloon Fest

✧

Opposite and above: For three decades, spectators have gathered at Bulldog Field in Provo to see more than two dozen hot air balloons launch and compete for prizes at America's Freedom Festival Balloon Fest. The three-day event brings pilots from around the nation who celebrate July 4 in an "inflated fashion."

Opposite and left: Orem Summerfest, one of many city festivals in Utah County each summer. Orem may be a growing city with a strong technological business base, but for at least one weekend a year, it has a small town feel when children get their faces painted, have balloon animals fashioned to carry under their arms and enjoy a carnival. Utah Valley communities—twenty-six of them—sponsor a city festival, and a constant presence at them all is a carnival for kiddies, teens and adults.

Orem Summerfest

✦

Above: The south end of the Orem Fest festivities hold dozens of vintage
and antique cars where proud owners display their restored vehicles.

Opposite: Carnival rides at Orem Summer Fest.

Orem Summerfest

✧

Opposite and below: In pioneer days Provo and Orem residents might have circled the wagons, but today more than a dozen vendors with decorated food trucks circle parking lots and historic sites to make an event out of fast food eating.

Huck Finn Days

✧

Left: Lindon, Utah, celebrates summer with Huck Finn Days. Every summer Lindon floods the stream in its city park and fills it with trout.

Bottom, left and below: Young fishermen get into the spirit of Huck Finn Days.

Major malls in Provo, Orem, the Shops at Riverwoods (see page 116) with unique stores and numerous restaurants, and the Traverse Mountain Outlet Mall in Lehi have done much to extend quality shopping. And the more than 600 restaurants range from the familiar to the unusual.

Numerous cuisines are offered because the residents have lived in many different countries (owing to service missions representing the Mormon Church), and their experiences are often reflected in the food. Consider tempting your taste buds with Peruvian tamales, Mexican squash soup or spicy ribs enchilada style.

✦

Above: The Outlets at Traverse Mountain during the holiday season.

Left: The Outlets at Traverse Mountain near Lehi greatly expanded Utah Valley's shopping options.

Opposite page: The Outlets at Traverse Mountain are part of the business and technology explosion occurring at the north end of Utah Valley. Many high-end retail stores have brought their businesses to this new outlet location.

✧

Clockwise, starting from the top, left:

The Shops at Riverwoods make running a 5K fun at the annual Santa Run.

The Shops at Riverwoods, a 120-acre village of retail space, residences, restaurants, and entertainment venues is a gathering place for festivals, concerts, splash pads, fire features and other entertainment. Set in a riverfront environment, it is designed to be community-centered and entertaining. To provide a summer experience year round, there is the Provo Beach Resort, a 50,000-square-foot entertainment center with, among other things, a carousel, mini golf and a surfing machine.

Nationally renowned fantasy artist James Christensen added a touch of whimsy to The Shops at Riverwoods with a selection of sculptures at its entrance and elsewhere.

The bright lights of Christmas make for popular shopping at The Shops at Riverwoods.

Above: University Mall in Orem, Utah, from the south side.

Right: Interior of University Mall, a thriving shopping area for more than forty years.

Below: University Mall has been a major shopping center in Utah Valley since 1973.

Provo is particularly attuned to changing attitudes and diversity. Its historic downtown has cultivated a decidedly urban feel and keeps generous crowds entertained with rooftop concerts, a film festival, comedy shows, and outdoor summer cinemas. Well-known bands such as Neon Trees, Fictionist, and Imagine Dragons got their starts on Provo streets.

SCERA
Shell Outdoor Theatre

SCERA SHELL OUTDOOR THEATRE

SCERA SHELL OUTDOOR THEATRE

✧

*Above: The cultural arts center in Orem for eighty years has been
the SCERA, (Sharon Cultural Education Recreation Arts),
which offers both indoor and outdoor theaters.
A recent popular concert filled the hill when
Kenny Loggins (right and opposite)
showed off his rock, folk, and
country styles.*

Another welcome entertainment addition is the Covey Center in Provo,
which offers anything from rock concerts and arts shows to ballet, comedy, and theater.
The SCERA Center for the Arts located a few miles north along State Street in Orem has been
a venerated home for the arts for eight decades, and its concerts and plays unfold in an historic art
deco facility or nested in a berm along the hillside of its Shell outdoor theater. Both the SCERA
and nearby Hale Center Theatre teach youth arts and performance classes.
And nearly every town has some sort of performance company.

Above: A quiet spot for contemplation at the gardens at Thanksgiving Point in Lehi.

PHOTOGRAPH COURTESY OF MARK PHILBRICK.

Opposite: Thanksgiving Point in Lehi becomes a mass of tulips every spring during its annual Tulip Festival.

PHOTOGRAPH COURTESY OF MARK PHILBRICK.

No sooner do you enter Utah Valley from the north than you reach an unusual complex called Thanksgiving Point, a popular tourist, educational and gardening mecca.

In the spring a quarter of a million flowers bloom on fifty-five acres during the annual Thanksgiving Point Tulip Festival. The gardens then become a spectacular array of perennial and annual flowers that reflect the seasons. During the festival, music, vendors, and food add to the festival atmosphere. Generous with their knowledge, a host of master gardeners teach gardening techniques through a series of Thanksgiving Point classes.

One of a Kind Destination Points: Timpanogos Storytelling Festival and Thanksgiving Point

6

Thanksgiving Point

✧

Below: Thanksgiving Point, a nonprofit farm, garden, and museum complex draws upon the natural world to cultivate transformative family learning. The familiar Thanksgiving Point tower beckons guests from the nearby I-15 freeway.

Opposite, top: Two of the primary buildings at Thanksgiving Point decked in holiday finery.

Opposite, bottom: The Tower Deli at Thanksgiving Point offers old fashioned floats, shakes and other soda fountain specialties as well as sandwiches, salads and desserts.

The site offers something year round: marathons, a championship caliber golf course designed by pro golfer Johnny Miller, a Scottish festival, Halloween Central, a reproduction of the first Thanksgiving, and a festival of spectacular holiday lights.

The newest attraction, the interactive Museum of Natural Curiosity, opened to capacity crowds in 2014 and augments the adventures in its other interactive gallery, the Museum of Ancient Life. Add a petting zoo, mammoth screen 3D theater, restaurants and emporium, and you have one of Utah's most must-do venues in the state.

For three days each Labor Day weekend Mt. Timpanogos Park becomes the largest storytelling festival in the West. The forty-four acre park, located a mile from Provo Canyon along Highway 189, was designed especially for the Timpanogos Storytelling Festival and includes plenty of grassy space for several large pavilion tents, picnic sites, and permanent fixtures such as restrooms, running water and electricity. The festival, now nearly a quarter of a century old, brings in storytellers selected from the finest national professions with experience performing to audiences young and old. An added bonus is the dazzling mountain scenery.

✧

Opposite, top: Popular to both visitors and local residents is the Thanksgiving Point gift shop and restaurant.

Opposite, bottom: What started out at a backyard event in 1990 has grown into the largest festival of its kind in the west and its own expansive story site near the mouth of Provo Canyon.

Above: Large pavillion tents set up to accommodate the many visitors at the Timpanogos Story Telling Festival.

Right: Participants listen to one of the many storytellers who have been enthralling listeners at the Timpanogos Storytelling Festival held the Thursday, Friday, and Saturday of each Labor Day weekend for more than a quarter of a century.

Timpanogos Storytelling Festival

Above: Halloween merchandise and candy is a big deal in Utah Valley and sales rival the Christmas holiday.

Left: As one of most popular holidays in Utah Valley, parents, children and grandchildren become creative and carve their own pumpkin families as well.

And if the valley did not offer enough of the good life, fifteen national parks, monuments, and recreation areas are within a half-day's drive of Utah Valley.

Unique to the Utah lifestyle is its high emphasis on religion. For families who want to play and pray together, Utah Valley offers so many churches, it is not unusual to see two large chapels that share a parking lot and then see another church, and another, a mere two or three blocks away. Founded by the Mormons, the predominant faith remains The Church of Jesus Christ of Latter-day Saints, and the region boasts four temples: one in American Fork to the north and in Payson to the south, and two in Provo, one of which, the Provo City Center Temple is being built from the remains of the historical Provo Tabernacle that was razed by an accidental fire. The influx of new timpanoyees and companies, however, is adding to other faiths, and nearly two dozen other religions are represented. In a country where a little more than half the population affiliates with a religious congregation, nearly ninety percent of Utah Valley residents participate with a church.

Utah Valley features superb public school and higher education systems, and the presence of two major universities in the valley's two largest cities contribute much to the academic atmosphere and advantages available. Among several on-campus museums are two prestigious art museums, a peoples and cultures museum, life science museum, and paleontology museum.

Students who attend Brigham Young University learn in a environment that fosters both spiritual and secular education. Thirty-three percent are from Utah, but students represent every state in the union and 105 different countries. Courses are available in ten colleges and through Continuing Education.

Education

Opposite, top: Patio at Springville Museum of Art.

Opposite, bottom: Constructed in 1937, the Springville Museum of Art is the oldest museum in Utah for the visual arts.

Below: Studio C, a sketch comedy show produced by BYUtv on the campus of Brigham Young University, is designed to showcase clean, family-oriented comedy for a national audience. Now in its fourth season, the troupe has also become a YouTube favorite with hundreds of thousands regularly checking in to see the antics of the young comedy team.

Nearly 70 percent of BYU students speak a second language—about 16 percent speak three—and 111 languages are spoken on campus. The high percentage is reflected, in part, because more than 50 percent of its students have served LDS Church missions, many of which require a second language. At any one time, 55 languages are taught on campus, and another 30 are available when interest warrants it. Its international reach is seen through a strong Study Abroad Program with 133 programs and 55 countries.

In a sampling of recent academic rankings, BYU's accounting program was named number one by *Businessweek*, and its master of accounting program got the third place ranking from *Public Accounting Report*. National rankings in the top ten include best value for a private law school, graduates with the least debt, graduates who go on to earn doctorates, graduate and undergraduate entrepreneurship, and best value school. Among other honors, *New York Times* magazine wrote a major feature on BYU's animation program, and its most recent class received the fourteenth first place award in the animation category of the College Television Award, commonly called a "student Emmy."

✧

*Above: The BYU Centennial Carillon Tower, constructed in
1975 when Brigham Young University turned 100, is a symbol
of the dedication and sacrifice of those who helped found BYU.
The tower holds a practice room, clavier room and a belfry.
The fifty-two bells play a chromatic scale and weigh 26,695
pounds. Both the tower and Y Mountain are familiar
BYU symbols.*

PHOTOGRAPH COURTESY OF MARK PHILBRICK.

*Left: The Y on Y Mountain, located 1.2 miles from the
mountain's base, (seen here behind the Carillon Bell Tower)
was built more than 100 years ago and is the nationally
recognized insignia for Brigham Young University—and
the reason the school is called "the Y." Made of concrete,
it measures 380 feet high and 130 feet wide (even larger
than the Hollywood sign in Los Angeles). Special events such
as freshman orientation, Homecoming, and April and August
graduations are celebrated with a Y lit by strands of bulbs
placed around its perimeter.*

BYU's advertising program is also noteworthy and won the National Collegiate Effie, the crown jewel of college advertising awards this year. Much honored, the BYU Ad Lab became the first team from the United States to win the Global L'Oreal Brandstorm competition in Paris, and beat thirty-eight other teams for the honor.

Their performing arts companies travel the world, and Cougar athletics have a large and enthusiastic fan base with football and basketball, but also experience national success in such sports as soccer, volleyball, cross country, baseball, and rugby.

✧

Nearly 65,000 football fans fill BYU's LaVell Edwards Stadium.

PHOTOGRAPH COURTESY OF MARK PHILBRICK.

This page: Utah Valley University has grown from the Central Utah Vocational School in 1941 to the largest public university in the State of Utah. Each of its forty-eight buildings uses the same style of unfinished concrete with all ten of the major buildings connected by thirty-foot concourses. The reflecting pond pictured above is one of two on the west side of campus. The site also includes a stream and runs through the east part of campus.

In many ways Utah Valley University is the little engine that could—and after it could, it became an overachiever.

Its roots are humble. UVU began in 1941 as a small vocational school in Provo, and with a current enrollment of well over 33,000 students, it recently became the largest public university in the State of Utah. When combined with BYU's student population, tens of thousands of people are earning an education in Utah Valley.

UVU's range of programs is extensive and ranges from aviation, psychology, ballroom dance and wildlife land management. Its Wasatch Campus in nearby Heber City (near Park City, a popular resort town) adds to the curriculum with bachelor's degrees in business management and secondary education and associate degrees in accounting, behavioral science, business management, elementary education and general education. The main campus also offers master's degrees in education, business and nursing.

Its 8,500-seat Events Center holds concerts, basketball and football games, trade shows and expos. A high focus on arts is evident in three theaters and the Woodbury Art Museum, and a Center for the Arts is under way. And it is especially pleased with its Digital Learning Center with networked computers, labs, computer reference area, media center, thirty-one study rooms and wireless internet throughout the building.

Thanks to the generosity of Toyota dealership owner Brent Brown, Utah Valley University has had a baseball stadium since 2005 that holds 5,000 people. The field is home of the minor-league Orem Owls and Utah Valley Wolverines, a team in the NCAA Division 1 Western Athletic Conference.

A Style All Its Own

—Steve Densley

While nearly everyone living in Utah Valley has a stunning backyard view worth staying home for, residents are also within easy driving distance of many stunning national parks and red rock vistas throughout the state. And with a growing infrastructure, family friendly communities, and a unique social structure that retains traces of a rich Mormon heritage, Utah Valley has a style all its own.

I invite you to stay for a day or a lifetime. Like me, you may find it's your kind of place.

—Steve Densley

✦

Top: The backside of Mount Timpanogos provides a year-round glacier view for this lucky homeowner.

Left: Utah Valley twilight.

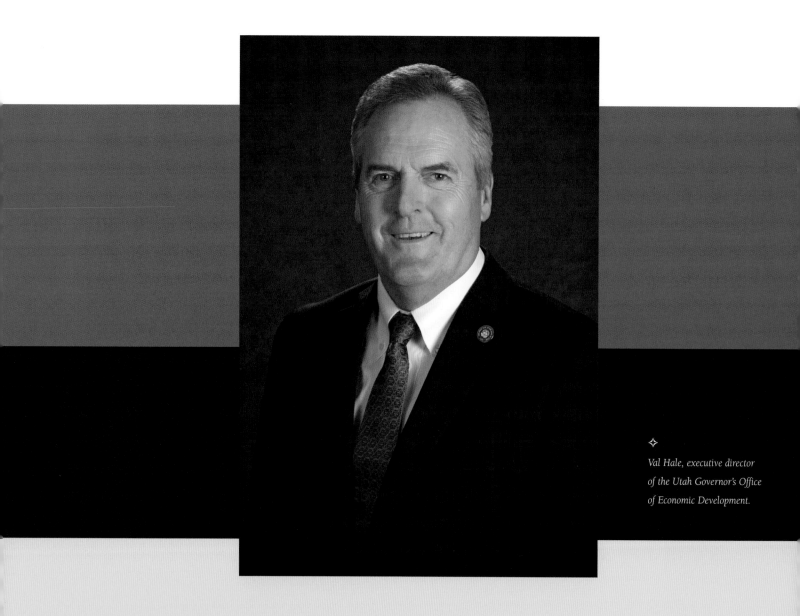

As recently as twenty-five years ago, Utah Valley was frequently left out of the discussion about Utah's economic prowess. But no more. For the past decade, the explosive growth of Utah Valley's economy has been the primary impetus behind Utah's ascension to the top of the nation's economic summit.

Several factors have contributed to the meteoric rise of prospering businesses in the county. Primary among them has been the presence of two outstanding universities: Brigham Young University and Utah Valley University. With more than 60,000 students between them, these institutions have spawned innovation and provided a significant, educated workforce for industry. Professors and students from these universities helped start and grow pioneering high tech companies like WordPerfect and Novell. Money and know-how spun out of those enterprises to help create a high tech cluster that has produced dozens of software and IT companies, several valued at more than a billion dollars today.

High tech's auspicious arrival to Utah Valley in the early 1980s came at precisely the right time. Geneva Steel, which had been the county's primary economic driver for forty-plus years, was on its deathbed, a victim of cheap, subsidized foreign steel production. Agriculture had been a mainstay of the economy from the mid 1800s to the 1970s. Utah Valley was famous for its bounteous fruit orchards, but by the late '70s, they were being pushed to the south end of the county by a burgeoning population.

> "For the past decade, the explosive growth of Utah Valley's economy has been the primary impetus behind Utah's ascension to the top of the nation's economic summit."
>
> —Val Hale

Today, Utah Valley's economy is more diverse than ever. In addition to high tech, agriculture and education, there is strength in manufacturing, healthcare, direct-sales companies, construction, and tourism.

One of the valley's strongest assets is its young population. In fact, no county in America is more prolific at procreating than Utah County. And that is a good thing. A young, growing population means there will continue to be available workforce as the county's population doubles in the next twenty-five years.

The economic outlook for the valley is bright. Venture capitalists have discovered that Utah Valley is fertile ground for entrepreneurs. Companies being birthed in the valley today tend to stay here instead of being purchased and moved to another state.

Critical to future economic growth are improvements in transportation and water infrastructure, as well as continuing emphasis on providing world-class education for our youth.

If we elect wise, forward-thinking local leaders, there is little reason to believe Utah Valley will not remain at the forefront of the state's economic activity.

—Val Hale
Executive director of the Utah Governor's Office of Economic Development (GOED),
which promotes state growth in business, tourism and film.

Utah Valley Partners

Profiles of businesses, organizations and families
that have contributed to the development
and economic base of Utah Valley

The Marketplace

Utah Valley's retail and commercial establishments offer an impressive variety of choices

BYU
BROADCASTING

A sophisticated, state-of-the-art broadcasting system one would expect to see in the nation's largest cities can be found in a university town a mere stroll from a major concert and performance hall, a basketball bounce away from a major sports arena, a homerun hit from a baseball field, and so close to a 65,000 seat football stadium you do not need to turn on the television to hear the roar of the crowd. And what is even more impressive is all of these incredible venues are fiber connected to this broadcast center, allowing for more than 1,000 hours of original broadcasts each year with over 600 hours of those being live sporting events.

It is the 100,000 square foot state-of-the-art high definition BYU Broadcasting studios on the campus of Brigham Young University. Consisting of four studios, production and post-production work spaces and a worldwide distribution operations center, BYU Broadcasting operates multiple local, nationwide and international television, radio and digital channels that stay true to its tagline of helping millions of people to "see the good in the world."

Visitors to Brigham Young University are encouraged to take a tour of BYU Broadcasting and see where the many different radio and television channels originate, including BYUtv, nationwide on satellite and more than 900 cable systems, BYU Radio on Sirius XM Satellite Radio, BYUtv International in Spanish and Portuguese (throughout Central

and South America, Mexico and the Caribbean), BYUtv Global in the Pacific Islands and other English speaking countries around the world, and the digital offerings of the BYUtv Roku, Amazon Fire, Xbox 360, iOS and Android channels. Daily broadcasts include a variety of programs that range from sports, reality, history and comedy to classical music, drama, and more. Visitors can enjoy scheduled behind-the-scenes tours or self-guided tours peeking in on many of the production studios at BYU Broadcasting.

✧

Right: The expansive lobby of Brigham Young University's BYU Broadcasting facilities.

Below: The exterior of BYU Broadcasting, a 100,000 square foot state-of-the-art complex that attracts industry professionals who help provide invaluable programming as well as mentoring to hundreds of students.

Employees of BYU Broadcasting are full-time professionals recruited from the likes of ESPN and Disney to those who have made their careers working for major Hollywood studios and networks. These broadcast veterans are paired with and mentor more than 350 student employees from the university learning all aspects of the entertainment industry.

Granite Flats was BYUtv's first foray into scripted drama. With a story arc spanning three seasons, *Granite Flats* was set in the 1960s with a backdrop of the Cold War during a period of intense political intrigue and paranoia. The series featured an all-star cast including Christopher Lloyd (*Back to the Future*), Parker Posey (*Waiting for Guffman*), George Newbern (*Father of the Bride*), Finola Hughes (*General Hospital*) and Cary Elwes (*The Princess Bride*). *Granite Flats* was produced and filmed entirely in Utah airing on both BYUtv as well as Netflix.

Other programming that has found particularly wide audiences are the more than 400 live sports shows and sporting events each year (including a live daily sports show), a reality show called *The Story Trek*, an American history offering called *American Ride*, and a comedy show known by millions as *Studio C*.

Take one look at the beefy, six foot two inch, 300-pound, denim-clad, ginger-haired and bearded biker wearing a skull rag; it is likely you would never guess Stan Ellsworth is a former football player and high school history teacher with a degree in history from BYU and a passion for United States history.

Above: BYU Broadcasting prepares for a pre-game football show.

Below: As the place to watch, analyze and learn about BYU sports, BYU Broadcasting airs 600 plus hours of live Cougar action each year.

Ellsworth, the host of the regional Emmy-winning *American Ride*, rides his custom Harley Davidson Softail Deluxe cross country and chronicles a 400 plus year saga of Americana. He tells tales that have been told many times, but his compelling delivery sets the program apart from other television history treatments. As a larger-than-life-character,

he delivers a one-of-a-kind narrative with enthusiasm and accuracy, which has helped him build a substantial fan base including history teachers, elementary, junior high and high school students nationwide—some now referring to Ellsworth as "America's History Teacher."

BYU Broadcasting visitors invariably ask if they can get a glimpse of the studio where the sketch comedy show, *Studio C*, is taped. When *Studio C* performs the seats are typically filled to capacity with up to 20,000 seat requests for each live taping. It is no surprise that *Studio C* has gained a large YouTube and television audience for wholesome, family-friendly comedy. The show is a hit and appeals to all ages and demographics with something not readily available on other channels—genuinely funny content that is not offensive or off color. Early on, the goal of the cast was to produce a video that reached a million views. Their reward would be pizza. They achieved

STUDIO C

Left: Millions of fans watch the Studio C troupe on television and YouTube and thousands more request the chance to see them perform live at BYU Broadcasting's headquarters on the Brigham Young University campus.

Below: The Studio C comedy troupe has attracted a viral audience online and an enthusiastic one on television. Millions of viewers tune in to see the antics of this funny, family-friendly team of players.

it with a parody on the *Hunger Games* movies. At the same time, however, along came a slapstick sketch about Scott Sterling, a hapless goalie, who repeatedly blocked the ball in a soccer shootout, unexpectedly—with his face. Total views of that sketch alone in just a matter of months exceeded thirty million. Extra toppings on that pizza for the goalie!

LARRY H. MILLER GROUP OF COMPANIES

In a state teeming with business triumphs and innovations, the thirty-five year old Larry H. Miller Group of Companies stands out not only as a certifiable business giant but also as a corporation with a legacy of enriching lives. The LHM reach permeates Utah and extends into nearly all fifty states.

LHM started modestly on May 1, 1979, with a single Toyota dealership in the Salt Lake City suburb of Murray. Larry H. Miller was by trade an automotive parts and operations manager when he and his wife, Gail, purchased their first dealership. Over time, more dealerships were purchased and the LHM Group has grown into one of the largest privately held companies in the United States.

With fifty-five new and used auto dealerships representing twenty-one automotive

brands in Utah, Arizona, Colorado, New Mexico, Idaho, Washington and California, Larry H. Miller Dealerships is the third largest privately held automotive group in the country. Also part of the company's automotive operations are Total Care Auto, which provides vehicle service contracts to consumers, and Prestige Financial, which provides financing solutions for both franchised and independent automobile dealerships.

If that represented the totality of the Miller brand, that would be impressive enough, but it merely represents a portion of the LHM enterprise. Larry (April 26, 1944-February 20, 2009) and Gail added sports and entertainment as well as philanthropy to their successful business ventures.

Today, under the direction of their son Greg Miller, CEO, the company is organized into six major areas: automotive, finance, insurance, real estate, sports and retail. The LHM Group of Companies has grown to more than eighty businesses and properties spanning forty-six states and employing more than 10,000 people.

The Millers successfully expanded their growing business empire in 1985 when they purchased the first half of the Utah Jazz, an American professional basketball franchise based in Salt Lake City. The following year, in spite of the professional and personal financial risk involved, they purchased the second half to avoid losing the franchise to an out-of-state buyer. They believed that keeping the team in Utah was extremely important to the economy

of the state and would provide its citizens with a unique experience only thirty cities in the United States can claim—a professional basketball team of their own to rally around.

Other properties include the MiLB Triple A Salt Lake Bees baseball team; Miller Performance, consisting of Miller Motorsports Park (which is a world-class race track), the Ford Racing School, Oneiro, an event management company; Fanzz sports apparel stores; KJZZ TV and 1280 The Zone Sports Network; Larry H. Miller Megaplex movie theatres throughout Utah and in Nevada; All-Star Catering; and the Tour of Utah, a yearly pro cycling race event.

In 1991 downtown Salt Lake City got a boost when ground was broken for a 20,000 seat sports and entertainment arena named the Delta Center (renamed Energy*Solutions* Arena in 2006). In 1993 the NBA All-Star Game was held in the Delta Center where Utah Jazz greats Karl Malone and John Stockton were named co-MVPs.

Many of the businesses are centered in Salt Lake City with the corporate headquarters located in Sandy, Utah. However, Utah Valley feels the Miller Group influence because it is the location of several Miller auto dealerships, Fanzz Stores and Megaplex Theatres.

Founded in 2007, the Larry H. and Gail Miller Family Foundation supports religious, charitable, scientific, literary and educational programs with an emphasis on issues that affect women and children's health and education. Whether it is sponsoring the Christmas Carol Sing-A-Long, providing help through its Day of Service, developing a program to help teachers improve the way history is taught in the classroom or giving donations to community fundraisers such as Make-a-Wish, the LHM stamp is found all over Utah. With their philanthropy, Larry and Gail donated to Brigham Young University the funding and construction of the Miller baseball and softball field facilities and continue to support many other programs at BYU.

The Miller family lives by the tenet coined by Larry himself: "Go about doing good until there is too much good in the world." They are devoted to "doing good" for a very long time to come.

FILLMORE SPENCER LLC

The legal team at Fillmore Spencer LLC.

When seeking an outstanding law firm that offers both quality and depth, consider Utah Valley's largest law firm, Fillmore Spencer LLC. Each of the firm's eight partners were educated at highly-respected institutions and have more than twenty years' experience in securing superb results for their clients. With a supporting cast of outstanding associate attorneys, the firm's bandwidth enables it to handle complex and general business transactions, large and small civil litigation, commercial contracts and intellectual property licensing, trademark registration and enforcement, Internet and technology law, estate planning, employment law, real estate matters, criminal defense (from major felonies to traffic tickets), family law issues (including divorces and custody disputes), immigration, bankruptcy (both debtor and creditor side), Social Security disability, and wrongful death, medical malpractice, and personal injury claims.

Fillmore Spencer, situated in the picturesque "River Bottoms" area along Provo's University Avenue, prides itself in serving Utah County in a unique way. The firm's attorneys care more about solving their clients' problems than generating large fees. Those they serve are not just clients, but become friends.

Because Fillmore Spencer's attorneys foster lasting relationships with clients, they stand side-by-side with them in defending their legal and business interests. They are strong litigators, and the firm's growth parallels the major population and business growth in Utah Valley.

Eager to help all—from start-ups and "mom and pop" companies to national and international businesses—the attorneys at this full-service law firm have traveled throughout the country and abroad for its clients. They have extensive experience before state trial courts, federal district courts, and appellate courts. They have argued nearly 100 cases before the Supreme Court and Court of Appeals for the State of Utah and various federal appellate courts and their persistent advocacy has resulted in the creation of new law and the settling of legal principles.

By way of example, one gratifying case involved the firm's defense of a small but growing Utah County company sued by a large national enterprise. Had the client lost the case, the family business would have been forced to close. Despite the odds and resource disparity, Fillmore Spencer's dogged defense succeeded. The saved business has grown into a $100 million company employing nearly 500 Utah Valley residents.

Utah Valley's vibrant entrepreneurial climate has achieved worldwide recognition, sometimes even being called the "next Silicon Valley." Fillmore Spencer attorneys find great fulfillment in assisting these innovative and emerging businesses and enabling their phenomenal growth and success. With experts in business formation, joint ventures, technology, human resource management, real estate, trademarks, trade secrets, securities, and funding, Fillmore Spencer can facilitate your participation in this fertile environment.

Fillmore Spencer clients include many large local, regional and national companies, as well as hundreds of smaller businesses and

individuals. Due to the firm's open and friendly attitude and well-deserved reputation, referrals are the firm's primary source of new business. Many clients were once adverse parties who wished that Fillmore Spencer had represented them, and then later chose the firm for their future legal needs.

Naturally, the partners and associates make their living through practicing law, but they work to make a positive difference in many other ways. They seek to live the firm's motto, *Serving our clients and community with excellence and integrity*. Their professional contributions reach deep into nearly every aspect of community activities, demonstrating their commitment to enhancing life in Utah Valley.

Fillmore Spencer attorneys can be found on many community boards, providing legal advice and other services to such entities as the Utah Valley Chamber of Commerce Board of Governors, America's Freedom Festival, the national board and executive committee of the BYU Alumni Association, Timpanogos Regional Hospital, the American Inns of Court, public school boards of education, local political parties, United Angels Foundation, and Kids Who Count.

The firm's attorneys are also involved in many other commissions, clubs and committees in Utah Valley, including the Saratoga Springs and Pleasant Grove planning commissions, the BYU Cougar Club (one partner serving as its National President), the Mapleton City Economic Committee, Provo Parks and Recreation, the American Red Cross, the Utah County Chapter of the Society for Human Resource Management, the Utah County Employers Committee, the Center for Constitutional Studies at Utah Valley University, the Utah Make-A-Wish Foundation, and the Strategic Advisory Council for the Utah National Parks Council. One partner

served in the Idaho State Legislature, and another has volunteered as a truancy court judge for the Nebo School District.

Fillmore Spencer has also been heavily involved in the national "Statue of Responsibility" project from its inception—the 300-foot statue originally envisioned by Viktor Frankl in his famous *Man's Search For Meaning* as a West Coast bookend to the Statue of Liberty in New York.

Fillmore Spencer recognizes that some cannot afford access to legal services. To promote justice for all, one partner was instrumental in establishing the Timpanogos Legal Center, which provides legal services to those who cannot pay. Another partner volunteered his time to travel to Europe and educate Ukrainian judges and prospective lawyers about Western legal principles.

Much honored, Fillmore Spencer has received the highest AV rating for legal ability and ethical standards by Martindale-Hubbell, and several of its attorneys have been distinguished as among "Utah's Legal Elite" by *Utah Business Magazine*. The firm has also been honored for "Best Legal Services" by the readers of the *Daily Herald*, and as the area's "Favorite Local Law Firm" by *Utah Valley Magazine*. Together with its other accolades, Fillmore Spencer's attorneys would be equally honored by your trust to resolve your legal needs. You may contact them at 801-426-8200 for a free consultation any time to determine if they can help you or stop by their office at 3301 North University Avenue in Provo, Utah 84604. Additional information on Fillmore Spencer is at www.fslaw.com.

✧

Above: The Fillmore Spencer LLC office, located along University Avenue in Provo, Utah.

FERRIN CAPITAL ADVISORS, INC.

✧

Top, left: James A. Ferrin.

Top, right: James T. Ferrin.

Below: Ferrin Capital Advisors.

Jim Ferrin is a man with a plan. He loves to invest—his own money and client money. He loves to help clients meet their financial goals and dreams. The president of Ferrin Capital Advisors, Inc. likes to say he is "saving the world—one investor at a time." Though said somewhat in jest, it reveals his passion for helping his clients to preserve and grow their money in an uncertain financial world.

Investors face a difficult challenge. Interest rates remain low. Stocks and bonds are high and volatile. Investment markets react to economic weakness at home and abroad. Nevertheless, a certain constant remains for us all: "We still need to preserve and grow our money," he says. "The challenge is how to do that now."

The solutions offered by some advisors are expensive, pre-packaged financial products. Others just say, "Buy and hold on...if it drops, it'll come back eventually." That might not be a great plan anymore. Perhaps what sets Ferrin apart most from all the rest is this: He knows the world has changed. "It isn't like the 1980s or 1990s anymore," he notes. "Today you have to pay close attention. Be flexible. You need a plan to manage risk, and a strategy to capture growth." Many advisors do not do that. Ferrin does.

With a finance degree from BYU in 1981, Ferrin has been helping Utahans with their investments for more than thirty-four years. Founded in Orem in 1993, his firm, Ferrin Capital Advisors, has staying power. From their start in borrowed office space to their beautiful new class-A office in Pleasant Grove, they have been a part of Utah Valley growth for more than twenty-one years.

Ferrin has deliberately kept the company small and profitable, employing him and three others. Still, the company has access to big firm systems and resources. Ferrin believes that in terms of money management systems and low, competitive costs, they are second to none. The company is pleased to help all investors. Those with investment portfolios of $500,000 or more will benefit most from the company's efficient, advanced systems.

A Certified Financial Planner™ professional, Ferrin is president and chief investment strategist. He is a member of the Utah Valley Chamber of Commerce, the Financial Services Institute (FSI) and a founding member of the Academy of Preferred Financial Advisors (APFA). Ferrin's son, JT, joined the firm in 2012 after graduating from BYU. JT counsels with his own clients as well as helps to serve all company clients. Lindsay Cook joined the firm over twelve years ago. She holds a bachelor's degree in business from the University of Phoenix. She works with the firm's growth initiative. Plus long time clients still know her as the one who can answer and address all of their account administrative concerns. Sydney Gardner is the "Director of First Impressions." Hers is the pleasant voice taking client calls. She also calls clients to schedule their review appointments. Sydney sets up and processes client accounts and arranges the transfers of funds from other companies. A UVU fine arts graduate, Sydney is also an instructor and coordinator at a local dance studio.

Clients of Ferrin Capital Advisors come from all walks—pre-retirees, executives, physicians, business owners, and more. Many have been clients from the beginning. "Our clients are smart, busy people but we don't expect them to be experts in monitoring, measuring, and managing investment markets," says Ferrin. "That's our job."

The company boasts a host of other "Gold Medal Services." These include an income tax return analysis, estate plan analysis, regular client review meetings, website account access, regular account reports, a quarterly economic update letter, an annual tax letter, client workshops, dinners, and special events. "Our goal is to treat our clients like they are our best friends, because they are."

Another important company goal is to provide great value to clients—to offer their services at the lowest possible cost. For example, as part of a company review last year they lowered their advisory fees across the board for all clients. Then, they did something rare among financial advisors—they published their low cost fee schedule on their website. "Why not?" asks Ferrin, "We are proud that we offer a great service at a low cost to our clients. It is value added!"

The challenges for investors remain the same—they want to retire—to be independent—to be good stewards of their wealth. They want to invest with confidence. Ferrin is the man with a plan. Ferrin Capital Advisors is a great Utah Valley business—experienced, ready, and able to meet the challenge.

Ferrin Capital Advisors, Inc., is located at 1955 West Grove Parkway, Suite 200, in Pleasant Grove, Utah. You may stop by for a visit, call 801-756-2220 or visit on the Internet at www.ferrincapital.com.

Securities offered through Triad Advisors, Inc. Member FINRA/SIPC.

✧

Left: Lindsay D. Cook.

Right: Sydney Gardner.

SQUIRE & COMPANY

More than forty years ago DeLance Squire and his son Joe opened an accounting firm in Orem, Utah, based on a conviction that success was more likely when they turned their clients into friends. They then kept them happy because their pencil sharp focus was all about service with competence.

✦

Above: Squire & Company (801-225-6900) is conveniently located at 1329 South 800 East near Orem's major shopping district, the University Mall.

Below: Working together to ensure excellent service are, from left, Kevin Johnson, Reuben Cook and Marc Andrus.

"DeLance used to say that when you became friends with those you served, you created a different, stronger relationship with them," says K. Tim Larsen, managing partner of Squire & Company. "I agree with that philosophy and we practice it today. People want you to be capable, and they like it when you are personable and interested in them beyond their business affairs."

As an example of early customer service, although the Squire tax fees were reasonable, —an individual tax return typically cost about seventy-five dollars and was meticulously prepared with paper and pencil— DeLance would frequently tell his clients just to pay what they thought the service was worth. They usually paid the full fee.

Squire prides itself on being at the forefront of emerging technology and has done exceptionally well. By 1978 it was using computers and helping others progress in their careers with a nurturing internship program. By 2000, Squire had split into specializations, and employees developed specific areas of expertise.

As one of the largest firms in the Mountain States, its fourteen partners and dozens of support staff work with customers and companies from throughout the world. And as a one-stop shop for personal and business financial needs, Squire & Company provides services in tax, audit, business advisory, technology advisory, payroll and accounting, and wealth management.

"Our clients started asking for additional services, and, eager to accommodate their expanding needs, we invested time and resources and added additional employees with specialized skills to meet those needs," adds Larsen.

Currently their business is composed of about one-third tax, one-third audits, reviews, and other attestation services and one-third advisory services. Their roots are still strong—they complete more than tax returns each year and audit services continues to be a solid base for the firm. However, more and more clients are requesting the additional areas of expertise that the firm has developed over the last few years.

"We like to take people who have a product or idea and help them develop a strategy for running a successful business," Larsen explains. "We are here to help others set and meet their financial goals."

Two parts of this process are critical: a lot of people do not know how to set goals and do not know where they are headed or why. Squire & Company is there to be their partner.

"We want to assist, and as we help others meet their goals, we are helped, too," Larsen adds. "At Squire it's a reciprocal relationship."

And it seems to be working. *Accounting Today* recently named Squire & Company among the top 100 mid-sized accounting firms in the nation, the only Utah firm so honored. The magazine has awarded this distinction five times. It frequently receives Best of Utah Valley Awards in the categories of best accountant, best tax service and best wealth advisors. As the only Premier Intuit reseller in the state, this has grown into a substantial portion of the advisory practice area.

Squire more than doubled its building size in 2006 and it sits in a prime Orem location at 1329 South 800 East.

"We needed the space to accommodate our expanding employee base," Larsen says. "Additionally, factors such as the recession have had very little impact on accountants since our services are needed more in economic downturns as our clients strive to manage what is going on in their financial worlds."

Among the many ways they help clients is to co-sponsor David Ramsey Financial Peace seminars. They partner with Zions Bank three times a year and share the financial specialist's conservative principles of financial responsibility.

They also offer Squire QuickBooks for business management and reports, and provide classes and Webinars that follow cloud, management, and desktop tracks.

Active in community life, Squire is part of the Adopt-a-Highway program and cleans a portion of University Parkway near their offices. They also participate in United Way's Day of Caring and Sub for Santa, and all professionals are asked to participate in a civic group.

While Squire has always been about service, one of the more unusual ways of taking care of client business occurred in the early days of laser printers. Although Squire used the premiere printer available, they had a machine that would only hold fifty sheets of paper at a time. This meant the machines had to be tended 24/7 to meet tax deadlines. Staff members brought floor pads and would lie down for a few minutes while the printers finished about six pages per minute. When the fifty pages were exhausted, they would get up, refill the machine and wait another eight or so minutes until they could refill the paper tray.

Squire & Company was willing to go to the mat then—and while it may not be an issue of paper trays now, they are still willing to go to the mat for their customers and business clients.

✧

Squire & Company has fourteen partners that include front row, from left to right, Tim Christensen, Shane Wood, Tim Larsen, Ray Bartholomew and Jonyce Bullock. On the second row, from left to right are Shane Edwards, Lynn Hillstead, Dwayne Asay, Paul Winward, Ray Chipman, David Archibald, Wayne Barben, Dave Brown and Doug Flake.

University Mall

University Mall opened in 1973 and was the first regional mall in the Utah County area. The mall is located in Orem, a suburban city north of Provo. University Mall is an award-winning, 1.77 million square foot, single level regional shopping center located at one of the state's busiest intersection—the intersection of University Parkway and State Street. University Mall is strategically located less than a mile and a half from two of Utah's largest Universities: Brigham Young University and Utah Valley University, together with over 75,000 students. The favorable market also includes an attractive population of over 750,000.

When University Mall opened, it was anchored by Utah-based ZCMI—one of the only major retailers owned by a religious organization, the Church of Jesus Christ of Latter-day Saints and JCPenney. One of the first major changes at University Mall was the addition of a north wing of retail space anchored by Mervyn's, a California-originated department store operated by Dayton-Hudson of Minneapolis, in July 1981.

In 1998, JCPenney closed their doors and moved to a new shopping center located in south Provo. Following JCPenney's departure, as part of a multimillion dollar renovation and expansion, University Mall secured Nordstrom as a replacement anchor to JCPenney. The Nordstrom store opened in a new building in 2002 following the renovation of the JCPenney building into additional retail space.

The multimillion dollar makeover upgraded appearances from floor to ceiling. Five different unique courts scattered throughout the mall representing the four seasons and nature features of Utah. Alpine Court features mountain springs and waterfalls. Village Court is an open air court with a leisurely living room atmosphere. Lodge Court has a big city style plaza with café seating and a large monumental fireplace and hearth. Canyon Court features a

"Canyonland" feel with rock outcroppings and walls, and standing cairns that glow. The treehouse court is an interactive "soft play" area for children featuring a large treehouse and slide. The food court area was expanded and the exterior of the mall was made over extensively with towers, glass windows and cobblestones.

The ZCMI store closed and a Meier and Frank store opened in 2001 after the Church of Jesus Christ of Latter-day Saints sold ZCMI to May Company in 1999. May retained the ZCMI name until 2001, when all of the ZCMI stores were either converted to May's Portland-based Meier and Frank nameplate or sold. The store at University Mall operated as Meier and Frank until shortly after parent company May was sold to Macy's in February 2005. Macy's converted all of the May nameplates, including this store, to their Macy's brand in fall 2006. Mervyn's closed at the end of 2008 when the company filed for a nationwide bankruptcy.

The Village at University Mall, an outdoor 'lifestyle' expansion debuted in 2008. Consisting of over 88,500 square feet of retail and entertainment space for fifteen stores, the Village is anchored by a 14-plex Cinemark theatre and allows patrons to shop outside and enjoy the beautiful mountain views and fresh air.

The future of University Mall is changing and expanding from a Regional Shopping Mall to a 130 acre urban mixed-use gathering place to be known as University Place. University Place is posed to be one of the most iconic places to do business in Utah. The center will continue to have the strong retail element that it now has with over 150 retailers, and will add the elements of high rise Class A office space, housing, a hotel, and residential units including apartments, townhomes and condos and will have a swim and tennis club on site.

At the center of the project will be a large park, which will be built to host a variety of programmed events for the public. Things from farmers markets, musical performances, exercise classes and other warm weather activities, to ice skating, Christmas events, and other winter activities. The retail office and residential elements of the project will

surround and compliment the park.

The unique combination of uses at the center will result in a destination that will have a competitive advantage over other large scale developments in the region. The mixture of uses creates a synergy—the retail benefits from the proximity of the office and residential while the office and residential likewise become more attractive because of the retail. Mixed-use development improves economic competiveness by making more efficient use of people's time. Employment centers, educational opportunities, residences, entertainment, services, and basic needs are all provided within walking distance of each other. At the core of its brand promise is the delivery of a compelling and iconic mixed-use environment offering relevant uses and experiences.

This development will attract business and visitors from Utah County and beyond. It is one of the most transit connected places in all Utah County. It boasts amenities that reduce the cost of doing business, provides convenience to employees, attract new employees, and help dramatically expand the public recognition and corporate distinction of the companies that locate there. The Center is an iconic and compelling address. It is the heart and spirit of Utah County's business and retail corridor.

KNEADERS

What do you when you retire after successfully running a Subway Sandwich franchise and quickly realize retirement is no fun? You find a new way to work with bread and develop your own, even more flourishing business.

That is what happened to Gary and Colleen Worthington who—after several discussions with their close friend Sherman Robinson of Lehi Roller (flour) Mills—decided Utah could benefit from amazing European-style hearth breads. They emerged with the idea for Kneaders, an award-winning bakery and café with thirty-two stores in five states that uses high quality ingredients to create fresh artisan breads baked on site, delicious sandwiches, homemade pastries, hearty salads, amazing breakfast entrees, and popular gift baskets.

The Worthingtons opened their first Kneaders in Orem, Utah, December 3, 1997, after several years of preparation. Prior to opening they visited the American Institute of Baking, the San Francisco Baking Institute, and attended multiple baking expos and conferences to learn how to make the best breads. They made contacts and established relationships among the finest equipment vendors and bakers found anywhere.

They tested flours and equipment in their garage and offered test samples to anyone who would take them. On opening day they sold breads, a few pastries, and some soups. Gary was the business' first baker and he,

along with a few assistants, prepared amazing breads in the wee morning hours.

It did not take the Worthingtons long to realize their bread would also be splendid for sandwiches, and their menu grew to include specialty sandwiches and beverages, a wider variety of pastries, soups and salads, and seasonal offerings, such as pumpkin bread.

Kneaders experimented with freshly roasted, hand-pulled turkey. In the beginning, they would daily roast and pull between four to six whole turkeys in each store for their sandwiches. Kneaders still roasts turkey every night, but now uses between eighteen to thirty turkey breasts.

Their most popular breakfast item came about because their son James, then a Brigham Young University student, wanted to impress some female students. He lived in a dorm with no cooking facilities, but female dorms across the street had kitchens. James picked up day-old loaves of Chunky Cinnamon bread and prepared French toast for the girls. As he was about leave for a two-year mission for his church he told his mom that his French toast was really good and that she should try it. After returning home, he realized his comment had made an impression. French toast had been added to the menu. Today it has evolved to include buttery syrup as well as strawberries and whipped cream and is Kneader's best-selling breakfast item.

From the beginning an added boost to their business was the use of a drive-through window. Not too many bakeries provide this option, but most Kneaders' stores have a window; forty percent of their business comes through the drive-through. A more recent enhancement was its 2014 online ordering system, www.kneaders.com, which was instantly successful. More than half of Kneaders' pie and roll orders at Thanksgiving came from their online business.

From the onset, Kneaders has been a family business built on the premise that they were going to delight guests in a way that creates loyalty. They do this not only with fresh products and outstanding ingredients but also with a hospitality model that creates long-lasting relationships with their guests.

Their son-in-law and CFO David Vincent joined the business in 2000 and their son James, now the company CEO, became the first franchisee when he opened a store in Midvale, Utah, in 2003. Son-in-law Curtis Smith and his brother Andrew, opened the Lehi, Utah, Kneaders in 2008, and Andrew helped expand the business by becoming a Kneaders Development Agent in 2009.

Kneaders employ more than 1,200 employees at its bakery/cafes plus another seventy-five who support the thirty-two locations. It serves about 3,000 customers weekly, and its revenues topped $63 million in 2014. With ten to twelve additional stores opening in 2015 and new locations planned in Utah, Arizona, Colorado, Nevada, Texas, and Idaho (and others under consideration), Kneaders is growing aggressively. Its sales have grown 375 percent in the past five years.

The family also looks forward serving their community every year with such events as the American Fork Canyon Half Marathon and the annual Evening with Santa to benefit children's hospitals. Kneaders have ongoing relations with the Utah Valley University Culinary Arts program where Colleen is a board member. The Worthingtons also sponsor the program's annual gala event as well as their annual golf tournament.

Much-honored, Kneaders has received a Best in State Award and national recognition from Technomic. Among the Worthingtons more prestigious awards are the 2013 leadership award from *Modern Baking* and a top ten ranking in the Future 50 brands by Technomic. In 2013, Kneaders was named Business of the Year by the Utah Valley Chamber of Commerce; Colleen recently was cited as a Women of Achievement, also by the chamber.

And Gary maintains his passion for bread. You can regularly catch him inspecting the loaves that bakers have produced and giving pointers and ideas from his expertise to pass on to their current generation of bakers.

✧

Above: Kneaders Red Velvet Mini Bundt Cakes.

Left: Kneaders makes fresh, homemade specialty breads every day.

Below: Turkey bacon avocado sandwiches and salads are among the popular Kneaders' menu items.

PHOTOGRAPHS COURTESY OF NICK BAYLESS.

WILL'S
PIT STOP

WILL'S
CANYON STOP

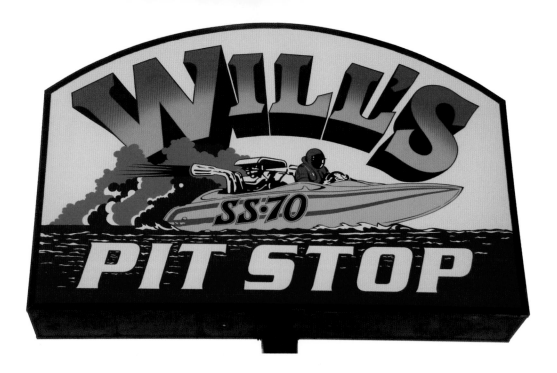

✧

Above: Wills Pit Stop sign has become a familiar landmark in Provo and Orem and depicts the owners' love of boat racing.

Right: Bill and Holly Faulkner operate Will's Pit Stop and Will's Canyon Stop.

Most people thought William and Marlene Faulkner were crazy when they announced their dreams of building a gas and convenience store on the family farm. Who would have guessed that the family farm was the prime location for such a store? Located in the beautiful river bottoms, Will's Pit Stop has become a community landmark and is iconic for its famous yellow cup, race boats, and as a point of reference for finding destinations.

In the summer of 1983, the family, with dad at the helm, began construction on what is now famously known as Will's Pit Stop. Will's opened January 9, 1984, and Will, who had been battling lung cancer, passed away nine days later. At only fifty years old, Marlene Faulkner found herself widowed, with three children still at home, and a new business to run. As their son Bill Faulkner describes it, "As a family we stuck together building the family business, each of us contributing where needed."

Marlene worked tirelessly to launch Will's Pit Stop. As a woman in a man's world, she put in many twelve hour days in the first years. "She taught us all that hard work and determination pays off in the end," says Bill. "Mom said people build a business in their home; I built a home in my business."

For them, Will's Pit Stop is not just any convenience store.

By design, they provide a family friendly atmosphere where everyone knows your name. "We have been blessed with the overwhelming support of our community and have the best customers in town," says Holly Faulkner, co-owner of Will's Pit Stop. "We wouldn't be here without them."

The family mission is to help those in need and to make a difference in others' lives.

"We have had the opportunity to help support many schools, auxiliaries, and non-profit organizations throughout the years." Bill explains. "And it brings us great joy."

Marlene not only put her heart and soul into Will's, she also strived to do her best, winning the prestigious Reed Smoot Award

and Outstanding Businesswomen of the Year in 1993. Many of Marlene and Will's posterity began their working careers at the family business, all learning the value of hard work and pursuing their own dreams. Their priority has been family, business, and then racing.

Marlene surprised her husband by naming their dream business, Will's Pit Stop after him. Its prominent sign shows off his love of boat racing, and the continued success of Will's Pit Stop has allowed the family to boat race all around the country.

"We have been active participants in the American Power Boat Association, winning numerous awards and recognition," Bill says. "We proudly display many race boats and memories on what we call our wall of fame."

From the beginning, the family has worked to continue a legacy of hard work, dedication, and integrity, which go hand-in-hand with building a successful business.

Bill's younger brother Lance was managing Will's Pit Stop when he was tragically killed in a boating accident on Thanksgiving Day in 2001.

"He had a contagious smile and warm personality, and we will miss him forever," Bill says. "He greatly impacted all he met."

With his death, Bill and Holly left their careers of more than twenty years and became partners with Marlene to continue the family enterprise. The trio brought different skill sets to the table, which allowed them to grow and develop together. They made changes to help increase profitability, decrease loss, and work more efficiently to help Will's expand and thrive.

In 2005, they added Will's Canyon Stop in Orem, which doubled the size, revenue, and work of the business. Having both locations gave them the opportunity to try new procedures, make necessary changes, and meet a new customer base.

"We love our Canyon location as well. We are fortunate to come to work every day and see familiar faces, touch the lives of others, and allow them to touch our lives," Holly adds. "We have had the opportunity to employ some of the most incredible staff anyone could ever want. Not everyone can say they have worked with their mother-in-law,

husband, and kids every day—and the life of a convenience store owner is anything but dull. We have seen and heard almost everything over the past thirty-one years."

Bill and Holly along with their family will continue to learn and improve every day; make changes and stay flexible in an ever-changing world. "The hyper markets and large chains have slowly been squeezing out the small businesses, but we hope to reinvent and grow so Will's can stay a household name in the community we love," Bill adds. "We like to think a small family business can make a difference, even if it's just one soda and one smile at a time!"

Will's has been an incredible journey for the Faulkners, who are grateful for the many doors that have been opened for them.

"We are thankful to our mom and hope to make her proud as we continue to develop and expand for future generations," Bill adds. "We are looking forward to more amazing memories and the opportunity to continue a family legacy."

✧

Two above: Boating has been a passion for several generations of the Faulkner family.

Below: The Faulkner family pays tribute to Marlene Faulkner, who worked tirelessly to make Will's Pit Stop successful and honored her late husband's memory.

SAVAGE COMPANIES

The history of Savage Companies began in 1946 in American Fork, Utah. Kenneth Savage had recently returned home from U.S. Naval duty at the end of World War II. He and his father purchased a KB-5 International stake body truck and began transporting coal, timber, cinder block and other materials in Utah under the name C. A. Savage & Son.

Kenneth's brothers Neal and Luke joined the business, which became Savage Brothers, and it expanded to include hauling more products to more locations. The brothers became known for their honesty and hard work, and their ability to always get the job done.

✧

Right: The company's first truck.

Below: Left to right, Luke, Kenneth and Neal Savage.

Today, Savage is a global leader in the creation and delivery of integrated services and systems designed to meet the unique challenges in each customer's supply chain. Savage customers quickly learn that they are working with a supply-chain solutions company built on innovation, collaboration, value creation and reliable service.

With thousands of employees in hundreds of locations, Savage supports a wide variety of customers in the production, manufacturing and distribution of energy resources and other essential commodities. The company offers capabilities that span rail, truck and marine transport, terminal and facility operation and design, and related services.

Savage retains the brothers' core values of providing high-quality, worry-free service to customers with a commitment to integrity, honesty and fairness. The company's vision and legacy statement expresses these values and the brothers' intent to have the company continue for future generations, pursuing opportunities for growth in business and for its employees.

Utah County has played an important role in the history of Savage Companies. Its first office was in American Fork, where Savage continues to have a trucking operation today. The Savage brothers attended American Fork High School and for many years Luke helped transport the American Fork High School Marching Band's equipment to their competitions throughout the country. Neal served as mayor of American Fork, where he initiated what became known as the Pageant of the Arts.

In 2015, Savage Companies established the Kenneth, Neal and Luke Savage Endowed Fund in Business at Brigham Young University in Provo. This endowed fund provides scholarships and other support for students at BYU's Marriott School of Management, with preference for students in the Global Supply Chain Management Program.

For more information about Savage, please visit www.savageservices.com or call 801-944-6600.

SUNDANCE MOUNTAIN RESORT

In 1969, Robert Redford purchased the land that is now known as Sundance with the vision of a community committed to the balance of art and nature. Sundance Mountain Resort is the place where all things Sundance began—where Robert Redford created an internationally renowned film institute, film festival, and television channel devoted to independent film. Still managed by the Redford family, Sundance Mountain Resort has grown into a destination resort with a difference, its original values still intact. The rustic simplicity of the Sundance Mountain Resort is graced by 5,000 acres of protected wilderness at the base of 12,000 foot Mount Timpanogos.

Sundance's commitment to the arts and nature is reflected in its year-round cultural programming that includes the renowned Summer Theatre, Bluebird Café Concert Series, and the Author Series. Its commitment to sustainability can be seen throughout the Resort from the intimate mountain cottages that are discreetly tucked into the mountainside, echoing the simplicity of the natural setting to the nature inspired eco spa that focuses on holistic wellness to bring the body, mind and spirit into balance. Even conference spaces showcase their natural environment with large windows looking out at spruce groves and mountain streams.

The Sundance Art Studio and Gallery offer classes in pottery, painting, jewelry making and photography. Sundance's Glassblowing program turns discarded bottles and glass into works of art that are sold in the Art Studio's Gallery and used in the restaurants. Mountain recreation includes year-round world-class fly-fishing in the Provo River, skiing, snowboarding and cross country skiing in winter, hiking, biking and horseback riding in summer. And in spring of 2015, Sundance introduced the longest zip line tour in Utah with the most vertical drop at 2,100 feet more than any other zip line in the country.

Sundance features award winning dining in The Tree Room, Sundance's fine dining restaurant and the Foundry Grill, noted by Zagat's for its "brunches to die for." The Sundance Owl Bar features the original 1890s Rosewood bar that was once frequented by Butch Cassidy's Hole-in-the-Wall gang, which was moved to Sundance from Thermopolis, Wyoming.

Sundance offers something for everyone, whether carving the mountain on a bluebird day, throwing a pot in the Art Studio, enjoying a summer concert or listening to a well-known author on a Saturday afternoon. Sundance provides the perfect blend of art, nature, and recreation.

For more information on Sundance Mountain Resort, please call, 801-225-4107 or visit www.sundanceresort.com.

✧

Above: The night sky over Sundance Mountain Resort.

PHOTOGRAPH COURTESY OF WILLIE HOLDMAN.

RUNNER'S CORNER

When Josh Lewis traveled from Colorado to visit family in Utah, he dropped off his suitcase and made a beeline for Runner's Corner in Orem. He planned to run a marathon and wanted owner Hawk Harper to help him with some pain issues.

"Hawk knew exactly what he was talking about, and his assistance far surpassed anything I have had from any other running store," he says. "He was personable and made me feel he had nothing better to do than work with me."

After specific guidance and some inserts, Lewis could run without pain.

"Hawk really gave me a leg up, so to speak." Lewis says.

This is a common reaction for customers who flock to Runner's Corner, a business Hawk and his wife Cheryl established twenty years ago to help runners have a better experience in their quest for fitness.

"We want others to feel the same kind of joy we get from running," Hawk explains. As the patriarch of what could arguably be called Utah's First Family of Running, the couple, their four children plus a daughter-in-law and son-in-law see the scenic wonders of Utah Valley from the perspective of running its hills, mountains, and trails.

Their store contains merchandise from apparel to sports nutrition. At the core, however, are the shoes. According to Cheryl, eighty-two percent of runners get foot injuries because of shoes poorly designed for the structure of their specific feet. They can discern whether a foot has a tendency to roll to the inside or the outside; whether the runners are wearing shoes that tend to cause bunions; if the footwear makes the heel land first, contributing to plantar fasciitis; and other foot problems. Trained employees work carefully with customers until the correct shoe is identified for each individual.

An additional benefit to Runner's Corner is Learn to Run, an in-store class with demonstrations to correct foot placement while running. Clients are videotaped and their running is evaluated. Foot placement affects neuropathy, runners' knee, shin splints, and IT band (outside the knee pain), which can be corrected by proper running form. The Harper's spacious new Orem building has an indoor track and an outdoor running area so customers can practice running techniques and try shoes before purchasing them.

Devoted to the community, the Harpers sponsor several charity races and support the Food and Care Coalition as well as local Spike Nights when a whole team gets fitted while the store provides pizza.

The entire family holds running records evidenced by a home bulging with trophies and medals. Their focus, however, is sharing their considerable knowledge with others in a comprehensive, personalized way.

Runner's Corner is located at 835 South 77 East in Orem and at www.runnerscorner.com.

Right: Runner's Corner, a full-service fitness center with a Wasatch Mountain backdrop.

Below: The Harpers, consisting of Crystal, Cheryl, Hawk, Summer, Amber and Golden, all championship runners who share their expertise at the Runner's Corner, the family's full-service fitness store in Orem, Utah. They analyze foot challenges and running styles, have a running track, a video room for taping, shoes, merchandise and more.

SUNDANCE MOUNTAIN RESORT

In 1969, Robert Redford purchased the land that is now known as Sundance with the vision of a community committed to the balance of art and nature. Sundance Mountain Resort is the place where all things Sundance began—where Robert Redford created an internationally renowned film institute, film festival, and television channel devoted to independent film. Still managed by the Redford family, Sundance Mountain Resort has grown into a destination resort with a difference, its original values still intact. The rustic simplicity of the Sundance Mountain Resort is graced by 5,000 acres of protected wilderness at the base of 12,000 foot Mount Timpanogos.

Sundance's commitment to the arts and nature is reflected in its year-round cultural programming that includes the renowned Summer Theatre, Bluebird Café Concert Series, and the Author Series. Its commitment to sustainability can be seen throughout the Resort from the intimate mountain cottages that are discreetly tucked into the mountainside, echoing the simplicity of the natural setting to the nature inspired eco spa that focuses on holistic wellness to bring the body, mind and spirit into balance. Even conference spaces showcase their natural environment with large windows looking out at spruce groves and mountain streams.

The Sundance Art Studio and Gallery offer classes in pottery, painting, jewelry making and photography. Sundance's Glassblowing program turns discarded bottles and glass into works of art that are sold in the Art Studio's Gallery and used in the restaurants. Mountain recreation includes year-round world-class fly-fishing in the Provo River, skiing, snowboarding and cross country skiing in winter, hiking, biking and horseback riding in summer. And in spring of 2015, Sundance introduced the longest zip line tour in Utah with the most vertical drop at 2,100 feet more than any other zip line in the country.

Sundance features award winning dining in The Tree Room, Sundance's fine dining restaurant and the Foundry Grill, noted by Zagat's for its "brunches to die for." The Sundance Owl Bar features the original 1890s Rosewood bar that was once frequented by Butch Cassidy's Hole-in-the-Wall gang, which was moved to Sundance from Thermopolis, Wyoming.

Sundance offers something for everyone, whether carving the mountain on a bluebird day, throwing a pot in the Art Studio, enjoying a summer concert or listening to a well-known author on a Saturday afternoon. Sundance provides the perfect blend of art, nature, and recreation.

For more information on Sundance Mountain Resort, please call, 801-225-4107 or visit www.sundanceresort.com.

✧

Above: The night sky over Sundance Mountain Resort.

PHOTOGRAPH COURTESY OF WILLIE HOLDMAN.

ZIJA INTERNATIONAL

Following a successful career in the health and nutrition industry, Ken Brailsford thought he had retired.

"Thought" is the operative word, because after watching a documentary about the Moringa oleifera tree—nicknamed nature's "miracle tree" because of its potential to enrich the health and vitality of people worldwide—he enthusiastically wanted to become involved.

✧

Above: A sampling of products offered by Zija.

Below: Among the most popular products Zija customers use is "Améo Essential Oils."

As Brailsford explains, "I was so moved by Moringa's potential to change the world; I just could not ignore it. I sought out the best scientists, nutritionists, and botanists to help me leverage Moringa and create products that best utilize it."

That was in 2005, nearly ten years ago. The result is Zija International, Inc., out of Lehi, Utah. He launched Zija Core Nutritionals, with high-quality nutritional supplement and energy beverages as well as a weight management system and skin care line, all of which utilize the nutrient-dense Moringa oleifera tree. The company later added two new product divisions in 2014: Améo Essential Oils and Ripstix Supplements.

Zija's mission to provide a life full of wellness and vitality inspired Rodney Larsen, Zija president and CEO, to be engaged in a company built on the four vital pillars of health and wellness, active lifestyle, financial freedom, and personal development.

Once the company launched, it was imperative for employees to wear many hats, whether it was educating distributors to ensure they believed in and understood the products or helping provide the vision to make Zija a billion-dollar company. The company quickly expanded to fifty plus markets worldwide, and, says Cathy Yeates, vice president of new market development, this means the company has had to be flexible and knowledgeable enough to adapt to each market's customs, culture, business style and marketing preferences.

The company's growth began in North America, quickly gravitating to several international markets. Only recently have there been many Distributors in Utah, but with the recent introduction of its Améo Essential Oils product division, business has exploded in Utah, and it has been fun to see friends and neighbors using and embracing all of the products.

The emerging news about Zija is impressive. It was named the fasted-growing company in Utah by *Utah Business Magazine. Inc. Utah Business* recognized its 906 percent growth, making it the thirty-eighth fastest growing company in the industry. *Utah Valley Business* named it among the fastest-growing and top revenue companies in Utah. Just as significant is its steady year-over-year growth.

Mindful of a responsibility to give back, Zija has established the Zija Miracle Foundation, which has been changing lives worldwide since it began in 2013. The foundation's charitable influence has been felt as far away as India, Japan and the Philippines.

PROVO MARRIOTT HOTEL AND CONFERENCE CENTER

Originally built in 1983, the hotel transitioned to the Marriott flag in 1998 becoming the Provo Marriott Hotel and Conference Center and has been a mainstay of the downtown area. The amenities offered in each of the 330 guestrooms feature luxurious Marriott bedding accompanied by plush pillows and down comforters, a thirty-seven inch LCD television, alarm clock, coffee maker/tea service, iron/ironing board and a hair dryer. Enhancing any traveler's stay is a spacious work area with data port hook-up, complimentary high-speed Internet access, and in-room dining. Executive rooms host additional features such as a larger living area and mini fridge. Safe deposit boxes are available at the front desk.

All visitors to the Provo Marriott Hotel and Conference Center may access the on-site business center, and relax in our Great Room with complimentary high-speed Internet.

Boasting twenty total meeting rooms encompassing approximately 28,000 square feet of banquet and meeting space, the Provo Marriott Hotel and Conference Center is the ideal location for any event. With over 8,000 square feet the Grand Ballroom can accommodate up to 1,000 guests for receptions. Additional breakout space for groups of ten to 250 guests is available with high-speed wireless Internet access in all our meeting rooms.

Our professional event managers are happy to oversee each detail of your event. We have an amazing, award-winning catering and banquet staff, and our in-house state-of-the-art audiovisual department is available for any questions or needs. Our very own on-site red coat service and direct meeting services app enables ease of access for meeting planner changes and requests. We also have off-premise catering available.

SLATE Restaurant offers American comfort food classics reinterpreted with a modern twist utilizing seasonal local ingredients. It is open for breakfast, lunch and dinner. SLATE Lounge brings guests locally crafted beers and a healthy selection of wines by the glass as well as classic cocktails in a comfortably sleek environment, with private tables and lively communal seating areas; open 5:00 p.m. to midnight.

SLATE Cafe proudly serves Starbucks coffee, hot chocolate, smoothies and grab-n-go food items including freshly baked pastries, healthy salads, sandwiches and other items. Open Monday through Saturday 6:00 a.m. to 4:00 p.m.; Sunday 6:00 a.m. to 12:00 p.m.

Recreation and leisure opportunities are available for all types of travelers who reside at the Provo Marriott Hotel and Conference Center. Our state-of-the-art fitness center offers complimentary twenty-four hour access with room key. Guests can easily relax in the indoor and outdoor pool. Just minutes away, horseback riding is available along with hiking and fishing, which can be experienced in Uinta National Forest.

Provo Marriott Hotel and Conference Center is close to a variety of attractions, such as Utah Lake State Park, Sundance Resort and Park City, Seven Peaks Water Park, Bridal Veil Falls in Provo Canyon, BYU Genealogy Center, Thanksgiving Point Golfing, Provo Towne Centre Mall/Movie Theater, Timpanogos Cave and more.

Nestled in Provo's city center, the Provo Marriott Hotel and Conference Center is an upscale hotel where views of Utah's striking Wasatch Mountains provide a tranquil and inspiring environment for a new generation of mobile business and leisure travelers.

BRENT BROWN TOYOTA

❖

*Above: The showroom at
Brent Brown Toyota.*

*Below: Brent Brown is standing in front
of his extremely rare restored 1963 Toyota
Landcruiser fire truck. All its systems
are operational and includes its original
ladders, axes and hoses. Brown uses it
for parades all over the state, including the
Days of 47 Parade in Salt Lake City and
the July Fourth Parade in Provo. When it
is not in parades, it remains in the Brent
Brown showroom for the enjoyment of
customers and their children.*

Brent Brown seems to have an innate gift for customer relations. "From the beginning, I really tried to give excellent service," he says. "I was the top salesman my first month working for an auto dealership, and when I broke the dealership's all-time sales record the second month, I thought this might be a great way to make my living."

Brown advanced in the business and in 1992 became the general manager/partner of what was Rick Warner Toyota. Toyota had ranked the dealership in the bottom twenty out of 1,250 Toyota dealers in customer satisfaction, and Brown immediately worked to improve buyer perceptions.

"At the time more than half the people in Utah County were leaving the valley to purchase their Toyotas," he says.

Eager to encourage residents to buy vehicles at home, he emerged with the slogan, "We'll bend over backwards to keep your business in Utah County." A billboard at the Point of the Mountain (the area where Utah Valley becomes Salt Lake Valley) used the slogan and featured Brown doing a back bend. It worked.

Seven years later, Brown purchased the dealership, now at 1400 South Sandhill Road in Orem, and uses a modified slogan—"We'll bend over backwards to be your auto dealer." It reflects the dealership's commitment that customers are first, employees second and profitability third.

It also helps that Brown has red customer service telephones in his dealership that ring directly to Brown, regardless of his location. And he takes those calls every time.

Brent Brown Toyota today is the number one metro dealership in a six state region in owner loyalty. It reigned as number one for service customer satisfaction in Utah for 2013, and this year it has broken its twenty-two year-record for sales three times. For many years Brown has received the highest honor Toyota bestows, the President's Award, for customer service and a well-run business.

Brown, a former Provo/Orem Chamber of Commerce board member, and past president of the Utah Auto Dealers Association, says he especially appreciates his selection as Ernst & Young's 2004 Entrepreneur of the Year. But he does not rest there. He recently finished a term on the State Board of Regents and serves on the Governor's Office of Economic Development.

Utah Valley Magazine recently named Brown's dealership one of its top three places to work. As part of a commitment to service, he and his wife Mona have become champions of children's education. Eleven years ago they started The Easter Basket Auction to raise money for the Provo School District. In 2014, their efforts yielded more than $200,000, raising in excess of $1.25 million to date. They also made a substantial donation to Utah Valley University, whose ballpark bears Brown's name.

VASA FITNESS CENTER

The bold, two-tone red V that dominates the exterior of eighteen buildings throughout Utah could just as easily signify "victory" as it does for its official name, VASA Fitness Center.

That is because Utah's premier new fitness facilities with locations from Bountiful to St. George—total of five in Utah Valley—are dedicated to making sure their 140,000 members become winners in the health and wellness arena. These friendly community centers live by a mission to UPLIFT those who live a VASA lifestyle. UPLIFT, an acronym for unity, passion, love, integrity, fun and trust, also supports a motto that says: VASA exists to help people find happiness through health and fitness.

VASA offers an excellent selection of fitness options to its members. Skilled instructors teach a range of classes including aerobics, cycling, step, Pilates, aqua (at locations with a pool—check the VASA website at www.VASAfitness.com for locations), hard core, sports conditioning, silver sneakers, pump, yoga, power yoga, kickboxing and Zumba.

Classes are conveniently scheduled throughout the day from 5:30 a.m. to 8:15 p.m. with a schedule published monthly on their website.

Cardio cinema rooms accompany workouts, and a team of knowledgeable personal trainers are available to tailor workouts specifically focused on individual needs.

Extra ads are found on their blog, which contains healthy tasty recipes, wellness tips from their trainers, support for the tougher times, such as holidays, vacations and the blah times of the year. It also contains minilessons for new or seasoned members and pages of excellent tips with photos.

When it comes to company fitness, VASA has developed a multifaceted HIPAA compliant program that educates, motivates, and provides health and wellness guidance to employees. Both effective and economical, it accomplishes prospective and ideal company growth.

VASA Fitness wellness coaches are equipped with a minimum four year health science related degree and develop a strong relationship with an individual on a one-on-one basis to help them reach health and wellness goals. The components of the Corporate Wellness by VASA Fitness include:

- Monthly personalized, onsite wellness coaching
- Inclusive memberships to all eighteen VASA FITNESS locations in Utah
- Biometric screenings including weight, body fat, BMI, and blood pressure
- Cholesterol testing
- Fitness testing
- Monthly educational classes
- Health fair promotion and planning
- Individualized healthy goal planning
- Individual usage reporting

Additionally, VASA Fitness's KidCare program offers child care up to ninety minutes per day while parents work out. Our KidCare staff undergo a rigorous screening and background check process. Also, they must be CPR and First Aid certified, as well as tuberculosis tested, before starting to work in the KidCare centers.

B. ASHWORTH'S, INC.

Many interesting people have slipped through the doors of B. Ashworth's, Inc., and they are almost as interesting as the shop at 55 North University in Provo that focuses on the best in rare books, manuscripts, books, art, collectibles, and curiosities.

One couple, for example, disguised in winter wear in ninety-eight degrees, visited the store. It was only when they shed their coats and the woman her wig that owner Brent F. Ashworth recognized them as comedian Marty Ingles and his wife, Academy Award-winning actress and singer Shirley Jones. As they spoke the couple was surprised when Ashworth knew the financier of the American Revolution (Haym Saloman). They also spoke about Hollywood for about half-an-hour after Ashworth showed them a dress worn by Marilyn Monroe he had acquired at an auction many years earlier.

Another time, he met an interesting steelworker and his family from the World Trade Center and a baseball player who played with the legendary Sandy Koufax. Radio personality Glenn Beck is also a client.

"I've met many people with interesting stories," Ashworth says. But few are as interesting as the collectibles he can find following more than five decades of collecting in many fields.

"After my own long experience with collecting, my wife Charlene and I felt it was important to share what we have learned and collected with institutions and with individuals who want to expand their own collections."

Because of Ashworth's extensive experience, he can help others by being aware of their individual and institutional needs and desires. He then selects the most appropriate avenues and venues available to match and acquire the desired items. "In short, we help them build and enhance their collections," he adds.

His firm deals primarily in rare Latter-day Saint and Western material but handles other significant items from around the world.

Ashworth strives to serve individual collectors and the collecting community with the most reasonable prices available. The Ashworths also assist in building corporate, university, institutional, and individual collections and strengthening the reputations of the collector in the collecting community.

When B. Ashworth's doors opened on June 6, 2006, Ashworth's father-in-law, G. R. "Mike" Mills, a veteran survivor of D-Day (June 6, 1944), cut the ribbon. Also on hand were his wife, Provo Mayor Lewis Billings, Miss Provo, and more than fifty families, friends, and community leaders.

Ashworth, an attorney by profession, is legal counsel of Zija International in Lehi, Utah. But B. Ashworth's has a big piece of his heart. "We have added a bit of class to the downtown in the objects we have gathered and the stories we have shared," he says.

"Our job is finding people jobs. We love what we do!" Locally owned and operated since 1989, Spherion's mission is to help local businesses work better, faster and more efficiently by rapidly locating the right talent. Additionally, Spherion aims to help candidates live the life they love by providing them with fulfilling career opportunities that utilize their unique talents and skills, while driving them toward greater success.

Dedicated to service excellence, owner Ron Zarbock knows it takes a personalized, high-response approach to service their clients and candidates. With offices located across the Wasatch Front, Spherion has become "Utah's Top Talent Resource" for companies ranging from small and mid-sized businesses to large, multinational organizations.

While most people view staffing services as temporary solutions, Zarbock has gone above and beyond to break the stereotype. As a true workforce leader, not only does Spherion provide a variety of employment services, they are also dedicated to workplace safety and helping companies create programs to operate efficiently and lower their workforce costs.

Zarbock, a native to the area and a twenty plus year veteran in the staffing industry, and his team love the people of Utah and are committed to providing the best talent and opportunities for their clients and candidates. Constant innovation in sourcing talent,

combined with their in-depth knowledge of the community and the talent that lives there, keeps them ahead of their competitors.

Proving their local roots run deep, Spherion has a strong relationship with the community and maintains an active partnership with many organizations that are committed to making our community better. Local partnerships include:

- The Great Kids Award—Annual Sponsor
- Young Entrepreneurs Academy Annual Angel Sponsor
- Utah Valley Chamber of Commerce member
- Women in Business Member
- Utah Manufacturer's Association member
- Wasatch Employer's Network member
- The local Society of Human Resource Managers (SHRM) Chapter

Zarbock is also involved in the humanitarian cause of building independence through enterprise (creating jobs) in Africa, Peru, Mexico, as well as locally. He currently sits as the chairman of Tifie Humanitarian (www.tifie.org.)

In his free time, he enjoys the outdoors and taking advantage of the great things Utah has to offer—from the mountains and deserts, to the beautiful canyons. Above all else, he enjoys helping the people who live here. When you love what you do, the fulfillment that brings spills over into every area of life.

For more information please visit Spherion online at www.spherion.com/Utah.

✧

Spherion owners, Ron and Jen Zarbock.

ELEVATE

As their business name suggests, Steve Anderson and Dan Vance promise to raise individual and organizational brands to new heights with a promise to "elevate your brand."

As experienced marketers, their team provides clients with a personal brand manager in addition to branding tools, which include a combination of promotional products, print, and design. Think event marketing, company stores, logos, creative thinking, branding strategy, and physical marketing such as screen printing, embroidery and custom apparel.

"We understand how important your brand is to your business," says Anderson, company CEO. "For us every client is a premier partner. With each project, we leverage our years of experience in promo, print, and design to give you creative solutions that work."

"We like to say, 'If you think it, we can brand it,'" adds Vance, president. "With Elevate you receive quick response time, headache-free ordering, on-time delivery, careful budgeting, quality products, and creative ideas."

Elevate takes company logos or brand designs and helps create a winning branding strategy. With a promise and a plan, an individual or corporate identity will have a recipe for success.

These Core Values drive Elevate to be the very best:
- The experience
- Let's talk
- Honesty
- Be the Solution
- Enjoy what you do
- Be the expert
- Know your clients
- Invest in your clients
- Surprise and delight

Elevate began out of necessity February 19, 2011. After several years of working together, Anderson and Vance found themselves part of a company downsizing. Rather than standing still, they saw an opportunity, so they retained a couple of great accounts, rented a room in Provo's Jamestown Square Business Park, and decided to create an exceptional promo business. When they brought Ricky Hacking on as marketing director, his first desk was a couch, and they all devoted their energies toward creating impressive ideas and notable products for their customers.

Within the first year they had acquired two Elevate branded trucks. In the years to follow they added a design team, added a website, acquired Moench Printing, and moved Elevate headquarters to Thanksgiving Point in Lehi, to better serve both Utah and Salt Lake Counties. By the end of year four, Elevate had grown from two guys in one room to a team of more than eleven brand managers serving thousands of brands!

Circumstances may have made it impossible for Elevate's founders to follow a beaten path, but so much the better. They created their own path and as part of their journey, they are working hard to plant their brand, and yours, into the hearts and minds of current and future customers.

Additional information is available on the Internet at www.elevatepromo.com.

For more than a century Bassett Home Furnishings has demonstrated how it is much more than your everyday furniture business, which is just as true for its Orem, Utah, location as it is for its 100 plus stores throughout the United States.

With skilled design consultants trained to take the guess work out of decorating, plus excellent craftsmanship and a well-earned reputation for quality custom furniture that can be made and delivered in thirty days or fewer, Bassett has a distinct advantage over its competition.

From the beginning, which began in the late 1800s in the foothills of Virginia's Blueridge Mountains, Bassett has offered a blend of style, comfort and value. The Bassett family ran the saw mill that supplied rail ties for the Norfolk & Western Line. With the completion of the line, the family needed new markets for its lumber. One of the Bassetts, traveling salesman John David (JD), began carrying lumber samples from the mill and made his first sale to a coffin company in North Carolina. On that trip JD learned there was a growing interest in solid wood furniture, which meant a growing demand for raw lumber.

He soon had orders for oak from several furniture companies in North Carolina. Factory orders soon expanded into New York and Michigan. JD began to think furniture could be made onsite in Henry County, Virginia, where he lived. So he and his brothers laid out a plan and opened the Bassett

Furniture Company in 1902. The company continued to grow, and at one time was the largest manufacturer of furniture in the United States.

Bassett places a huge emphasis on customized furniture. Customers can select a piece of furniture, pick from 1,000 fabric options, choose arm styles, back styles, and base options. Customers select the firmness of the cushioning plus add their flair of choice, such as nail heads and fringe.

"Domestic manufacturing allows us to make a particular piece just for you," says Rob Spilman, Bassett's CEO. "And we can tell customers they can have what they want. Our leaders like it, our reps like it, and it feels good doing it."

The Bassett belief that quality matters has made it one of the most recognizable brands in America. To personalize the buying experience, consultants help create custom furnishings, assist the customer in defining a decorating lifestyle, and establishing a budget. They will even make house calls, or simply offer an opinion...all free of charge.

"We invest our time, talent and resources into creating fresh living spaces," says Craig Werner, Orem's store manager/owner. "And we also believe a great makeover can bring smiles, comfort, and encouragement."

BASSETT HOME FURNISHINGS

✧

Bottom, left: Sutton customized furniture for the family room.

Bottom, right: Dublin is the customized collection for the bed and Harvest Bridle is the customized furniture for the bedroom.

RIVERSIDE COUNTRY CLUB

❖

Top: The Riverside Country Club with the golf course in the foreground and the impressive Wasatch Mountain range in the background.

Above: A warm and inviting conversation area inside Provo's Riverside Country Club.

Below: The meticulously maintained greens of the Riverside Country Club in Provo, Utah.

To look at the newly built, elegant Riverside Country Club today with its prestigious eighteen hole golf course that has hosted PGA, LPGA and other championship tournaments, as well as its impressive 42,000 square foot clubhouse and swimming pool complex, no one would suspect the creativity and determination it required to bring the prominent center to Utah Valley.

It started modestly enough as the Club Radar in 1945 on Springville Road as a social organization featuring excellent food and beverage service. Provo physician Robert Hammond considered a different possibility after visiting a colleague in Wenatchee, Washington, who took him to a country club for dinner with a view of the Columbia River. He thought, "Gee, Provo City is about the same size as Wenatchee…we ought to have a golf course and a country club and a place to sit like this when our friends come to town."

The idea percolated for a few years, and when the idea emerged at the Radar Club, Hammond jumped on it and became part of a committee to seek country club options.

They considered an inexpensive piece of property ultimately ruled unsatisfactory. They rejected some Mapleton farmland. They looked at Riverside, but because a train then traversed the property, they decided it would not work. Other properties looked appealing, but owners would not budge. Others would sell, but the asking price was too high. The committee went to the Salt Lake Country Club, and when they realized it cost $150,000 a year in water bills alone in 1956, the Riverside land looked more attractive with its many springs on the property.

Bits of land from different owners comprised the Riverside Country Club. A cornfield they needed had been an Indian camp in pioneer days. The land—free to the owner because his wife was Native American—became theirs after the committee provided the owners with a Lehi farm complete with hay, cows and house. They even got permission to shoot golf balls across the railroad tracks with a legal agreement that no one would sue if they got hurt. Club owners purchased furniture in exchange for having their names carved on a plaque on the furniture.

Riverside Country Club became a reality in 1960.

Newly remodeled, the stunning, full-service Pro Shop was voted Country Club Retailer of the Year in its first year of operation! Club amenities include dining facilities, private banquet and meeting rooms, a fitness facility with a massage treatment room, and a studio for Pilates, Zumba and Yoga classes, cardio and weight training, and first-class locker rooms. The pool area includes a 25 meter lap pool, 1 and 3 meter diving boards, a kiddie pool and splash pad.

Additional information is available on the Internet at www.riversidecountryclub.org.

Glen Ricks has experienced all aspects of life in Utah Valley, and he has done it through the lens of his camera.

Glen Ricks has photographed almost every board chairman for the Utah Valley Chamber of Commerce since Provo and Orem merged their chambers in the 1980s. He is a long time Rotarian. He served as head of photography for America's Freedom Festival at Provo for more than sixteen years. He has captured images of the winners of the Ernst and Young Entrepreneur of the Year award for nearly thirty years, and he has photographed most of the region's top CEOs.

Executives from well-known companies such as Franklin/Covey, Nu Skin, Do Terra, Merritt Medical, MonaVie, Intermountain Healthcare, Kneaders, and Little Giant Ladders and many others have benefited from Glen Ricks' considerable talents.

Equally important, are the families and individuals who have hired him. Ricks loves to help them create memories through family portraits, images of children, high school portraits, weddings and more. He specializes in large wall portraits.

Photography has been a lifelong passion. He caught the photography bug in Rexburg, Idaho, as a Boy Scout. He had a darkroom in his bedroom, and later moved it to a basement closet. Throughout high school and two years of college, he studied photography and worked for a local photographer as the main darkroom tech and camera salesman. By the time he came to Brigham Young University, he had advanced in his photography knowledge to the degree that there were few photography classes to challenge him—so he majored in business.

He open his first business as Ricks Photo Studio in 1979 out of his apartment; three years later he opened a store front in the Carillon Square in Orem. He remodeled it in 1991 and changed the name of his business to Glen Ricks Photography.

Ricks moved to his dream studio in 2002. It is a more than 100 year old Victorian home on Main Street in American Fork, and while he likes to take his clients to beautiful locations in Utah Valley, he also has a spacious camera room and portrait garden right on site. His passion is to create customized images that exceed customer desires. His portrait and wedding assignments have taken him as far away as Hawaii and Mexico City.

His beautiful work speaks for itself, but it also helps to be recognized by professional groups and peers. Glen Ricks is one of a handful of Utah photographers to hold the degrees of: Master Photographer, Photographic Craftsman, and Certified Professional Photographer. He has won many awards for photographic excellence, including the prestigious National Kodak Gallery Award.

Rest assured—you can trust Glen Ricks to capture those special times of your life in portraits.

GLEN RICKS PHOTOGRAPHY, INC.

✧

Above: Glen Ricks has been a professional photographer in Utah Valley for more than thirty-five years.

Below: Glen Ricks converted a more than 100 year old Victorian house in American Fork into his professional photography studio.

RUNNER'S CORNER

When Josh Lewis traveled from Colorado to visit family in Utah, he dropped off his suitcase and made a beeline for Runner's Corner in Orem. He planned to run a marathon and wanted owner Hawk Harper to help him with some pain issues.

"Hawk knew exactly what he was talking about, and his assistance far surpassed anything I have had from any other running store," he says. "He was personable and made me feel he had nothing better to do than work with me."

After specific guidance and some inserts, Lewis could run without pain.

"Hawk really gave me a leg up, so to speak." Lewis says.

This is a common reaction for customers who flock to Runner's Corner, a business Hawk and his wife Cheryl established twenty years ago to help runners have a better experience in their quest for fitness.

"We want others to feel the same kind of joy we get from running," Hawk explains. As the patriarch of what could arguably be called Utah's First Family of Running, the couple, their four children plus a daughter-in-law and son-in-law see the scenic wonders of Utah Valley from the perspective of running its hills, mountains, and trails.

Their store contains merchandise from apparel to sports nutrition. At the core, however, are the shoes. According to Cheryl, eighty-two percent of runners get foot injuries

because of shoes poorly designed for the structure of their specific feet. They can discern whether a foot has a tendency to roll to the inside or the outside; whether the runners are wearing shoes that tend to cause bunions; if the footwear makes the heel land first, contributing to plantar fasciitis; and other foot problems. Trained employees work carefully with customers until the correct shoe is identified for each individual.

An additional benefit to Runner's Corner is Learn to Run, an in-store class with demonstrations to correct foot placement while running. Clients are videotaped and their running is evaluated. Foot placement affects neuropathy, runners' knee, shin splints, and IT band (outside the knee pain), which can be corrected by proper running form. The Harper's spacious new Orem building has an indoor track and an outdoor running area so customers can practice running techniques and try shoes before purchasing them.

Devoted to the community, the Harpers sponsor several charity races and support the Food and Care Coalition as well as local Spike Nights when a whole team gets fitted while the store provides pizza.

The entire family holds running records evidenced by a home bulging with trophies and medals. Their focus, however, is sharing their considerable knowledge with others in a comprehensive, personalized way.

Runner's Corner is located at 835 South 77 East in Orem and at www.runnerscorner.com.

CHRISTOPHER ADAMS PHOTOGRAPHY

Chris Adams had his photography beginning influenced by his father at an early age. He would watch his father take photos using a 35mm Argus C3 camera using transparency slide film, then project the processed images on a large projector screen. The old "family vacation slide show" became a regular thing for the family, and Chris loved the large colorful images that came from Kodachrome film. As such, years later his favorite photography method is using a personally restored 1960s Graflex 4X5 field camera shooting on Velvia transparency film. This is a slow and thoughtful process, which is the best personal therapy for him. The new digital photo world of today is quick and easy, which he does use, but his passion lies in the artistry of true chemistry photography.

He grew up surrounded by artists, and was always encouraged to become involved with many hobbies. His mother is an award-winning oil and canvas painter, as well as a quilter and other home-spun arts. His older brothers always had interests in model building and mechanical work, musical instruments, woodworking, old cars and business entrepreneurial adventures. These many family influences have shaped Chris into what he has become today.

Chris has been a professional photographer since 1996. He has studied nature photography as well as portraiture, architectural work, and commercial photography. The majority of his success lies in photographing weddings and family portraits. He is a past member of the Intermountain Professional Photographers Association, as well as earning awards from the BYU Monte L. Bean Museum of Natural History and has served multiple years as chief photography judge for the American Fork Arts Festival Photo Contest.

He enjoys spending time outdoors with his wife of thirty-three years, and being involved with numerous hobbies. Almost anything he can do to build and create with his hands is what you will find him doing. He and his wife are the parents of three children and currently have four grandchildren. Chris can be reached at 801-380-1120 or via the web at www.chrisadamsphoto.com for information about weddings, family portraits or commercial work.

❖

Above: Christopher Adams.

✧

Right: Bridal Veil Falls adds to the scenery in Provo Canyon.

PHOTOGRAPHS COURTESY OF CHRISTOPHER ADAMS.

Christopher Adams
Photography 2007

Quality of Life

Healthcare providers, school districts, universities and other institutions that contribute to the quality of life in Utah Valley

CENTRAL UTAH SURGICAL CENTER

Many physicians looking for an alternative and more desirable way to care for their patients found their answer in Provo nearly twenty years ago when Central Utah Surgical Center opened its doors.

Since 1995, CUSC has provided a way for physicians, surgeons and patients to have a greater say in how they will work with each other—and healthcare professionals have more choices on how to conduct procedures and what resources to use.

Although fully accredited as an ambulatory service center by Medicare and the Joint Commission on Accreditation of Health Care, CUSC is free standing and does not affiliate with any hospital. That is one of its strengths. The medical team is at liberty to offer its own robust model of excellence.

At its core the Central Utah Central Center is about service and exceeding expectations, according to Jill Andrews, RN BSN CNOR, a hands-on administrator who has directed the facility since 1997.

"We benefit our community by working hard to ensure patient and physician satisfac-

tion. We work with all types of patients: self-pay, insured and uninsured," she says. "Additionally, we do whatever possible to help the patient and affiliate with several community care programs that help people with limited resources."

She recognizes that some insurance companies will only cover certain procedures through a hospital but emphasizes that when doctors have a choice, they choose Central Utah Surgical Center.

"We know there are other options for medical care, and we work hard to ensure that CUSC is the top choice," Andrews says.

And they are busy, working more than 1,000 cases a month. In 2014, for example, the Center finished 12,770 procedures. For the past three years, Andrews has attended the *Outpatient Magazine* OR Excellence meetings, an invitational event for the country's 100 busiest administrators of hospitals and ambulatory surgical centers.

To make it desirable for physicians to use CUSC, it is conveniently located at 1067 North 500 West across the street from Utah

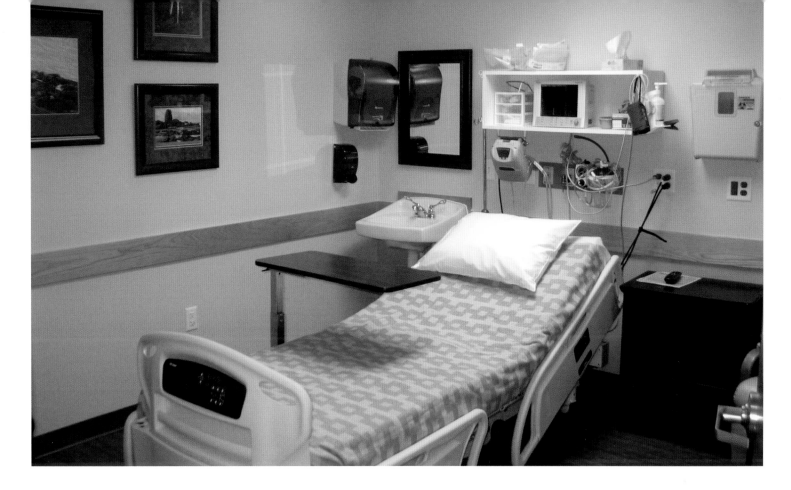

Valley Regional Medical Center and is within a twenty mile radius of four other hospitals. It also provides flexible hours for physicians and clients.

CUSC is a facility designed to provide the best in outpatient surgery, and is well equipped for such services as gastroenterology, orthopedics, hand surgery, ophthalmology, general surgery, ear, nose and throat procedures, urology, podiatry, gynecology, cosmetic and reconstructive surgery, oral surgery, pediatric dental surgery and pain management surgery.

In short, Andrews says, "We can handle any surgical need for a patient who does not require a hospital stay." And even then, the facility has a twenty-three hour stay option for patients who do not meet the criteria for going home immediately after surgery.

"It's very cost effective to use an outpatient facility," Andrews adds. "It is not uncommon to provide savings to the patient, insurance companies and government agencies, such as Medicare and Medicaid." Among the other bonuses is its one-stop shop approach that puts the administration and management on site. Answers come quickly when the coding, billing and insurance office is part of the surgical center.

An additional key to the CUSC's success is its personal touch.

"We have a culture of caring," Andrews says. "We are extremely careful about whom we hire and we seek employees whose overriding objective is exceptional patient care. Ours is a collaborative effort and it works. I surround myself with great people and great things happen."

Among the strengths is a hardy Infection Control program. Administrators meet quarterly with an infectious disease physician to discuss any issues in that department with him. The infection rate for the 2014 year was 0.042 percent. This statistic is well below the Centers of Disease Control national infection rate for hospitals, which a few years ago was 1.9 percent.

Central Utah Surgical Center gives tax dollars back into the county, and as a locally owned and operated business, CUSC employees believe what they offer is neighbors helping neighbors.

"As long as the operating rooms are booked and efficient and as long our physicians and patients are happy, Central Utah Surgical Center will remain the desired place for outpatient surgery," Andrews adds. The motto at Central Utah Surgical Center is "We measure our success by your satisfaction."

UTAH VALLEY UNIVERSITY

Student success is the heart of every program, and every class taught at Utah Valley University. The university's formula for promoting student success is a powerful combination of intellectual and professional seriousness, engaged learning experiences and an inclusive spirit of welcome for all.

UVU was founded in 1941 when the nation was slowly recovering from the Depression of the 1930s. The shadow of war was creeping closer, and the need for arms and ammunition by the Allied forces demanded skilled craftsmen. Many citizens had benefited from the federal work programs during the Depression but needed more training to qualify for better jobs. Vocational classes were taught at various shops and businesses throughout Utah and Heber Valleys under the direction of the State Vocational Office. In fall 1941, under the direction of Hyrum E. Johnson, those vocational training courses were moved to a central location in south Provo and named Central Utah Vocational School.

After World War II, ninety percent of the school's budget was lost with the cancellation of war production training funds and a bill introduced in the 1943 Utah Legislature to make the school a state-supported, two-year vocational school failed. Cutbacks followed with fewer classes offered until the college received a $50,000 operating costs appropriation for 1945-1947. The appropriation was strongly opposed by local two-year colleges and the two local universities because it posed a threat to the money they received from the Legislature. In 1947 the school was permanently funded as a state institution.

During the summer of 1945, Johnson was given a leave of absence. Following a short transitional period, Wilson W. Sorensen, the school's former purchasing agent, was appointed director. Sorensen was instrumental in obtaining a thirteen acre site for the school in Provo, purchased by Provo City, Utah County, and the four local school districts with the understanding that the state would finance new college facilities.

In 1952 the state appropriated $400,000 for the first phase of the Provo campus. Built in three phases and completed in 1963, the campus was designed for 1,200 students. In 1961 enrollment neared 1,000 students; by 1971, it increased to nearly 2,000.

Growth brought many changes. During the Sorensen years, the name of the College changed several times to reflect these dynamics. In 1963, it changed from Central Utah Vocational School to Utah Trade

Technical Institute. In 1967 it became Utah Technical College at Provo, and with this change, the college received authority to confer associate degrees. Space demands sent college officials searching for land, and 185 acres of farmland were purchased in southwest Orem adjacent to I-15. The first phase of the new campus used state and student funds for the first buildings and a $1.5 million federal grant for landscaping. This initial campus was dedicated in March 1977 with a business and administration building. A learning resource center and trades building were added as soon as the state made funds available.

In 1982, Sorensen retired after forty-one years, thirty-seven years as president. J. Marvin Higbee, former president of Snow College in Ephraim, Utah, was named third president. President Higbee broadened the college's image and scope by offering expanded educational opportunities to all facets of the community. In 1987 the Legislature changed the school's name to Utah Valley Community College to reflect this expanded mission.

Expansion efforts continued. Not only were major building projects initiated, but several education programs were also added to help keep pace with local demand. Higbee emphasized the need for community support of UVCC by focusing the involvement efforts of the Development Office, the Utah Valley Community College Foundation and the Alumni Association.

Kerry D. Romesburg was appointed president in 1988 and led the college into an era of incredible growth. President Romesburg analyzed student needs and directed his efforts toward filling those needs. The president

initiated the conversion of the college to a semester calendar, the first state school to do so, and also placed emphasis on international education, arts and humanities, and short-term training. UVCC became among the first community colleges to sign an exchange agreement with Soviet Russia. Additional exchange agreements were created with China, Hong Kong, Taiwan and Germany.

During President Romesburg's tenure from 1991 to 2002, student enrollment skyrocketed. Some 8,700 students walked the halls in 1991, while more than 23,000 were enrolled in 2002.

In 1992 the Utah System of Higher Education and the Board of Regents proposed an initial offering of four-year degrees at UVCC. Business Management, Computer Science and Information Systems, and Technology Management were the first three bachelor degree programs offered.

After noting the institution was growing and expanding its focus, the Board of Regents changed the name to Utah Valley State College in 1993.

The rest of the 1990s saw significant growth for the new state college. More bachelor degrees were added to the institution's offering plate, and by 2003 the total was thirty-three. More than fifty associate degrees were also offered, along with certifications, diplomas and concurrent enrollment programs.

The Center for the Study of Ethics was created in 1993, with an emphasis on training

✧

Top: Freshman Convocation where students and parents are welcomed to the UVU experience.

PHOTOGRAPH COURTESY OF UVU MARKETING.

Above: A convocation ceremony at Utah Valley University.

PHOTOGRAPH COURTESY OF UVU MARKETING.

✧

Top: UVU's unique Capitol Reef testing station in a Utah national park.

PHOTOGRAPH COURTESY OF UVU MARKETING.

Above: Engaged learning where every student is designed to leave with a resume is represented by this student conducting DNA research.

PHOTOGRAPH COURTESY OF UVU MARKETING.

ethical leaders. In 2001, UVSC was awarded the Theodore M. Hesbergh Award, a $30,000 cash prize rewarding innovative ethics curricula that inspired similar initiatives at other schools. In 1996 the David O. McKay Events Center for special events was completed and dedicated on the Orem Campus. UVSC, a member of the National Junior Collegiate Athletic Association, saw not only many Utah Valley athletic events but also many community trade shows, concerts and conferences. In January 1997 the single-game attendance record for an NJCAA team was set at 8,063 in the McKay Events Center.

The late 1990s and the early 2000s saw extensive campus construction. UVSC announced the Liberal Arts Building, and the Utah County Journal Building, on the southeast side of campus, was purchased and remodeled.

Other campus expansions included the Wasatch Campus in Heber City. In 2002, President Romesburg left for another administrative position and William A. Sederburg was

chosen as the fifth president of UVSC.

That same year, the school received provisional status in the NCAA Division I athletic competition. UVSC started D-I play in the 2003-2004 school year. A wrestling program was added and continues to be the only one of its kind in Utah. Other intercollegiate programs include men's baseball, basketball, cross country, golf, and track and field, and women's basketball, cross-country, golf, soccer, softball, track and field, and volleyball. A new baseball stadium was added in 2005. That year the former Vineyard Elementary School was remodeled to house the School of Education.

In September 2006 ground was broken for a library to be completed in 2008. In February 2007 the Utah Legislature unanimously voted to make Utah Valley State College a university on July 1, 2008. With the new name came a new mission and set of core values to guide the university in the future. The Capitol Reef Field Station opened in October 2008 as a unique learning facility within a national park.

In August 2008, President Sederburg officially resigned as president of UVU to fulfill new responsibilities as Commissioner of Higher Education in Utah.

Under President Sederburg's leadership, a strategic planning model was developed that aligned planning with budgeting and accountability. The number of bachelor degrees offered went from thirty-one in 2003 to fifty-eight in 2009. Today the university offers 66 bachelor degrees, 62 associate degrees, and 31 certificate programs. UVU began offering master degrees in the fall of 2008 with the Master of Education. In the fall of 2009, the Master of Nursing was added, and a Master of Business Administration was added in 2010.

In 2009, Dr. Matthew S. Holland became the university's sixth president. President Holland has established a reputation as a respected educator, savvy problem-solver and master communicator.

UVU was granted official NCAA Division I membership in 2009, after a seven year provisional process. UVU became a member of the Great West Conference and received three consecutive Commissioner's Cups for highest performance of all athletic teams. New facilities were added for track, soccer and softball. On 2013, UVU began a new era in the Western Athletic Conference.

President Holland realized the need for additional facilities with the burgeoning student population. In March 2010 the Utah Legislature approved funding for a Science Building, which was completed April 2012. Also approved were the Facilities Building, Noorda Theatre, Business Resource Center, expanded Wee Care Center, Student Life & Wellness Center, and Classroom Building.

The University made changes to the institution's schools and colleges with the move to university status, including: Woodbury School of Business, School of the Arts, School of Education, University College, College of Humanities & Social Sciences, College of Science & Health, College of Technology & Computing, and College of Aviation & Public Services.

During Holland's first year, he developed four themes—student success, inclusive, engaged, and serious. Holland was instrumental in UVU's designation as an All-Steinway School, the development of a Business Engagement Strategy, the addition of the Freshman Reading Program and Presidential Lecture Series, the implementation of a strategic enrollment management plan and strategic planning advisory council, the development of the University Project and the creation of the Women's Success Center and the Center for Global & Intercultural Engagement to support the institution's inclusive focus.

Structured enrollment was instituted fall 2012 to maintain UVU's historical role as an open admission institution while increasing the seriousness of the university experience. Enrollment in fall 2011 topped at 33,395 students.

"Utah Valley University is building a two-for-one institution that is without peer in its efficiencies while attracting an ever more accomplished faculty and producing an ever more dazzling set of students," says Holland. "The world does not quite know it yet, but UVU is one of the great educational success stories of the nation."

UVU is the provider of higher education for more Utahans than any other state institution, and remains steadfastly dedicated to student success. And today, it continues to serve as a critical driver of the region's academic, economics, and cultural activity.

✧

Above: With the only Division 1 soccer team in Utah, Utah Valley University's popular sport brings in capacity crowds.
PHOTOGRAPH COURTESY OF UVU MARKETING.

Below: Family Fun Fair, an alumni event that welcomes students, alumni and friends to campus each year.
PHOTOGRAPH COURTESY OF UVU MARKETING.

ALPINE SCHOOL DISTRICT

When the newly organized Alpine School District opened its doors a century ago, few would have predicted it would swell to become the largest school district in the state. It had fewer than 5,000 students districtwide and getting to school usually meant traveling in horse drawn wagons or perching on the top of hay bales in a farmer's truck.

Despite transportation challenges, school was a valued part in the lives of Utah County youth, and much of the credit goes to dedicated personnel from the Alpine School District.

"Clearly the organization of the Alpine School District was an important step in building a system that would ultimately strengthen the member communities, prepare the rising generation to be good citizens, develop an educated workforce, and promote the general welfare of residents within the district," says current Superintendent Vernon Henshaw.

Many things have changed since its May 16, 1915, creation but the constant that has characterized ASD for 100 years is an ongoing commitment to its students. This ideal even preceded the formal creation of the district as typified by former Superintendent C. W. Whitaker of American

Fork Public Schools, who wrote in 1914, "Not only does the thriving city of American Fork boast of being a leader in social and commercial life, but she is also justly proud of her school system, which she feels stands second to none in the state." Being the first city in Utah to adopt the 'Free School System,' her citizens, ever loyal to the educational cause, have spared neither effort nor means to keep in the forefront of educational advancement in our fair state.

The pride in the quality of North Utah County's education was sufficiently rooted that many residents opposed consolidating under the ASD umbrella. Yet most people accepted the move as proper.

In 1915, Orem, Lindon, Manila, American Fork, Lehi, Highland, Alpine and Cedar Fort comprised district borders that now include the newer cities of Cedar Hills, Saratoga Springs, and Eagle Mountain. Starting with a modest student population of 4,906, growth in the early years was limited—such as from 1919 to 1930 with an increase of only forty-four students, or during the years of the Great Depression. But a better economy, an influx of industries, superior teachers, and continuing community growth has given the district a robust environment that fosters excellence.

One of the first initiatives in the school district was to establish standards and educational programs with a sense of unity. Board members historically have supported professional growth for teachers, sound leadership, and a challenging curriculum. As a result, today ASD maintains a strong identity focusing on improving the lives of young people.

While showcasing 100 years of highlights has its challenges, the constants include growth, creative use of limited funds, and pride in achievement.

A certain sweetness characterizes some early events. Students participated in "Alpine Days" beginning in 1922. Every spring all senior high school students gathered at one campus for activities and athletic competitions. When the older students began participating in extracurricular events year round, the tradition remained, but "Alpine Days" became a junior high school activity.

The 1920s were fairly progressive and schools emerged as a primary source of community pride and activity. Three high schools opened, the district instituted a free immunization program, bus service began, and schools went from six years of elementary and six years of secondary learning to a model that included junior high school.

When the stock market crashed in November of 1929, however, schools were deeply affected by a decade of uncertainty. The Alpine School District was not immune and adapted the national philosophy of "use it up, wear it out, make it do, or go without." District resources were strained, but the district kept school doors open and welcoming.

As the 1930s began, the student population remained small. Several schools closed but some bright spots remained. Orem City created the family-friendly Sharon's Cultural Educational Recreational Association (SCERA) and the district launched a public summer kindergarten that eventually became part of the regular school program.

With the construction of Geneva Steel, an inland steel plant built during World War II, the tax base increased; this major employer provided a healthy income to local residents and spurred the local economy. The fear of the era was polio, and the district even shut down its schools at times because of the fear associated with the disease.

Utah Valley, with its elaborate American's Freedom Festival at Provo celebration every Fourth of July is known for its patriotism, but this was also evident in the Alpine School District in the 1940s—and beyond.

Dale Kirkham, Lehi High Class of 1943, reported that: "It was an unusual period of time. Everybody was patriotic. Everybody was buying war bonds, but money was tight. The lack of funds meant that the class did not get to have a yearbook, yet the class banded together to purchase one of the bonds in order to leave a class gift to the school. The bond matured ten years later and the class purchased an oil painting."

Major growth characterized the 1950s, reflecting the nationwide post-World War II baby boom. Several schools opened, ASD added driver's education courses, launched adult education classes, added French and Spanish to the curriculum, provided classrooms for children with disabilities, and upped the expectations for math and science courses. After the Soviets launched the *Sputnik* satellite into space, ASD and others received Utah Board of Education funds for the sciences to become competitive in the space race.

The 1960s ushered in many changes. Brick and mortar development continued, and eight new schools opened their doors. Among the innovations was team teaching in open classrooms. President Lyndon Johnson declared war on poverty by signing the Elementary and Secondary Education Act of 1965. This effort attempted to narrow the gap between privileged and underprivileged children, which teachers applauded.

The 1970s advances were dramatic. In a decade, ASD was named the second fastest-growing school district in Utah and student enrollment climbed from 17,742 to 26,969.

✧

Opposite, top: Built in 1910, the Cedar Valley School in Cedar Fort was one of about twenty schools in existence when Alpine District was formed in 1915.

Opposite, middle: ASD's first superintendent and board of education. Front row: Samuel I. Goodwin, Superintendent W. Karl Hopkins and Eli J. Clayson. Back row: Charles G. Johnson, George A. Goates, S. E. Bunnell and Alfred Anderson.

Opposite, bottom: Initially called the wolverines, students at Lehi High School suit up for the school's first football game in 1924. The mascot was later changed to the pelicans, and ultimately to the pioneers.

Above: Just two years after kindergarten became part of the regular school program in Alpine District, this picture was taken at Windsor Elementary School in Orem, in 1959.

Left: Susan McDonald and Brent Scear mix bread dough during a foods lesson for eight year olds at Greenwood Elementary School in American Fork.

✧

Above: Upper grade students stack up the slide in 1985 at Highland Elementary School.

Below: Students at Traverse Mountain Elementary School in Lehi learn to demystify computer science during "Hour of Code" in 2013.

The district added nine schools. A major acquisition was the purchase of Clear Creek outdoor education camp. Discovered by district supervisors who were transporting milk to a temporary facility south of Scofield, the buildings were part of the Mountain Fuel Company. Students learned about ecology, biology, geology and other subjects in an outdoor setting. The acquisition of Clear Creek was referred to as "one of the most exciting innovations in education in the last decade." (8/15/73 *Herald*)

Students, looking to the culture of rock and roll, challenged dress and hair codes. Girls finally were allowed to wear slacks, and hair length mandates were dropped in favor of the more general "well groomed and clean." Educational options expanded and included programs for students with disabilities, a young mother's high school, and an alternative high school.

This was a decade of innovative thinking with computers being introduced into the elementary schools in 1978. Other improvements included a Spanish Immersion program and school accreditation. The one constant was more students. With approximately 1,500 new students added to the district annually, two or three new schools were needed every year.

The district charted a course of excellence in the 1980s marked by attention toward improved curriculum, instruction, and parental involvement. The history of ASD has been characterized by limited operating funds offset by a great work ethic and spirit of volunteerism, exemplified by its Parent Teacher Association. In 1987 the Alpine District Region PTA received recognition for having the most volunteer hours in the State of Utah, exceeding 100,000 hours.

Student growth, school construction, and increased emphasis on literacy, especially reading and writing expanded in the 1990s. The district, through bonds, a leeway and donations, built a much needed district office.

Student success and employee satisfaction were hallmarks of the 1990s. Certainly, increased emphasis on technology and continued efforts to provide educational services for students with disabilities were critically important.

The district maintained the distinction through the decade as one of the fastest growing but least funded districts in the nation.

Student growth in the 2000s doubled from that of the 1990s—an upsurge of nearly 20,000 students. Population increases meant building nineteen new schools, as well as renovating older ones. Yet, ASD grew in more ways beyond numbers. Teachers had opportunities for unprecedented professional learning targeted at increasing student achievement. Despite significant outside pressures, such as high-stake testing (under the No Child Left Behind Legislation of 2002), competition for student enrollment (with the increase in charter schools), and reduction in funds (resulting from the recession of 2008), the dedicated members of the ASD team emerged with a focus on student learning and well-being.

Today, a culture of K-12 collaboration, with an emphasis on student learning, is a hallmark. What else would explain ten consecutive years (2003-2013) of steady increases in the percentage of students passing year-end language, math, and science tests?

The magazine, *District Administration*, compared Utah's three largest school districts in 2011 (Alpine with 68,275 students, Granite with 67,736, and Davis with 67,736) with their largely urban New York counterparts, which are more than 2,000 miles away and a world apart in per-pupil spending. The report concluded, "While the Utah districts annual per-pupil expenditures are barely a third of New York's districts, they have achieved some impressive results—from graduation rates between eighty-five to ninety-two percent, to AP scores that rank in the nation's first quartile, to a spate of innovations designed to get more bang for their limited bucks."

For 100 years, Alpine School District has made a significant return on the biggest investment made by its communities, embodied in the mission statement: "Educating all students to ensure the future of our democracy." Countless educators have helped prepare young people for productive, responsible roles in families and society. "Our communities created public schools to develop citizens and to sustain our democracy," writes Diane Ravitch. "That is their abiding purpose. This unique institution has the unique responsibility of developing a citizenry, making many peoples into one people, and teaching our children the skills they need to prepare for work and further education" (2013). Continued staff development and partnership with families will ensure that Alpine School District helps prepare students into the next century and beyond.

✧

Above: Caitlin Sorensen and friends cheer on the Bruins of Mountain View High School in Orem in 2014.

Below: Orem Junior High School principal Joe Jensen fist bumps students at lunchtime in 2013. OJH is one of twelve schools in the district to receive federal Title I funding to help close the achievement gap.

TIMPANOGOS REGIONAL HOSPITAL

The short history of Timpanogos Regional Hospital is punctuated by continuous change and challenge. Named after the towering mountain that dominates the landscape, Timpanogos Regional Hospital opened its doors January 28, 1998, and as the hospital's reputation grew, so did its services.

It was evident from the start that the hospital was undersized in Women's Services. The facility—projected to perform thirty deliveries per month—achieved that number the very first week! The first expansion moved the nurses' lounge to create an additional patient care room.

In 2000 a cardiac catheterization lab with its resultant service line opened. In 2005 a dedicated cardiovascular operating room, open heart surgery, and cardiac rehabilitation capabilities further expanded cardiac service. A year later Women's Services added a fourteen bed postpartum wing and a five bed Newborn Intensive Care Unit (NICU). A second cardiac catheterization lab was purchased in 2008, and electrophysiology services began in 2009.

To accommodate growing services and to match the community standard of private rooms, the hospital added a third and fourth floor. During this addition, the second floor was remodeled to include a second intensive care wing. In total, fifty-eight beds were added; increasing the total bed count in 2009 to 105. In 2011 the Level III NICU expanded to total twenty-four beds.

Timpanogos also remodeled operating room suites in 2013 to better accommodate robotic surgical capabilities. It has become the fourth largest employer in Orem with 600 plus employees.

Above all else, Timpanogos Regional Hospital is committed to the care and improvement of human life. To deliver high-quality, cost-effective healthcare, Timpanogos Regional Hospital offers a vast array of services.

Expert cardiologists consult and evaluate using advanced diagnostic and therapeutic techniques in the following areas:

- Stroke
- Coronary heart disease and disorders
- Heart failure
- Open heart surgery
- Heart attack and chest pain
- Electrophysiology (EP Lab)
- Peripheral vascular disease
- Cardiac cath lab

We work closely with local paramedics to receive 12-Lead EKGs, allowing us to better serve patients. When a 12-Lead is received, our team acts even before the patient arrives. As a result, we are the only Utah County hospital system with the Chest Pain Center accreditation. Timpanogos Regional Hospital has been recognized with a disease specific certification in AMI and as a Center of Excellence in AMI Care by The Joint Commission.

Timpanogos Regional Hospital specializes in Women's Services and cares for high-risk, premature and "well baby" deliveries. It delivers more than 2,000 babies per year. We welcome all types of birth plans. The Labor & Delivery unit maintains a quiet atmosphere for mothers to enjoy their new infants in peace.

The NICU offers services for babies born at twenty-four weeks gestation and older and can deliver babies as small as a pound and a half. The NICU offers twenty-four beds with state-of-the-art technology (HeRO Monitoring System, body cooling) to allow physicians to better treat the tiniest patient.

The pediatric unit uses the HUGS security monitoring for medical and surgical pediatric patients 0 to 18 years. Pediatric patients are cared for by pediatricians, family practice physicians, and surgeons. Common diagnosis are respiratory illness, gastroenteritis, and dehydration, and appendectomy. Babies 0-3 months needing ICU level care for medical issues can be admitted to the NICU by the neonatology staff.

Our pediatric unit is decorated to the delight of children, and our dedicated pediatric all-RN nursing staff (supported by expert ancillary employees [RT, Radiology, etc.]), give exceptional care to each patient. In addition, areas of the ED, SDS, radiology and lab are geared to treat our smallest patients.

Timpanogos Regional Hospital offers the most advanced equipment and highly trained radiologists. The result—faster imaging exams, more accuracy, and low radiation doses. We offer a dedicated Women's imaging area for mammography, bone density, ultrasound as well as biopsy for maximum convenience. It also offers expertise in the areas of:

- CT
- Nuclear medicine

With a goal of greater results, smaller incisions, and faster recoveries, we provide consultative and surgical services for out-patients and inpatients and offer advanced surgical technologies in:

- General surgery
- Neurosurgery & spine
- Orthopedics, including joint replacement
- Urology
- Open heart
- Minimally invasive procedures using the Da Vinci surgical robot

Timpanogos Regional Hospital is proud of its excellent patient care track record. The healthcare facility annually earns national and state recognition from third party healthcare ratings. They include:

- Hospital Accreditation; Top Performing Hospital–The Joint Commission

- 4 Disease Specific Certifications–The Joint Commission
  - Prematurity
  - Spine surgery
  - Acute myocardial infarction
  - Primary stroke center
- Accredited Chest Pain Center–Society of Cardiovascular Patient Care
- Grade "A" Hospital Safety Score–The Leapfrog Group (only Utah hospital to achieve)
- GWTG Gold Plus Quality Achievement Award for Stroke Care–American Heart Association
- Level IV Trauma Certification–State of Utah
- Patient Safety Excellence Award–Healthgrades
- 5-Stars for Maternity Care–Healthgrades
- Maternity Excellence Award–Healthgrades
- Ranked among the top fifteen percent nationally and five-star rated for stroke treatment
- Consistently ranked among top hospitals nationwide in achieving zero vascular complications and treating coronary blockages (American College of Cardiology)

In 2015 Truven Health Analytics identified Timpanogos Regional Hospital as one of the Top 100 Hospitals in the United States.

✧

Clockwise, starting from the top:

Nurse and newborn.

An MRI machine is prepared to scan patients and determine the severity of certain injuries.

Patient is readied for a CT scan, (also known as a cat scan.)

Timpanogos employee is working in the cath lab.

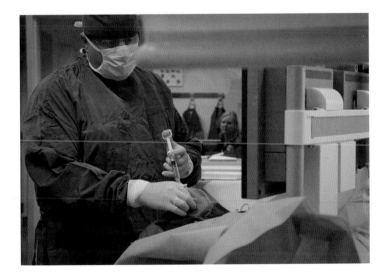

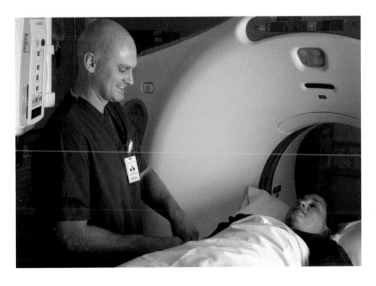

MOUNTAIN VIEW HOSPITAL, MOUNTAINSTAR HEALTHCARE

✧

Above: Mountain View Hospital.

Below: A mother enjoys her newborn in the maternity ward at Mountain View Hospital.

Bottom, left: A patient receives conscientious orthopedics care at Mountain View Hospital.

Bottom, right: Part of the Mountain View Hospital medical team working in the Cath Lab.

Mountain View Hospital in Payson, Utah, honors its commitment to the care and improvement of human life by treating every patient as if he or she is a close family member. It combines the warmth of a small town feel with the sophistication of a modern, up-to-date medical center.

Hospitals are complex organizations, and it takes an entire team to provide great care. The medical staff and employees at Mountain View Hospital work together to provide the highest quality healthcare possible. From independent physicians who determine the best course of treatment and the volunteer who greets you at the door to the highly trained nurses in ICU, the entire team at Mountain View Hospital collaborates to provide an excellent facility. The combination of a first-rate staff of physicians, the latest technologies, and homegrown compassion is the key to Mountain View Hospital's success.

Payson's first hospital opened in 1914 by local physician, A. L. Curtis and his wife, Annie. Soon, the hospital contained fifteen beds with two physicians. In 1922 a tonsillectomy was provided for five dollars, and the delivery of a baby cost thirty dollars. The hospital was able to break even with the help of the local Relief Society ladies of The Church of Jesus Christ of Latter-day Saints, who canned fruit and vegetables and assisted with the preparation and serving of patient meals.

In 1936, Payson City built a thirty-five bed hospital at the urging of Dr. Curtis. The hospital expanded over time to serve the needs of a growing population. In 1977, HCA purchased the facility and began construction of a new ninety-four bed hospital east of town that became known as Mountain View Hospital. Its name was a natural choice, because most patient rooms have a commanding view of the surrounding Wasatch Mountains. Subsequent expansions have increased inpatient capacity to its current level of 124 beds.

Mountain View Hospital now provides all the state-of-the-art services expected of a twenty-first century facility. It has won multiple awards and accreditations, being chosen nationally as one of only 147 Joint Commission-accredited hospitals recognized as a Top Performer on Key Quality Measures™ for four consecutive years. It has also achieved the Maternity Care Excellence Award for three consecutive years (Healthgrades 2012-2014). It is ranked among the top ten percent in the nation for Maternity Care (Healthgrades 2012-2014). Mountain View Hospital also achieved the Health Insight Quality Award for six consecutive years (2009-2014). In 2013, Mountain View Hospital was designated as an Accredited Chest Pain Center (Society of Cardiovascular Patient Care 2013). It is certified as a Receiving Facility for both Trauma and Stroke by the Utah Department of Health. Additionally, it won the Get With The Guidelines-Stroke, GOLD PLUS Achievement Award from the American Heart Association.

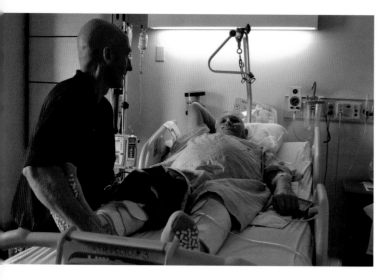

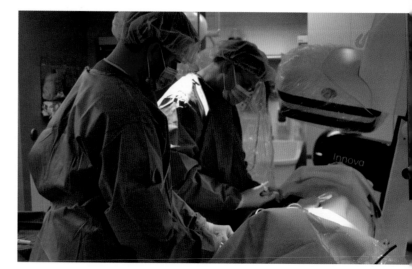

Jeff Anderson, CFO of Center for Change in Orem, had his first exposure to eating disorders when he got married. The stress of being accepted by a new person in her life, when there had been so much rejection and abuse in her history, pushed his new wife quickly down the road into an eating disorder. "It took her years to trust that I was committed to her and wouldn't leave her or hurt her," he explains. "I felt helpless at times as I'm sure she did."

When she was securely on the path to recovery, Jeff knew they needed to be involved in this work by doing what they could to help others suffering with this disorder.

"Eating disorders present a beautiful and significant challenge," says Dr. Michael Berrett of Center for Change. "You don't know where it's going to land. What you do know, is you're going to do your best to give 100 percent and hope like crazy the clients will match it, so that working together they will be able to get better. I learned to love these clients and to relate to them, and I have been taught by them. I've been doing it for thirty years."

Founded in 1994, the leaders at Center for Change know that an eating disorder is a complex illness, but with the right kind of treatment most can transcend the illness.

The Center offers Inpatient, Residential, Intensive Day and Evening Programs, Independent Living, and Outpatient Programs. All treatment starts with an extensive evaluation and assessment of each patient's strengths, struggles, and needs. Treatment Plans from the assessment create a road map to help clients transcend illness and reach their needs, goals, and their deepest desires. They "get their life back!"

All treatment is focused on breaking self-defeating patterns, overcoming eating disorders, becoming physically, emotionally, and socially healthy, improving body image, improving self-image, setting goals, facing fears, finding internal peace, preventing relapse, and living life to the fullest.

In December 2005, Center for Change was acquired by Universal Health Services, Incorporated, with headquarters in King of Prussia, Pennsylvania. Three of the original founders, Michael Berrett, psychologist, assumed the role of CEO, Jeff Anderson, a businessman, became the CFO, and Julie Clark, psychologist became a clinical director.

Center for Change continues its mission to help those suffering find recovery and healing "from the inside out." The message, "A Place of Hope and Healing," can be found woven through the entirety of the treatment experience, which has provided help and healing for so many clients over the years.

For additional information on Center for Change, visit www.centerforchange.com.

✧

Above: For twenty years the Center for Change has achieved significant success battling eating disorders.

Left: The courtyard view at the Center for Change.

Below: The beautiful Wasatch Mountain range is reflected in the back windows of the Center for Change building.

LEHI CITY

With an enviable business climate and rock-hard family values nested solidly among a range of ruggedly beautiful mountains overlooking the landscape, it is no accident Utah Valley is often cited as one of the most favorable places to live anywhere. And it is also no accident that Lehi City sits at the center of that praise.

Lehi has become the heart of Utah's "Silicon Slopes," so nicknamed because of an abundance of high technology companies such as Adobe, IM Flash, Microsoft, Xactware, and Oracle that have situated their businesses in Lehi and employ thousands of residents from Lehi City and throughout Utah. It is the fifth fastest-growing city in the United States and is estimated to nearly triple its population of 54,382 in the next fifty years.

At the same time, a drive through the historic downtown district of the city will show small town business loyalty with small town charm. Many descendants of settlers more than a century-and-a-half-ago still call Lehi home. Even some of its enterprises are open for business at the same location. Broadbent's, a gift and goods store started by Sarah Broadbent, for example, has operated in Lehi for more than 100 years. Porter's Place, a decades-old dining establishment, gives a nod to the late Orrin Porter Rockwell—a legendary figure in Mormon folk lore and body guard of that faith's first prophet, Joseph Smith.

Lehi's spirit of community is typified by activities that bring together new and established residents alike. Winter features a snowman building contest and polar plunge in the chilly waters of Utah Lake (to support Special Olympics). In summer residents enjoy Foam Day, a Pioneer Day celebration that cools people down with spraying foam and free watermelon. A longstanding Lehi summer tradition is the Lehi Roundup Rodeo, which preserves Lehi's Western traditions. A touch of small town America remains in this growing, sophisticated city.

In 1996 the northwest end of the city began its explosive growth that continues today. The growth began with the construction of Thanksgiving Point, a nonprofit family learning organization. The complex contains museums, restaurants, gardens, classes, a movie complex and interesting one-of-a-kind shopping options and activities. In fewer than twenty years it has become a major city landmark.

Lehi's current growth represents quite a change from a settlement incorporated in 1852 and named after a prophet in the Book of Mormon. Lehi's settlers felt that just like Lehi—a prophet who led his family from place to place—they, too, had moved often. Lehi's pioneers found sagebrush-covered landscape intermingled with greasewood, bunchgrass, sunflowers and Indian paint brushes. Meadow grass, cane brakes and rushes surrounded Utah Lake. And few except historians remember anything about the unusual smell of the water that led to it being dubbed Sulphur Springs, or that the Overland Stagecoach Route, the Pony Express Trail or that the Transcontinental Telegraph all passed through or near Lehi during the peak of their use.

Water access made population and economic growth possible. A seven mile water canal, dug from the mouth of nearby American Fork Canyon, helped farmers produce viable corn and wheat crops, and eventually led to a highly successfully sugar beet industry from which molasses was made. Twenty years after Lehi was incorporated, the Utah Southern Railway built tracks through Lehi, which opened up business opportunities.

The town experienced some lingering flavor of the Wild West when war erupted after

Lehi's Main Street retains much of the charm of a small town despite its development as a major business center.

Native Americans were killed south of the city, in Springville. The Lehi Militia was called to arms in support of what became known as the Walker War. Lehi even built a fort in the center of town, and one of its canons, an artifact of the conflict, now sits in a Salt Lake City museum.

Throughout its history, Lehi has believed in shaping its future with an enterprising spirit while preserving a vibrant family-oriented and business-friendly environment.

To support this dynamic community and manage its vigorous growth, Lehi City is a full-service organization with a budget of nearly $122 million that provides vital services to its residents and businesses. These services include:

- Administrative services providing leadership and support for the city's operations;
- Legal services to execute proper legal affairs of the city in civil, criminal, and risk management matters;
- Planning department to ensure that the city's general plan, development code and design standards are adopted and followed;
- Development services department that helps facilitate the city's economic development;
- Public works that supervise water, parks, and streets;
- Leisure services that offers recreation, library, literacy center, senior services, and museum opportunities to the city's residents and surrounding areas;

- A full-time fire and police department to ensure public safety; and
- A power department that provides electricity to Lehi's residents and businesses.

"Lehi has always represented the best of each generation," says Mayor Bert Wilson. "Today high tech companies from across the nation have come to embrace our lifestyle of opportunity and optimism. With plenty to entertain, enlighten, and inspire, Lehi is a place for families today and tomorrow."

✧

Above: A look at Lehi City with its farming heritage in the foreground, business in the center, and new residential development in the rear is typical of the rapid growth the city is undergoing.

Below: Thanksgiving Point has become a destination place for shopping, museums, movies, abundant gardens, golfing, hands-on adventures, and more.

UTAH VALLEY REGIONAL MEDICAL CENTER

❖

Above: Utah Valley Regional Medical Center began as a modest community hospital in the late 1930s.

Below: As a major medical facility, Utah Valley Regional Medical Center is the only designated Level II Trauma Center south of Salt Lake City, and serves as the regional tertiary-care referral center for all of central Utah and much of southern Utah.

More than seventy-five years ago, Utah Valley took a giant step forward in providing professional healthcare for Central Utah southward when Utah Valley Hospital opened its doors September 10, 1939, with 55 beds, 12 bassinets, and 38 physicians.

The entire state had a pressing need for better medical facilities. Utah had only three small county hospitals, and seeing a specialist meant traveling to Salt Lake City—a considerable distance, particularly for rural areas where patients had to travel state roads in the pre-freeway era.

Today, Utah Valley Regional Medical Center is licensed for 395 beds and has a medical staff of more than 600 physicians. UVRMC is recognized as the only designated Level II Trauma Center south of Salt Lake County and serves as the regional tertiary-care referral center for all of Central Utah and much of Southern Utah. Other areas of excellence include heart and vascular services, the newborn intensive care unit, cancer services, and stroke services. Included are such specialty areas as emergency, critical care, neurosurgery, women's and children's services, diabetes management, weight loss surgery, diagnostics imaging, psychiatric services, medical air transport, speech, hearing and balance, family medicine, hyperbaric medicine, and the Utah Valley Rehabilitation Center.

Maturing from a modern, but modest facility in 1939, to a major medical center today occurred in stages in response to the growth of the valley. In 1943 an average of three babies was born in the hospital each day. By the middle of April 1944, the hospital had accepted its 10,000th patient. With the addition of Geneva Steel and other industrial businesses, population in the Provo area exploded in the mid- to late-1940s, and it soon became apparent that the hospital needed to expand.

Construction of a much-needed addition was completed in December of 1950, and the hospital bed count rose to 112. In 1953 the hospital's board of directors approved the transfer of ownership to The Church of Jesus Christ of Latter-day Saints, which meant a name change to Utah Valley Hospital of The Church of Jesus Christ of Latter-day Saints.

A growth spurt in 1958 prompted new services and treatments. The bed count increased to 160, and the facility added five new operating rooms, four emergency rooms, an x-ray therapy room, and a pharmacy. The medical staff increased to seventy-five. This reflected the growing population, to be sure, but it also meant that specialties were being added to provide more comprehensive medical care. For example, the first cornea transplant took place December 1, 1956. In 1969 the hospital opened a new laboratory, and by 1975, the department performed at least one million tests annually. At the same time, the hospital opened an emergency center, increased the beds in coronary intensive care and expanded the surgical wing. The hospital's first neurosurgeon arrived in 1975, and with 260 beds filling the facility, it was clear a major expansion was in order.

In 1974, The Church of Jesus Christ of Latter-day Saints donated its extensive hospital holdings to the community, and Intermountain Healthcare was created. The LDS Church had two stipulations—it would become a model healthcare organization, and it would remain a not-for-profit entity providing care for all. Groundbreaking ceremonies took place at UVRMC on October 7, 1975, for a seven-story tower completed in 1978. Bed capacity reached 389 beds.

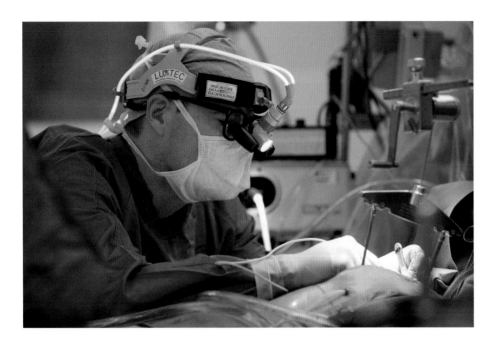

Utah Valley Regional Medical Center (its new name in 1984) began fulfilling its promise as a major medical center. Open-heart surgeries were added, the first oncologist arrived, and an updated CT scanner and other equipment were added. The West Building opened in the late 1990s, providing much needed space for Newborn Intensive Care, Labor and Delivery, Mother/Baby, and the Intensive Care Units. In 2005 the South Building added room for a hyperbaric chamber and allowed many support services to come together in one location. The Outpatient Center was completed in 2008, creating a new space for same-day surgery as well as out-patient services such as imaging and laboratory.

The hospital's Newborn Intensive Care Unit is the largest in the state. This facility knows how to take care of its precious little ones. More than 4,000 infants are born here annually, and in one unprecedented year, 6,206 babies took their first breaths at UVRMC.

Approximately 3,300 people work for the medical center, making it one of the largest employers in Utah County. It has kept its promise to extend services regardless of a patient's ability to pay, and from 1990 to 2014, Utah Valley Regional provided $222,365,000 in charity care.

As administrators and hospital leaders look toward the future, it is evident that as the population continues to soar, it must assist the needs of a growing region. Looking ahead for another seventy-five years, UVRMC is preparing to replace the existing seven-story tower and other aging buildings. The replacement project is set to begin in mid-2015 and be completed in 2018.

Although the changes from 1939 to today are considerable, one message has remained constant: the mission of Utah Valley Regional Medical Center is and always has been to help people live the healthiest lives possible.

✧

Above: The quality of medical care in Utah Valley during the past seventy-five years can be measured in part, by substantial additions to its surgical staff and their diverse specialties.

Below: A mother and nurse share in the joy of a healthy newborn at Utah Valley Regional Medical Center.

PROVO CITY POWER

On April 1, 1940, Provo City Power began electrical generation as its own public power utility. It was a pivotal moment in Provo's history and was a turning point in the economic development for the City of Provo.

Although there was electricity available during the late 1800s and early 1900s, electricity was a luxury item that not everyone could afford. In 1916 the only electrical provider along the Wasatch Front was Utah Power & Light (UP&L). At that time, electricity was in the process of becoming not the plaything or luxury of the rich, but a potential necessity within the reach of all consumers.

In 1939, Mayor Anderson (who became the mayor in 1935 for four consecutive terms) along with the work and dedication of several committees made up of Provo citizens won a seven year legal battle in the Supreme Court that ruled in favor of Provo to own and operate what is known as "Provo Power." The mayor and committees worked tirelessly conducting several surveys, investigating financial options, and petitioned residents to sign and vote for public power to overcome major opposition and lawsuits from private investor-owned companies.

So what does having public power actually mean? Public power is:
- Locally owned
- Locally controlled
- Reliable electrical service
- Competitive rates

A testament in history of what the vision of public power was supposed to be, Judge Ballif is quoted as saying: "I am of the opinion that voters of Provo are in a position to, and should declare what they want for themselves without interference at least from this court."

Another major benefit of public power is the reduced tax burden. Profits are not paid to private investors or stockholders, rather annually, Provo City Power transfers eleven percent of revenues (about $6 million dollars) to the City of Provo for the use in city services including police and fire, city infrastructure and equipment. Without the annual transfer, taxes would have to be raised to help cover the costs associated with running the city and having resources available.

History has played a huge part in the success of Provo City Power, but we also recognize the employees of Provo City Power who have contributed immensely in that success as well. There is a sense of pride and ownership by all employees, board members and city leadership.

Provo City Power celebrates providing competitive, reliable public power to the residents and businesses of Provo for over seventy-five years.

Right: Provo City Power Plant, c. 1949.

Below: Current Peaking Power Plant for Provo Power. The smoke stacks were decommissioned over twenty years ago.

PHOTOGRAPH COURTESY OF BRAYDON BALL.

"Welcome Home"—a heartfelt expression of a community connecting with newcomers, residents and businesses alike. A place where people feel at home!

Provo, the third largest city in the state, has a population of 115,000. The area is also home to 60,000 university students attending both Brigham Young University (BYU) and Utah Valley University (UVU). These institutions are catalysts to Provo's startup business environment with their entrepreneurship and innovation classes. The entrepreneurial spirit is robust and startups are encouraged and nurtured. Resources like Google Fiber give startups a competitive edge.

In March 1849, Mormon Prophet Brigham Young called some early Utah pioneers to establish a settlement near Utah Lake. These pioneers built Fort Utah along the banks of the Provo River and over time the fertile valley was teeming with commercial, social, industrial and cultural activity. Two markers of development were the cooperative stores set up on the east and west ends of the Center Street commercial district and the Provo Woolen Mills, the largest woolen mill in the west in the early 1900s.

Downtown Provo has combined the quaint atmosphere of retail and commercial business of the past with forward thinkers and entrepreneurs of the future. Renovations to the late nineteenth and early twentieth century buildings downtown keep the feeling of historic Provo. Even as tech startups, coding campuses, and other local entrepreneurial minds have found a niche on the second and third floors of those buildings, Downtown also boasts fifty-three independently owned, unique restaurants, including Station 22, Black Sheep Café, Mamacitas, Communal and Slate.

Downtown is experiencing a resurgence of growth and vitality. Notable additions to the downtown skyline are the Nuskin Innovation Center, Provo City Center Temple, 63 East Condos, the Utah Valley Convention Center and Provo City Recreation Center. The 100 block on University Avenue offers a music night scene highlighting the home grown, nationally acclaimed talent of the valley such as The Strike, Neon Trees, Fictionist, Joshua James and Ryan Innes. A storefront lineup of big draw venues guarantees large crowds and hubs of activity on most weekends.

The new Frontrunner Station offers convenient travel up and down the Wasatch Front and connects to light rail lines throughout the Salt Lake Valley. Provo Airport provides access to regional hubs including Los Angeles, Oakland/San Francisco and Mesa/Phoenix through scheduled air service. Duncan Aviation continues expanding its full-service corporate jet and aircraft maintenance facility.

From the center of Provo, you are ten minutes from a lake or a canyon, fifteen minutes from a ski resort, and three to four hours from five national parks.

✦

Above: The Strike, performing at The Shop at Riverwoods.

Below: Downtown—the Heart of Provo.
COURTESY OF BRYANT LIVINGSTON PHOTOGRAPHY, 2014.

PROVO CITY SCHOOL DISTRICT

Since 1890, Provo City School District has been responsible for the education of Provo's children. It is a responsibility that is taken with much thought and care. All work in the district is undertaken with students in mind.

In January 2010 it was determined that Provo City School District would develop a plan that would drive education efforts in the district for the next decade. The intent would be to create a plan that will deliver

superior performance, have a distinctive impact and will achieve lasting endurance. Most importantly, the desire to deliver exceptional results will be framed by two simple words: CHILDREN FIRST.

The resulting 20/20 Initiative is the first of its kind in the State of Utah. This is a forward-thinking approach that has and will continue to enhance the Provo City School District school system, create the best learning environments and give students the best education absolutely possible.

The 20/20 Initiative provides a set of guiding principles that all district employees implement into their job duties. These guidelines directly contribute to the success of the education of each of our students.

Excellence—We are absolutely and unequivocally dedicated to highly effective teaching with superior learning outcomes. We have high expectations for the adults who lead, support, and teach our students, as well as for student learning. We strive for excellence in all areas of our organization.

Partnerships—We believe the educational needs of children can best be met through a strong partnership with families. We welcome families into their children's schools, and encourage and expect their full participation in the education of their children. In addition, we believe strong community partnerships strengthen our schools.

Individual Potential—We believe all children have potential. We believe this potential is magnified when children and adults are treated with dignity and respect, are motivated by interest and engagement, and are given broad opportunities to develop their talents and gifts.

- Advocacy—We cherish all children and will advocate for their inclusion in the full spectrum of educational and developmental opportunities.
- Thinkers and Learners—We believe our increasingly complex future requires us to expect and encourage the development of individuals as thinkers, learners and problem solvers. This is essential to being part of the human conversation. Life-long learning is essential for all members of our educational community.

- Literacy—We believe literacy, the ability to effectively read, write and communicate in all content areas, is the gateway to critical thinking, reasoning, and problem solving, and therefore deserves our focused attention at every level of the district.
- Civic Engagement—We believe a primary purpose of public education is to prepare students to govern themselves and contribute to the vitality of our community and nation. We hold this public trust sacred. We will model and cultivate integrity and reasoned discourse. We will expect mutual trust, respect, civility, and humility in our interactions.
- Climate and Safety—We believe a school's climate can have a powerful effect on the behavior and performance of teachers and students. Children learn and teachers teach best in a safe environment.

In alignment with the 20/20 initiative, Provo City School District consistently strives to focus on anything that will enhance student achievement and learning. This takes commitment from each administrator, teacher and staff member. While not 100 percent comprehensive, this commitment has resulted in:

1. A strong focus on student safety and school security. Provo City School District has formed a Safety and Security Committee to continually evaluate all aspects of safety and security in its schools.
2. A strong focus on financial transparency. The business office of Provo City School District has consistently been nationally recognized by the Governmental Finance Officers Association and the Association of School Business Officials.
3. A strong focus on technology. Technology is the future of education and Provo City School District is working hard to provide its students with the technology they need to be successful.
4. A strong focus on capital needs. Provo City School District addresses the challenges presented by old buildings and ever changing building requirements.
5. A strong focus on student learning. The Teaching and Learning Office of Provo City School District provides support, training

and professional development to teachers, administrators and parents with the goal of enabling students to gain the academic knowledge and skills necessary for success in their careers and in college.

6. A strong focus on student health and well-being. The Child Nutrition Program of Provo City School District has been honored with the Best of State award for five consecutive years (2010-2014).

The work and improvements do not end. It is a continuous effort to make the education of Provo's students successful and rewarding. Provo City School District is committed to excellence in all facets of education. It is a job that must be done in order for students to achieve the maximum from their education. Provo City School District has that job in mind with everything it undertakes.

United Angels Foundation

✧

Above: United Angels Foundation's largest annual advocacy event is their annual Walk With Angels day.

Below: Chantelle Bailey and her son Sebastian who has cerebral palsy at a Walk With Angels event.

When their daughter Aubrey was born, Mark and Amber Leck were only in their early twenties and had every reason to expect a perfectly healthy firstborn child. Despite having all the routine prenatal examinations and tests, no one detected their baby was going to have a genetic disorder.

The day Aubrey was born, the Lecks were shocked to discover she had Down syndrome. This unexpected news was difficult, but the parents received much needed support from Kathy, a caring nurse who visited them while their daughter received care in the newborn intensive care unit. She said she understood what they were experiencing because she, too, had a child with Down syndrome. As she answered key questions geneticists and other specialists could not answer (because they were not parents of children with Down syndrome), Kathy also assured them Aubrey was going to be a great blessing.

Inspired, the couple shifted their perspective, embraced their newborn, and looked for ways to support others.

"We realized not all parents of children with special needs are fortunate enough to meet their own 'Kathy,'" Mark says. "So Amber and I decided to start a foundation to help others."

The original plan was a Down syndrome-specific organization, but their friend Grant Bigler, who had a child with a rare birth defect, inspired them to organize a foundation that encompassed all special needs.

"Grant had experienced the same emotional roller coaster we had, but unlike us, he didn't have a large support community because his child's condition was so rare. Realizing our experience as parents was similar, despite our children's different conditions, we broadened our scope," Mark explains.

The result is United Angels Foundation, a nonprofit parent-to-parent support group that supports parents and families of children with special needs.

The Lecks readily admit that United Angels would not be what it is today were it not for incredible volunteers. Their executive director, Jill Austin, whose daughter Joby has Down syndrome, has been essential to United Angels' success. She had served the special needs community for several years before meeting the Lecks, and when she learned what they were planning, she jumped right in to help.

"We had no idea how much there was to learn from each other," Jill says. "Parents of children with Down syndrome benefit from behavioral research occurring within the autism community, and we see the autism community leveraging reading techniques originally developed within the Down syndrome community. Also, therapies and technologies originally adapted for the deaf are helping all children with special needs. It's amazing!"

A few years after starting United Angels, one of Mark's sisters gave birth prematurely, and her baby was diagnosed with cerebral palsy. Mark and his sister learned firsthand the benefits of United Angels' inclusive vision.

"We also discovered many special needs children had multiple conditions, like Down syndrome and autism, and that some families had multiple children with special needs,

but with different conditions," adds Mark. "With United Angels, they all belong." One of their member families has adopted several children with varying conditions. Recently Bigler, who had persuaded the Lecks to enlarge United Angels, had another child born, this time with Down syndrome.

The foundation supports families through interaction, education, and resources, including newborn visits, parent lunches, online chat forums, youth and family activities, and parent education seminars. As of 2015, United Angels actively supports over 1,087 families in ninety Utah cities.

United Angels prides itself on being entrepreneurial. A great example was the launch of iPads4Angels in 2013. Inspired by feedback from member families, the foundation sought a way to provide iPads—powerful technology aides for special needs children—to Utah special education classrooms.

Since the 2013 launch of the iPads4Angels' technology grant program, 75 special education classrooms in 52 schools have received iPads—affecting more than 1,000 students in five counties. Shortly after launching, Apple® reached out to United Angels and invited them to its headquarters in Cupertino, California, to discuss the program and ways to work together. In 2015, they collaborated on adaptive technology training for Utah Special Ed Educators, the first of its kind in Utah.

United Angels has provided more than fifty educational seminars designed to address parents' concerns and struggles. Examples include estate planning, IEP training, occupational and physical therapies, behavioral interventions, ASL training, marriage classes, and leveraging technology when educating children with special needs.

Hundreds of parents have received home or hospital visits upon diagnosis of their child's condition. United Angels sends a parent of a child with the same condition to offer support, mentoring, and information. More than 700 families have received support phone calls from another special needs parent. Nearly a dozen families have been supported through UAF's annual Sub4Santa program. In one instance, their Sub4Santa gift helped a single mother move her family

from a friend's spare bedroom by locating an apartment and making a deposit. Another family received much needed dental work, while another received therapy for their son.

The foundation offers more than forty networking, family and educational events annually. Families interact and learn from one another and gain access to information and resources to help them better serve their child. Since organizing in 2007, more than 20,000 people have attended events, and United Angels was recognized by Intermountain Healthcare in 2010 as part of its Select 25 Awards and by Red Cross in 2014 as Community Heroes.

United Angels headquarters is located at 1411 West 1250 South, Suite 310, in Orem and at www.unitedangels.org.

✧

Above: Mark and Amber Leck with two of their four children. The Lecks established United Angels after their first child was born with Down syndrome.

Below: Jill Austin, executive director of United Angels, and her family, Joby, who has Down syndrome, Jeff and Jalen.

NEBO SCHOOL DISTRICT

The Nebo School District is nationally acclaimed for its successes in academics, operations, and extracurricular activities and is recognized on the state and national level for quality programs and innovative concepts that focus on students.

Nebo School District continues to be a growing district and experienced significant growth the first decade of the twenty-first century with approximately 1,000 new students each year. Nebo School District's commitment to a quality education continues today for more than 32,000 children in 42 schools and 3 specialty programs, encompassing nearly 1,315 square miles including 21 communities from Springville to Elberta. Nebo is in the top ten percent of large districts in the nation and is the sixth-largest school district in Utah and second-largest school district in Utah County. With approximately 4,000 employees, Nebo School District is the fifth-largest employer in Utah County.

Nebo continues to build on its mission: "We engage, empower and collaborate to ensure student success." Nebo School District focuses on preparing all students to succeed in school and life and prepares students for active participation in school and the global community. Nebo also empowers students to acquire and develop knowledge, skills, and talents and works to promote safety, involvement, and student achievement.

"Through engaging, empowering and collaborating, Nebo School District will ensure student success," says Rick Nielsen, superintendent. "We have strong, innovative programs in everything from reading to technology, and we are confident we are preparing our students for the twenty-first century."

Nebo students are consistently represented in state and national honors in fine arts, academics, career, technology, and athletic competitions. Nebo students also consistently score above state and national norms on beginning and end-of-level assessments.

Nebo's graduation rate is 91 percent, significantly higher than the state average of 83 percent and the national average of 80 percent. Nebo students receive more than $8.7 million in scholarships every year. Additionally, Nebo District belongs to the Utah Valley University K-16 Alliance and is a member of the Brigham Young University Public School Partnership.

Nebo's academic programs are designed to reach every student from early childhood

through high school graduation and include career and technology options, summer enhancement classes, and young adult and adult/community education programs.

Every Nebo student can be a college- and career-ready student prepared to succeed in college and workforce training. Students can earn college credit through Advanced Placement (AP) and Concurrent Enrollment classes. Nebo is recognized on the AP Honor Roll for significant gains in AP access and student performance.

Career and Technical Education (CTE) programs help students explore a variety of careers through course work in business, agriculture, marketing, information technology, health science, technology, engineering, family and consumer science, building construction, drafting, and skilled and technical program areas. CTE programs also provide industry certifications including computer programming and repair, digital media, video production and medical science. Nebo continues to emphasize technology integration in classrooms to engage teachers and students in twenty-first century teaching and learning.

Utah keeps the top ACT spot in the nation among states testing all students. Nebo students' ACT scores exceeded the national and state average scores in every category— English, Mathematics, Reading, Science, and Composite.

Nebo School District strives to balance the needs of the student with the needs of the taxpayer. Nebo continues with a strong financial position as recognized by the AAA bond rating issued by Moody's and the AAA bond rating issued by Fitch. Nebo consistently receives superior ratings in the financial integrity rating system.

Supportive relations with the business communities through school and volunteer partnerships represent significant contributions in hundreds of thousands of dollars' worth of resources, finances, talent, and time. This support helps the Nebo Education Foundation award grants to teachers and students for innovative classroom projects each year.

Nebo School District's success is directly attributed to the parents' and community's expectations for quality education, the sound decision making and planning from the faculty, staff, administration and school board, as well as the students' thirst for excellence. Parents and patrons have confidence in Nebo's school system.

Nebo School District is strongly committed to effective communication and communicates regularly with parents regarding attendance, school events and emergencies. Please join Nebo by going to www.nebo.edu, LIKE Nebo School District on Facebook and FOLLOW us on Twitter @NeboDistrict for announcements, events and further details about Nebo School District.

✧

Opposite, top: Nebo educators put a high emphasis on the arts.

Opposite, bottom: Literacy is a major focus in the Nebo School District.

Above: The Nebo School District takes pride in its technology advancements.

WASATCH MENTAL HEALTH

For nearly half a century, Wasatch Mental Health "WMH" has embraced the ideal of wellness among individuals with chronic mental illness. It prides itself on its dedicated and deepening reach into the community as it offers an array of acute and chronic care services for children, youth, adults, families, and individuals covered by Medicaid.

✧

Above: Wasatch Mental Health at Westpark in Provo, Utah.

Below: The Wasatch Mental Health team is committed to helping others achieve better mental health.

WMH wants the residents who live in Utah and Wasatch Counties to know the services exist to improve the quality of life for individuals who need their care.

From the beginning the administrators and support team at WMH worked towards the provision of excellent, supportive services to help integrate people into their local communities in Utah County and, since 2013, in Wasatch County. This goal of re-integration continues to be met with substantial success, according to executive director Juergen Korbanka, Ph.D., who adds that excellent mental healthcare, outstanding customer service and an emphasis on employee development are vital to its accomplishments.

When WMH first began, it operated as an inter-local agreement among several counties and operated this way until 2003 when it became a Special Service District that focused on Utah County residents. Not surprisingly, as the population in Utah Valley has exploded, so has the need for WMH, which has experienced consistent growth to respond to increasing mental health needs.

Four hundred employees annually provide services to about 9,000 Utah and Wasatch County residents. At any one time over 4,000 clients are assisted. For eleven years (the years for which WMH has solid data), there has been a consistent rise in clients served. And for the past four years, the cost per client has decreased. This demonstrates the organization's increased efficiency and cost savings.

"A strong community and allied agency network, which enables us to respond quickly to community needs has been essential to our efficiency and success," Korbanka emphasizes. "For instance," he adds, "in 2004, when essential funding was lost to treat individuals who are un- or underinsured, the State appropriated a fraction of the funds to provide much needed services. Wasatch Mental Health developed the Wellness Recovery Clinic, based on an innovative treatment delivery structure to greatly reduce costs and provide much needed services to the un- and underinsured. This program was recognized with an innovative program award by the State and the program was subsequently visited by then Governor John Huntsman."

More recently, WMH adopted a mobile crisis team to respond to mental health emergencies in the community and a "bridge" team to provide supportive services to severely mentally ill individuals, thus enabling them to maintain independence in the community. Additionally, the Utah County Child Abuse prevention team awarded WMH with an Excellence in Service Award.

A sampling from the past year demonstrates the expanded reach and services WMH provides:

- Aspire Youth Services opened in January 2014. This sixteen bed residential facility is located in Orem and serves girls in state custody.
- Mountainlands Health Clinic opened a physical health clinic in June 2014, greatly enhancing much needed access to physical care for WMH clientele.
- Mountainlands also opened a full-service pharmacy, which helps clients with their prescriptions.
- Mountain Peaks Counseling, a clinic for clients with commercial insurance, opened in late 2013.
- WMH increased the number of Utah and Wasatch County residents served from 8,122 in fiscal year 2013 to 8,922 in fiscal year 2014. This ten percent increase represents the eleventh consecutive year where WMH experienced an increase in clients served.
- After starting to provide mental health services to nursing homes and assisted living homes in 2013, it has increased the services from fifty-nine persons to 141 persons in 2014.

"We are genuinely committed to assisting everyone who needs what we offer, including the uninsured and underinsured residents in Utah and Wasatch Counties," Korbanka says. "This year we provided more than $1.4 million worth of services to them, representing an increase of more than fifty percent." In total 1,500 individuals benefited.

WMH services are amplified by excellent collaborative partnerships, thus helping WMH facilitate a seamless array of community service. And they have expanded significantly. Utah Valley Regional Medical Center, for example, in collaboration with WMH, hired a client advocate to enhance and facilitate access to care for uninsured persons. WMH has worked closely with Hope4Utah to train communities on suicide prevention and participated in the "Walk for Hope" Suicide Prevention Walk. When Orem City presented an awareness event after the surprising suicide of actor Robin Williams, WMH was there to discuss suicide prevention. In Wasatch County, the WMH clinical staff collaborated in the creation of the Wasatch County Suicide Prevention Coalition.

Additionally, WMH's partnership with the Provo Police Department has increased significantly and a representative from WMH attends the department's weekly meeting to coordinate responses to mental health crises in the community.

Not content with its already substantial growth, WMH plans to add a fifth classroom for its Giant Steps Autism preschool; to remodel its South Provo facility to house a psychiatric nurses station and several offices; hire a grant writer/coordinator; add a facility in Payson for several clinical programs; and bring an electronic records system online to boost its Human Resources Department.

✧

Above: Members of Wasatch Mental Health at a retreat at Aspen Grove in Provo Canyon.

Below: Wasatch Mental Health follows a strategic plan to embrace wellness.

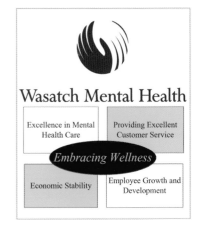

MOUNTAINLAND APPLIED TECHNOLOGY COLLEGE

Mountainland Applied Technology College (MATC) knows that education should be more than just studying out of a textbook. Students benefit from real life hands-on experience in labs, classrooms, and industry sites that provide the skills students can apply to a resume and to life. MATC gives students more than just a chance to learn about their future career, they get a way to experience it firsthand.

Mountainland Applied Technology College is a fast track educational path for career milestones, continuing education opportunities, financial improvement, and self-development. MATC helps individuals raise the bar on their educational level, quality of life, and earning potential.

MATC combines hands-on training and focused career-skills to quickly get individuals the training and certifications they need for employment in a variety of career fields.

Students may choose from more than forty different career opportunities in fields such as: healthcare, service trade professions, manufacturing, computer systems, business technology, transportation, and apprenticeship professions.

Mountainland Applied Technology College, a Utah College of Applied Technology Campus (UCAT), is accredited by the Commission of the Council on Occupational Education (COE).

Students gain experience through hands-on-training. Students are taught by instructors who have industry experience. This hands-on

 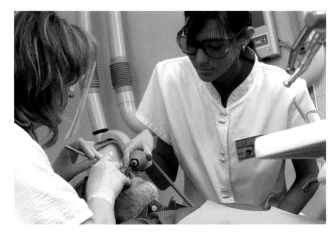

environment allows students to learn in a way that gives them work experience well before they graduate.

Most MATC programs can be completed in less than twelve months. These focused training plans enable students to gain skills and experience. There is no time wasted on unnecessary classes that do not pertain to their careers.

MATC focuses its training on the end goal of helping students obtain employment. The hands-on, skill focused environment prepares students for future careers. The mission of MATC is to increase the number of quality of skilled workers in Utah County.

MATC adult students experience one of the lowest tuition costs in the State of Utah. High school students attend tuition-free! MATC is dedicated to getting students an education they can afford without burdensome debt!

Mountainland Applied Technology College is located in Thanksgiving Point, Orem and in Spanish Fork and at www.mlatc.edu.

STEVENS-HENAGER COLLEGE

With more than 120 years of experience behind them, Stevens-Henager College has found winning strategies to help students graduate and obtain better jobs.

The focus is clear.

The college, accredited by the Accrediting Commission of Career Schools and Colleges, wants to educate people for rewarding careers in a timely manner.

"We accomplish this through tailored programs, scholarships for those who qualify, accelerated programs, flexibility, convenience, certifications and career services," says Regional Director Kenneth Plant.

Tuition goes directly to programs and services to help students graduate quickly and begin working in the fields of healthcare, business, information technology, or graphic arts. Stevens-Henager offers hundreds of scholarships annually and actively seeks scholarship donors. But its commitment goes deeper. Through Good Neighbor Initiatives, Stevens-Henager offers free programs and services to help people who may not otherwise be able to move toward obtaining a college degree. GED® preparation classes and other services provide a bridge to degrees that can improve lives. These free services are not within the institution's scope of accreditation.

What appeals to many students are the college's accelerated programs, which make it possible to earn an associate's degree in twenty months or a bachelor's degree in thirty-six months. Students are encouraged to work toward certification programs. (Certifications and licenses may require additional study and cost and are not awarded by the college.)

Flexibility and convenience are an added bonus. Students need not wait for the beginning of a year or semester to enroll. Stevens-Henager's flexible course options enable students to get started almost immediately in day, evening or online courses and continue working while going to school.

Of high value is Stevens-Henager's commitment to programs packed with career-specific knowledge and skills, including critical thinking, communications, problem solving, and technology. One of the best reasons to select a Stevens-Henager education is its dynamic Career Services Department. The career services staff helps students write resumes, identify job opportunities, and practice for interviews, including what to say (and even how to dress), and set up interviews. Of course, the college offers employment assistance, gaining employment is the graduate's responsibility.

Stevens-Henager College celebrates future success from the beginning by giving each student a new laptop to help them during their college experience. Students use the laptops while in school and are able keep them when they graduate.

Provo/Orem is one of the school's seven campus locations in Utah and also located in Boise, Nampa, and Idaho Falls, Idaho. Students who do not live near a campus can take a variety of programs online through the college's affiliated institution, Independence University.

Please visit www.ucanmakeithappen.org or www.stevenshenager.edu for more information.

UTAH VALLEY CHAMBER OF COMMERCE

The Utah Valley drew settlers to its rich soils and plentiful agriculture throughout the second half of the nineteenth century. Wilson H. Dusenberry recognized the need to create an organization that would support and promote business in the area. In September of 1887, he joined with James Dunn and A. A. Noon to create the Provo Chamber of Commerce. Within the first year, the chamber united sixty members, and boasted of its unparalleled success in economic development and support.

Provo's original chamber members referred to the region as the "garden city" and basked in the revels of its abundant agriculture. At the time, the Chamber of Commerce excitedly pushed along projects like the building of the Provo Tabernacle and promoting the beautiful Provo Opera House. Members of the chamber made commitments to promote the growth, development, and success of its resident businesses. One of the first chamber members commented that Provo and the surrounding area was "destined to be a great city, none who know her opportunities, or who appreciate the extent of her resources can doubt."

The Provo Chamber of Commerce continued to grow as a member business network for nearly a century. In 1985 the Provo and Orem Chambers merged to form the Provo/Orem Chamber of Commerce, which was led by Steve Densley for thirty years. Densley worked tirelessly to promote positive business relationships with local companies. In 2010 the chamber transformed yet again; it became the Utah Valley Chamber of Commerce, spreading to include twenty-five cities throughout the area.

Shortly after this change, Val Hale became the chamber president for two years. He was followed by Rona Rahlf, who is the chamber's current president and CEO. Today, the Utah Valley Chamber of Commerce still sits in Provo, the heart of the county, but it reaches to serve and support the entire Utah Valley area.

Today the chamber is heavily involved in community and local business. The chamber maintains positive relationships with many businesses in the area, including Utah Valley University and Brigham Young University. The Utah Valley Chamber of Commerce provides resources and events for all groups within the community, from small businesses and start-ups to women in the professional workplace.

The Utah Valley area has undoubtedly evolved over the past 128 years, but the heart of the chamber remains the same: its mission is to build relationships, advocate principle-based public policy, and promote business and community prosperity. The chamber welcomes all who are interested to help fulfill its vision of making Utah Valley a better place to live, play, and work. For more information about the Utah Valley Chamber of Commerce, visit www.thechamber.org or call (801) 851-2555.

✧

Top: Board of directors, 2015.
PHOTOGRAPH COURTESY OF GLEN RICKS.

Above: Utah Governor Gary Herbert, Pillar of the Valley Event, 2015.
PHOTOGRAPH COURTESY OF GLEN RICKS.

Below: Executive Summit at Sundance, 2014.

CHRYSALIS

In 1985, a special education teacher in the Alpine School District founded Chrysalis, a program with a mission to improve the lives of people with intellectual disabilities and acquired brain injuries. The program started with fourteen people in a sheltered workshop and small group home in the quaint town of Heber City, Utah. Given this simple beginning, who would have anticipated the monumental growth throughout Utah over the next three decades!

With support from the State of Utah, Chrysalis' goal was—and is—to provide residential, day, behavior and clinical services to people with intellectual disabilities, autism, and acquired brain injuries. Breaking the trend of institutional models, Chrysalis' primary objective is to integrate people with their local communities.

From a single home, Chrysalis has become the largest provider of services for people with disabilities in Utah. Moreover, their reach has expanded into Nevada and Texas. With approximately 250 homes in the three states, Chrysalis employees are making a difference. Chrysalis' corporate headquarters are located in Orem, Utah, and offices are statewide in Logan, Riverdale, Murray, Park City, Provo, Price, Nephi, Cedar City, and St. George. Nevada offices are located in Reno, Carson City and Las Vegas and Texas offices are in Austin and Houston.

Chrysalis' 1,600 employees provide services to more than 700 individuals every day.

Services are tailored to each individual's needs and wants and are typically provided in homes with one to four individuals and/or in day programs.

Chrysalis is aptly named, because much like the chrysalis, or hard shell spun by a caterpillar in which the transformation into an appealing butterfly takes place, this organization changes lives through transformative processes. Its mission is to make a difference daily, a charge Marc Christensen has guided for more than twenty years. Just like the individuals are in the process of becoming, so is the company. It has enjoyed consistent and steady growth for years, an indicator of accomplishing their goal to improve people's lives.

"We plan to continue making a difference every day in Utah for decades to come," Christensen says. In the past few years Chrysalis has expanded its services to include early intervention services for children with autism and their families. With their fun and exciting programs the company is seeing huge strides with children.

"Our team of employees does amazing things for people every day and is the backbone of our agency!" Christensen states. They seek to enrich the lives of individuals with disabilities by providing support and opportunities where they can live, work and participate more fully in the community. Their programs are wrapped around core values embodied by mentoring, accountability, respect, safety, and fun.

"Everything we do is designed to make the lives of people with disabilities better," Christensen adds.

✧

Below: Chrysalis works hard to improve the lives of people with special needs.

Bottom: Through early intervention, Chrysalis is making substantial inroads helping children with autism.

The Utah Valley Convention & Visitors Bureau (UVCVB) is the official destination marketing organization for Utah Valley. The slogan of UVCVB is "Bring everyone together," and the mission of UVCVB is two-fold:

1. Promote Utah Valley as a business destination for conventions, meetings, and events.
2. Highlight the tourism and leisure activities in Utah Valley for both visitors and locals.

UVCVB has combined efforts with community partners and the Utah Office of Tourism to promote the festivals and events in Utah County like the Utah Valley Marathon, Tulip Festival, America's Freedom Festival, the Timpanogos Storytelling Festival and more. UVCVB national leisure campaign efforts alone resulted in 15,709 visitors spending $3.4 million. Additional campaigns throughout the year encourage visitation to BYU and UVU sporting events, museums, world class skiing and outdoor adventure at Sundance Mountain Resort.

"With the recent growth of Utah Valley, more and more people are coming here to visit," said Utah Valley Convention & Visitors Bureau President and CEO Joel Racker. "Most of these visitors that come here are purpose-driven, meaning they're attending a specific event, visiting family members, or dropping off a family member at school. Whatever the reason may be, these visitors are positively impacting tourism growth by staying in our hotels, eating at our restaurants, and purchasing tickets to local attractions."

Local billion-dollar tech companies like Vivint, Qualtrics, and Domo have helped place Utah Valley on the radar for business travelers. Utah Valley has now established itself as prominent tech hub with a rapidly-growing population that is home to quintessential business, musical innovation, outdoor adventure, and unique dining options with more than 600 restaurants. Several of these restaurants are independently-owned eateries, featuring anything from local flavor to authentic, international cuisine.

Last year, thousands of visitors were introduced to Utah Valley through attendance at conventions and tradeshows hosted at Utah County venues such as the Utah Valley Convention Center (UVCC) in downtown Provo. Corporate, Sports, and Association groups are all finding interest in hosting events here through UVCVB sales efforts with 114 bookings in 2014. Among those groups include Nu Skin, Adobe, Mary Kay, Tough Mudder, Mettle Wrestling-The Rumble, Wrangler Champions Challenge, and Shingo.

In 2014, UVCVB launched the new UtahValley.com. This website builds awareness of destination amenities, events, hotels, and restaurants, and is great for visitors and locals alike. Going forward, UVCVB will continue to market Utah Valley as the ideal place to "bring everyone together."

UTAH VALLEY CONVENTION & VISITORS BUREAU

ROCKY MOUNTAIN UNIVERSITY OF HEALTH PROFESSIONS

❖

Top: RMUoHP campus located at 122 East 1700 South in Provo, Utah.

Above: Commencement ceremony in Provo.

Founded in 1998 by retired Navy physical therapists, Dr. Richard P. Nielsen and Dr. Michael Skurja, Jr., and a Brigham Young University professor, Dr. Larry Hall, the mission of the Provo-based Rocky Mountain University of Health Professions (RMUoHP) is to educate current and future healthcare professionals for outcomes-oriented, evidence-based practice. The University demonstrates mission fulfillment through the quality of its education and success of its students in academic programs that develop leaders skilled in clinical inquiry and prepared to effect healthcare change. RMUoHP's vision is to advance the quality, delivery, and efficacy of healthcare.

The University provides unique and meaningful graduate healthcare education grounded in evidence-based practice principles. RMUoHP's academic programs promote student success through the strategic fusion of best contemporary clinical and educational practices, technology, and a faculty of over 130 nationwide experts. The high quality, rigorous program outcomes improve healthcare and develop leaders across a diverse student population from all fifty states. For example, RMUoHP constituents have over 700 publications in approximately 250 peer-reviewed journals.

RMUoHP offers traditional (residential) and non-traditional (hybrid) academic programs, both utilizing technology-rich environments to support diverse face-to-face and distance learning. Areas of study are constantly growing and presently include physical therapy, occupational therapy, nursing practice, physician assistant studies, speech-language pathology, athletic training, clinical electrophysiology, health promotion and wellness, human and sports performance, pediatric exercise science, rehabilitative science, and more! Various continuing education programs are also provided for healthcare professionals.

Dr. Nielsen, RMUoHP president, shared his insight regarding the selection of Utah Valley as the University's home, "This community is a special place. Besides the obvious beauty of the outdoors, Utah Valley is an excellent place to work and live. While our academic programs are timely in supporting the healthcare needs of the area, the University has greatly benefited by associations with incredible people who have supported us as talented employees, dedicated students, and visionary community leaders. We are thankful to be in Utah Valley and look forward to our mutual growth!" In 2014 the University relocated to a larger Provo facility at the beautiful East Bay Technology Park, where it doubled square footage to include additional classrooms, laboratories, office spaces, and larger student areas.

The University is accredited by the Northwest Commission on Colleges and Universities (8060 165th Avenue Northeast, Suite 100, Redmond, Washington 98052-3981), an institutional accrediting body recognized by the Secretary of the U.S. Department of Education. Additional programmatic accreditation and general university information may be found at http://www.rmuohp.edu.

IVY HALL
ACADEMY

Ivy Hall Academy was established in 1988 when James Lindahl and Alan Osmond rented a few rooms in Provo's Ridge Raquetball and Tennis Club, hired teachers, and began with twelve junior high students. Since that day, Ivy Hall has grown, expanded, and touched the lives of thousands of students, enabling greatness.

There is nothing "common" about Ivy Hall Academy. As concerns surface about common core, mandated in all public and charter schools, Ivy Hall Academy maintains academic excellence.

Ivy Hall Academy teachers are concerned about each student's learning rather than teaching "down the middle" on a prescribed schedule. The school motto is SOAR, which stands for See Others and Respond. This approach encourages children to notice the needs of others around them and then jump in to help. The Covey Leadership Program helps produce students who are able to make wise decisions, interact successfully with others, and confidently face life's expectations.

"Our small classes allow for individual attention from caring teachers," says Susan Kirby, director of Ivy Hall Academy for the past twenty-five years. "We utilize a combination of advanced learning and solid values to enhance each child's development. Our four areas of focus are: Scholarship, Leadership, Citizenship and Faith."

Parents trust Ivy Hall Academy to deliver the finest education for students from preschool to eighth grade, encompassing prayer, the Pledge of Allegiance, a comprehensive curriculum, and a safe environment.

An eighth grader asked if she could stay at Ivy Hall Academy until she was twenty. Another chimed in and said, "We all feel that way."

The school's mascot is the eagle—soaring high and alone at times, discovering its wings and seeing the big picture. Those who see farthest, fly highest.

Ivy Hall Academy encourages members of the community to visit the school at 1598 West 820 North in Provo or on the Internet at www.ivyhallacademy.org. The faculty and staff are sure the things that are important to you are important at Ivy Hall.

Above: Ivy Hall Academy, a private school in Provo, Utah, for children pre-kindergarten through grade eight.

Left: Whitney Harken, one of the teachers at Ivy Hall Academy in Provo, Utah.

Below: A highlight of Ivy Hall Academy is class size, which is limited to eighteen students. Here Nicole Nielsen assists several children.

SCENICVIEW ACADEMY, INC.

ScenicView Academy, Inc. (formerly ScenicView Center, LLC) was organized in early 1999 and opened its doors in 2001. Concerned parents Ray and Tye Noorda had been searching for an establishment committed to the betterment of adults with learning differences while simultaneously encouraging a clean, uplifting lifestyle. After exploring all the available options, however, they struggled to find anything that would meet their child's needs. Pondering the situation, the thought occurred to Tye, "If not me, then who?" This idea propelled the Noordas into building their own school where individuals with learning differences could discover their true potential. In their quest, they found many interested families and professionals who shared their vision. Facilitated by the support of other community partners, the Noordas created a unique residential and day program designed to "Remember the One."

Built on nineteen and a half acres at the base of beautiful Cascade Mountain near the mouth of Provo Canyon, ScenicView Academy has a capacity to serve up to eighty students. As a residential school, it features fifty-four apartment and dormitory-style housing units for both male and female students, with staffing for an additional twenty-six daytime students. ScenicView Academy supports a values-based growth experience and admits students regardless of their religious preferences or ethnic origin.

As a nonprofit organization, ScenicView Academy serves adults diagnosed with Autism Spectrum Disorders, ADHD, Executive Functioning Deficits, Dyslexia, Dyscalculia, Dysgraphia and other learning differences by helping them gain skills that lead to more independent and fulfilling lives. Thanks to the Noorda's generous endowment and gracious donations from other community sponsors, scholarships are available to students who are unable to pay the full tuition.

The ongoing, program-wide goal at ScenicView is for every student to graduate as they demonstrate they can live independently in the community and maintain a steady income. To accomplish this, students practice self-advocacy, selecting or requesting courses based on their individualized transition goals. Classes, tutoring, therapy, and coaching revolve around what each student needs. Every student is part of a team where he or she works closely with a case manager, a psychotherapist, teachers, employment specialists, recreational therapists, and a variety of other professional staff. ScenicView Academy also works diligently to encourage students to develop the independent living skills necessary to succeed throughout life.

ScenicView Academy's distinctive programming helps students in eight "Balance of Life" areas: creative, educational, emotional, social, vocational, independent living, physical, and spiritual. It offers high school diplomas, college support, pre-vocational training, clinical services, fine arts, conflict resolution, health and fitness, cooking, money management, recreation, social skills training, and other services tailored to the needs and goals of the students.

Employment Services provide training and a work environment that will prepare students

to pursue career-level employment and earn a livable wage. Students progress through in-house employment, apprenticeships, and community internships to develop and sharpen work skills such as dependability, positive interpersonal skills, initiative, and producing quality work. ScenicView Academy employment staff partner with Vocational Rehabilitation and Workforce Services for job assessments, skills training, and job placements.

Clinical Services deliver opportunities for students to increase emotional, social, and cognitive skills. Recreational Services provide training to help each student develop healthy leisure activities, important social skills, and to interact outside of a structured campus environment.

Educational Services ensure that students learn how to learn. Through classes and tutoring, students are prepared and empowered to understand their personal learning style, accommodate for individual learning challenges, progress in reading, writing, math and other needed educational curriculum, utilize relevant technology, gain a healthy understanding of self, and pursue further learning based on their personal and professional goals.

Case Management Services design a service plan based on each student's strengths, needs, and challenges. They provide regular coaching and core management services to set and achieve personal goals. Additionally, they offer tutoring in independent living skills such as budgeting, personal hygiene, cleaning, shopping, and cooking. Case Managers coordinate outside services for the student and support them in processing applications and documents for financial entitlements. Personal fitness and healthy lifestyles are emphasized as students have access to a personal trainer, a well-equipped fitness room and regular sports opportunities.

ScenicView Academy believes in strong community involvement. Staff and students demonstrate good citizenship with ongoing service to local organizations such as United Way of Utah County and Hale Center Theatre of Orem. Additionally, ScenicView Academy supports local service organizations' fundraising efforts and initiatives, partnering with others which include Community Action, Spectrum Academy, Heritage School, Clear Horizons Academy, and the Food and Care Coalition. ScenicView Academy plays a leading role in the Autism Resources of Utah County (ARUC). Each year, ScenicView Academy helps sponsor its spring respite program and balloon launch, as well as its summer carnival and BBQ. ScenicView Academy invests much time and effort in community education and outreach programs to enhance services for autism in Utah through its involvement with the Utah Autism Initiative, UVU Passages program, internship programs at local universities, conference presentations, workshops, planning committees, the Learning Disabilities Association of Utah, and its own R.E.A.C.H. program, which offers social skills training and experiences to transition age youth. ScenicView Academy students also work in a variety of internships with community partners, which help to increase an understanding of autism and build employment and social connections.

ScenicView Academy is certified by the National Commission for the Accreditation of Special Education Services. It is licensed by the State of Utah and is a member of the Provo/Orem Chamber of Commerce.

At the heart of all its activities and objectives, ScenicView Academy strives to live up to its mission statement, empowering students to gain skills "that lead to interdependent and fulfilling lives by developing best methods and practices for the benefit of 'the one.'"

For more information about ScenicView Academy please visit www.svacademy.org.

CAREER STEP

✧

Above: More than eighty-eight percent of Career Step graduates work within their field of study after graduation.

Below: Career Step's online training makes it easy for students to balance other responsibilities while still training for a new career.

Thousands consider Career Step training essential to their professional success. In fact, more than 85,000 people throughout the United States and the world have gained the skills needed for life-changing employment opportunities with the comprehensive online education and corporate training programs offered by Provo-based Career Step.

Career Step was started by a single mother twenty plus years ago. Because she was able to support herself and her daughter as a medical transcriptionist, this single mom wanted to help others in similar situations. This led to the creation the first Career Step training program, which was unique because it focused on helping students gain exactly the skills they needed to get hired and be successful as medical transcriptionists—by training them on real-world files.

In the past two decades, Career Step has grown to offer a number of additional

courses, many similarly focused in healthcare. Available programs include: medical coding and billing, pharmacy technician, medical office manager, medical transcription and editing, medical administrative assistant, health information technology, computer technician, and executive assistant.

Students can enroll directly through Career Step or one of the school's 150 plus college and university partners nationwide. Career Step training is also used by some of healthcare's most respected employers to provide long-term educational opportunities for their employees.

Career Step training is different because it focuses on teaching students exactly the skills employers are looking for within specific, growing career fields, all within a relatively short timeframe (programs can be completed in a year or less) and at an affordable price. For less than $3,400, students can go from having no experience in the field to graduation as a confident professional prepared to earn relevant industry credentials and excel in their first job and beyond.

Career Step's mission centers on improving the lives of its students. The company's employees strive to live by eight core values—ownership, integrity, execution, customer focus, innovation, quality, teamwork, and personal fulfillment—in a coordinated effort to offer the best services possible. More than a quarter of Career Step's staff is solely focused on helping students on a daily basis through one-on-one instructor, graduate, and other support services, and the primary objective is to help students successfully complete their training and prepare for improved career opportunities, giving them the skills they need to change their lives.

Career Step leadership also strives to make a difference in the lives of their employees. The company is currently working toward the goal of being one of the best places to work in Utah by offering best-in-class benefits, various health and wellness activities and initiatives, charitable opportunities, and a positive company culture.

More information on Career Step, visit www.careerstep.com on the Internet or call 1-800-246-7836.

The vision of American Heritage School's founders was to create a school where faith, virtue, and character education would be taught as the foundation for excellence in all other areas of life. Over the last fifty years, that vision has come to fruition at the school, which is located in American Fork, Utah on an eleven-acre campus at the foot of the Wasatch Mountains in beautiful Utah Valley.

American Heritage blends faith, reason, and plenty of fun by offering outstanding academics, athletics, music, and extracurricular programs. The student experience culminates in impressive portfolios, project-based learning, teamwork, oral presentations, and experiential learning for graduates, virtually all of whom attend four year universities or serve LDS missions following graduation.

The school feels strongly that strengthening faith in Christ is indispensable to properly educating the hearts and minds of the rising generation. In addition to regular morning devotionals, prayer, and use of scripture as a foundational reference text in every subject, the AHS Honor Code focuses on the two great commandments to love God and neighbors "with all thy heart, and with all thy soul, and with all thy mind" (Matthew 22:36–39). Every student and faculty member at the school commits to uphold the highest standards of moral conduct whether they are on or off campus.

The school serves approximately 800 students on-campus in grades K–12, plus 280 students in afternoon extracurricular orchestra and choir programs, and approximately 4,000 homeschooling and distance education families living in 50 states and 45 countries and territories. The student body represents diverse ethnic, racial, religious, and socioeconomic groups.

The administration, faculty, and staff consist of more than 110 highly qualified personnel with many holding advanced degrees.

Rigorous courses are offered in fine arts, business fundamentals, English, foreign languages, family science, leadership, mathematics, wellness, biology, chemistry, physics, history, geography, social studies, speech/debate, drama, choir, orchestra, technology, and more.

Extra-curricular activities include basketball, soccer, cross country, Boys/Girls State, choir, drama, orchestra, science fairs, service learning, speech competitions, student government, experiential learning, and travel study.

AHS graduates typically score well above state and national norms on college entrance exams, including the ACT and SAT, for which the school offers rigorous preparation as a part of the standard high school experience. AHS graduates are prepared for, and have been admitted to, many of the finest colleges and universities around the country.

American Heritage School is open for tours by appointment. Interested parents are encouraged to explore how the school's unique approach can support their family's learning goals (visit www.american-heritage.org).

AMERICAN HERITAGE SCHOOL

REAGAN ACADEMY

For almost its entire existence, the Ronald Wilson Reagan Academy in Springville, Utah, has reached its 675 student capacity and maintained a waiting list. Obviously demand for the independent public school serving grades K-8 is high.

This reflects its focus on founding principles of American society, an emphasis on personal responsibility and moral integrity, and an excellent academic foundation.

The Reagan Academy was founded July 1, 2004, less than a month after the death of its namesake, the fortieth President of the United States. His vision of a community working hand in hand with schools inspired school founders to establish the school motto, "Partnership in Education." To recognize the leader whose term saw a restoration of prosperity at home with a goal of achieving peace through strength abroad, each graduating eighth grader visits the Reagan presidential library and President Reagan's ranch every spring.

The first students arrived for the 2005 school year, even though teachers, students, and parents were ready for the first day of school, the building was not. School started late, and once the building passed inspection, faculty and volunteers worked feverishly to get classrooms ready.

Because the school was organized without its building, planning and recruited meetings took place throughout Springville. Especially useful was the basement of the Springville Art Museum, where students registered and participated in early testing. Today Reagan Academy's art program is at the forefront of elementary and middle school art programs, including annual art shows at BYU. Some have mused that the humble beginnings in the museum must have laid some of this foundation.

Before the school opened, overwhelming volunteer support and fundraising helped establish the school and its traditions. An early fundraiser still beautifies the school. Students and families purchased and decorated tiles later organized into a colorful display called the Heritage Tile Wall. Parents helped raise funds for a fully functioning kitchen that provides free and reduced lunches for between thirty to forty percent of Reagan students.

Of special note is a large auditorium. Its guests have included a holocaust survivor; Gail Halvorson, the candy bomber; a secretary to Ronald Reagan; several children's authors; and local and state politicians. It has also provided a venue for concerts and plays.

Reagan has used real-time student performance data to design individual instruction for students, thus increasing chances for classroom success. In the past five years, Reagan has received 2 NAMM national music awards; 4 High Performing Title I School designations; 2 Best Charter School awards; and has scored in the top ten percent among Utah elementary schools for student achievement.

President Reagan reinvigorated America. By design, the Reagan Academy, also aims to reinvigorate…by reinvigorating education.

Domestic abuse statistics for men, women, and children can be heartbreaking and are getting worse every year. Battering results in more injuries to women than accidents, muggings and rapes combined. Forty-two percent of Utah homicides are related to domestic abuse, and eighty percent of prison inmates grew up in abusive homes. Unfortunately, most domestic violence cases go unreported.

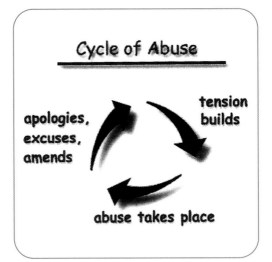

Most victims have no idea where to turn for help, which sadly perpetuates the problem. Children who witness domestic violence are much more likely to pass the behaviors down through the next generation. Cycles, however, can be broken, which is the major conviction of the ChainBreaker Foundation, a Utah-based, nonprofit entity that helps empower victims through education, guidance, and support.

The ChainBreaker Foundation was founded in 2002 as an all-volunteer organization. No one in the foundation is paid, and many volunteers are well-known community members who spend countless hours helping others. Some have been victims themselves and are now turning around to help others. As they say, "Together we can break the chains of domestic abuse."

The foundation offers services designed to help victims liberate themselves. Stepping forward to help are educators, therapists, financial advisors, and many others from the community. Every Tuesday night the foundation provides a free self-improvement class that helps victims develop self-confidence and skills that can facilitate healthy living. Professionals from throughout the state willingly give their time to educate others by teaching classes that cover a broad range of topics, such as Understanding Abuse, Anger, Depression and many, many more.

Believing that outward confidence is also important, the foundation provides new and like-new clothing, hair vouchers, DI vouchers, and numerous other donated items. The foundation has a library of educational and motivational books, an informative website, connections to the WISP Scholarship (funded by Warren Buffet) and many other services.

Founder and director Joan says, "Most victims are ordinary citizens carefully hidden beneath the wreaths on their front doors. When they get the necessary information and assistance, they change their lives and become 'chainbreakers' in their own families."

The foundation, designed to help their clients help themselves, lives by an ideal: "We cannot liberate victims, we can only educate them. They must liberate themselves."

For a list of available services or upcoming events, visit www.chainbreakerfoundation.com or contact directly at 801-900-3518.

CHAINBREAKER FOUNDATION

FREEDOM PREPARATORY ACADEMY K-12 CHARTER SCHOOL

✧

Above: Freedom Preparatory Academy.

Bottom, left: Creativity in group learning is included in a Freedom Prep education.

Bottom, right: Winners of a Freedom Preparatory Academy spelling bee.

Freedom Preparatory Academy was founded on the vision of Utah families who believed that a better model of K-12 education could be created. It opened its doors in September 2003. Now, with well over a decade of distinguished progress and achievement, this vision has been realized and thousands of students have flourished in their pursuit of educational excellence.

Empowering students to become effective communicators and critical thinkers is Freedom Preparatory Academy's goal. It is also their objective to mold ethical and passionate leaders through a broad, rigorous curriculum, participation in school activities, and community outreach. With a focus on college preparation and life-long learning, students will experience a challenging atmosphere while building a foundation for global success.

Freedom Preparatory Academy focuses on making a positive and measurable impact in the local community and beyond by providing an education of the highest quality to students who will go on to become leaders in their family, community, business, and society.

Lynne Herring, executive director of Freedom Prep, came onboard in July of 2004 after the first year. She continues to head the 1,000 plus student body, faculty and staff. Her experience from traditional schools in Arizona prepared her to plow fertile ground for change and rebirth in the U.S. educational school system. A risk-taker at heart, Lynne believes that anything is possible when careful research, design, teamwork and realistic goals are incorporated.

Early on, the administration realized that parents were definitely hungry for a new model of education. The time was right for forging new territory in educational opportunities.

Transitioning from a small initial setting in a warehouse in Provo's East Bay with only 350 students to a magnificent two school campus in central Provo, Freedom Prep has continued to meet the expectations and

desires of conscientious parents seeking a personalized, parent-involved educational organization. Finding leaders, governing board members, teachers and employees who pioneer new paths and work together to build, create and support a twenty-first century vision and mission continues to hallmark their thriving and growing K-12 organization today.

Parents were highly involved in the earliest days building walls, installing carpet, painting, and putting together desks the night before the first opening day. The ducks at the East Bay Golf Course became frequent visitors on the school property in the early years and charmed the students.

In the winter of 2005 they purchased an eight-acre park that was dilapidated, overgrown, and frequently used by drug dealers and the drifter population. This once beautiful park, which was owned by the Geneva Steel Retirement Association, now needed a new tenant to bring it to life again, and that was Freedom Prep.

Freedom Preparatory Academy hired a builder, obtained bonding, and in the fall of 2007 opened the doors of a beautiful 65,000 square foot modern building that added much to the surrounding neighborhood. That same year they welcomed seventh and eighth grade students to their population.

The canal running through the old Geneva Park was moved to the back edge of the property, partially buried, and then fenced to prevent access. It flows freely today and fosters water fowl and other creatures along with beautiful trees and plants.

In 2009 parents began requesting that the administration and the governing board further expand the already successful education model through high school. Approval came in 2010. Freedom Prep expanded from a K-8 to a K-12 over a four year period by adding grade 9 in the 2012-2013 year, grade 10 in the 2013-2014, and so forth, until they had a complete K-12 program by the 2015-2016 school year. Originally, the architects said that expanding on the current site was feasible. However, outcry from the neighbors concerning increased traffic and population impact on the same

school property prompted the school to locate a site a half-mile west of the existing school. Today this is the secondary campus, housing grades 7-12 in a striking 60,000 square foot facility.

Parents choose Freedom Prep for a variety of reasons and they come from many backgrounds. The demographics reflect wide diversity and Freedom Prep embraces and welcome all cultures. Parents quickly learn that the expectations are very high and that academics are a priority. At each phase of a child's education at Freedom Prep, the curriculum is individualized to inspire and engage the students to do their best and push their own personal envelopes to achieve their highest potential.

A glimpse at demographics reveals a comparison of data from the first year to today's student population. In 2003: 350 students, 16 percent minority, 25 percent economically disadvantaged, 9 percent special education. In 2014: 1062 students, 39 percent minority, 41 percent economically disadvantaged, and 9 percent special education.

Ever cognizant of continued growth in the state, Freedom Prep is exploring the possibility of future growth in the county by adding satellite schools.

Freedom Prep continues to provide a rich and challenging college prep educational program for Utah Valley families. Please visit the schools and see what Freedom Prep can offer your family.

✧

Above: Learning is more fun when taught by an "historical" figure.

Below: Executive Director Lynne Herring met Senator John Valentine at Utah's State Capitol.

Bottom: Science projects are hands on at Freedom Preparatory Academy.

CITY OF OREM

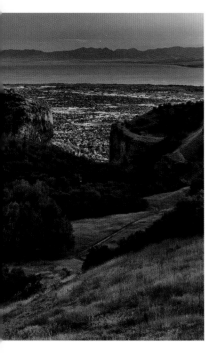

Top, left: A view of Orem City in the distance framed by the nearby mountains.

Top, right: Sleepy Ridge Golf course in Orem City.

Below: Baseball is a popular city sport in Orem, Utah.

The City of Orem calls itself *Your Place to Grow* and is a great place to live, work and play. It attracts a thriving blend of people passionate about making it a progressive community for raising families. Located on the eastern shore of Utah Lake, Orem extends on the east to the foothills of Mount Timpanogos and is bordered on the south by Provo. The bustling commercial, retail and technological center for Central Utah ranks among the fastest-growing metropolitan areas in the United States. Housing, educational, and employment opportunities continue to be in high demand, and when Orem's population passed 91,000 residents in 2014, it became Utah's fifth largest city.

The seeds of Orem were planted in 1919 with the idea that this was a place of growth. Independent thinking helped a desert grow into an oasis. Lush orchards and farmlands helped an oasis grow into a community. Abundant resources and cutting edge technology helped a community grow into a city that has captured the imagination of the world. Today we are planting opportunities and growing businesses. We are planting individuals and growing families. We are planting the seeds of economic growth by reimagining our community. It all goes back to the notion that Orem is a place of growth!

Orem boasts ever-expanding businesses, restaurants, a large shopping mall that has remained as robust in 2015 as it was when it opened in 1973, a fine school district including various charter schools, and Utah Valley University, which began as a technical college, but, under the direction of forward-looking leaders, has grown into Utah's largest state university. Orem has ever-expanding residential neighborhoods, schools, senior centers, hospitals, and more.

Long known as Family City USA, its annual summer festival celebrates family values, and its more than eighty year old historic SCERA Center for the Arts provides a learning center for youth and teens to participate in all aspects of the arts from technical stage production to acting, singing, dancing, classes and successful participation in regional and national competitions. Orem is also home to the highly popular Hale Center Theatre, a flourishing theatrical company that began in California and expanded to select Utah locations.

Its close proximity to Provo Canyon invites tourists and natives to hike, camp, and mountain climb. Just up the road is Sundance Ski Resort, which is famous for its slopes in the winter and a world-famous film festival. The Provo River offers fast rafting and great trout fishing, lazy walks along its shores, and tiptoeing across its rocks. Orem overflows with outdoor activities and the sunshine in which to enjoy them.

Welcome to Utah County, the Heart of Utah. Located in the center of the state, Utah County is the place people are choosing to work, live and visit. Consistently, hailed as one of the top five places in the U.S. for business, Utah County leads the nation in job creation, cost of living and cost of doing business, income growth along with an amazing quality of life that attracts a young educated workforce.

Utah County is the Heart of Utah Educationally with two nationally recognized universities, Brigham Young University and Utah Valley University. Both committed to producing students that not only graduate, but come out of college prepared to work in high tech and other industries. Utah County's young and well educated workforce has a huge impact on why businesses decide to locate here with both UVU and BYU providing trained and talented employees.

Utah County is the Heart of Utah Economically. G. Scott Thomas of the *Philadelphia Business Journal* reported that the "Provo/Orem metro area, which includes most of Utah County, was No. 1 in the nation for economic vitality. There's no doubt the economy in Utah County is booming with great things taking place."

Often referred to as Silicon Slopes, the county is a recognized leader in the high tech world. "The number of private sector jobs has expanded by 4.9 percent since 2008, providing the fifth-best growth rate in the nation. Shops and restaurants are booming, where retail employment has grown by 6.6 percent during the past year alone. Job growth was top in the nation coming in last year at 5.3 percent. Utah County job growth ranked seventh best in the nation over the past five years with an unemployment rate at a microscopic 3.2 percent.

Utah County is the Heart of Utah when it comes to Quality of Life. Families take priority with quality primary and secondary public and private educational opportunities. Beautiful neighborhoods, friendly people, up-to-date public and private transportation options all contribute to a desirable place to live, work and raise a family.

Outdoor opportunities too numerous to mention serve to attract educated, young professionals. A system of urban and mountain trails appeal to those who love to hike and bike the scenic byways of the county. Camping and fishing, public parks, outstanding golf courses and easy access to national forests along with youth programs of all types contribute to a quality of life that is second to none.

Utah County attracts tourists from throughout the U.S. as well as internationally. Whatever your reason for visiting be sure and take note of Thanksgiving Point's Children's and Prehistoric museums, Sundance, BYU, or any one of our spectacular canyons.

So whether you are looking to expand your business, find a new job, or just looking for a better place to put down roots—consider this your invitation to visit and explore Utah County, the Heart of Utah.

PLANNED PARENTHOOD ASSOCIATION OF UTAH

Planned Parenthood Association of Utah has been a respected health organization in Utah Valley since 1989 seeing over 6,000 patients a year. In 2009 the agency outgrew the facility they had occupied and built a new health center. As part of Planned Parenthood's effort to be a "green" organization and to reduce our carbon footprint, the health center was built according to the nationally set standards for design and construction. PPAU directed the design team to "do the right thing" for the clients, the staff and the greener environment. As a result, the building was certified as a Platinum level Leadership in Energy and Efficiency Design (LEED®) building, the highest ranking available. Not only was it the first LEED® certified building in Orem, but the first to incorporate cutting edge sustainable design strategies such as

a living roof, integrated renewable energy systems, storm water management, ground-source heating and radiant cooling. The building served as an education tool for city planners and inspectors and opened the door to a smoother process for future projects. It was designed by Principal Angela Dean of AMD Architecture where sustainable design has been at the core of their projects since inception in 1997. AMD has been an advocate of the LEED® rating system for building owners, to ensure accountability from their hired professionals. It was built by Paulsen Construction Company, a local fourth generation construction company that became LEED® qualified during the construction of the clinic.

The clinic is a model for the relationship of beauty, function and environmental responsibility. Passive solar design provides comfortable day lit spaces that are warm and inviting. The natural materials and finishes create a pleasant, non-clinical feel for staff and visitors alike. The clinic is used as an educational tool for clients, staff and interested individuals wishing to learn more about green building. Along with teachings about the building design and systems employed the education program also includes posters hanging throughout the clinic that explain behavioral changes and are integrated with actions that are healthier and environmentally responsible.

As a healthcare organization, patient health as well as the health of staff and all those involved with the project was the primary driving force. Within the building, materials and equipment systems provide optimum patient and staff health through elimination of harmful chemicals and pollutants in specified products; control the intrusion of outside pollutants post construction with an enhanced ventilation system. In a broader context, materials and construction systems were selected with the health of those finding them, manufacturing and constructing in mind.

The resulting design for the clinic was a direct response to the Planned Parenthood Association of Utah's mission "...to live in peace with our planet."

SCERA

In 1933, Orem was a sprawling town of 3,000 struggling through the devastating effects of the Great Depression. Many had lost lifetime investments in farms and homes, and spirits were low. Concerned about the citizens' morale and well-being, local leaders pooled resources to create the SCERA, which they envisioned as the community's gathering place—a place for neighbors and families to come together, create friendships, have fun, and be enriched and uplifted.

From those humble beginnings has come a nonprofit organization dedicated to the arts, family, and youth. With a focus on family-friendly entertainment, the SCERA has remained dedicated to serving and unifying the community through involvement in the arts. SCERA's educational programs and performing arts seasons have been enjoyed by millions of Utah County citizens for more than eighty years.

SCERA was founded in a spirit of volunteerism and loyalty that remains today. More than 400 young people twelve and older—adults and seniors, too—serve annually at SCERA facilities, sharing talents, learning skills and developing a love of community service. More than 500 volunteer cast members perform in stage productions, and each year nearly 1,000 volunteers give more than 172,000 hours of service. The SCERA also offers educational programs in all areas of the arts for more than 18,000 people annually.

As SCERA grows and improves, the dream of the founders has become an evolving reality that continues the family tradition and dedication to the arts. The SCERA has a saying: "Every time the curtain rises, so does the quality of our lives."

The historic SCERA Center for the Arts, which opened in 1941, is the longest-standing facility and has two theaters: the remodeled XanGo Grand Theatre and Showhouse II.

A sundial, bronze sculptures, giant cheese board and plaques with inspiring quotes grace an outdoor courtyard. The interior lobby showcases stained glass windows depicting eight areas of the arts: theater, dance art, architecture, song, music, art and film and well as two floor-to-ceiling custom stained glass pieces by artist Tom Holdman.

The Orem Heritage Museum, which for many years was located on the second floor of the SCERA Center, moved to a new home on the SCERA campus in November 2012.

Located in Orem's SCERA Park under the backdrop of the beautiful Wasatch Mountains, the SCERA Shell Outdoor Theatre is a one-of-a-kind outdoor venue, perfect for summer evening plays, concerts, and movies. The large and open grassy slope can accommodate more than 4,000 patrons. Audience members can bring a blanket or rent a chair specially cut to sit on the hill.

SCERA also has a shop building for the costume, prop and scenic department plus the SCERA Art Studios, an educational building dedicated solely to visual arts classes.

For additional information on SCERA and its many programs, visit www.SCERA.org.

✧

Top: The SCERA Center for the Arts, remodeled several times since it was built nearly seventy-five years ago, is a community gathering place for the arts in Utah Valley.

Above: The historical SCERA Showhouse, built in 1941, has been a key center for cultural arts in Orem since opening.

Below: Vocal Point, a popular BYU a cappella group, performs at the SCERA Shell Outdoor Theatre.

Manufacturing/ Technology

Utah Valley is rapidly becoming a high tech corridor for the state of Utah, led by software development and manufacturing

TEMKIN INTERNATIONAL, INC.

✧

Above: Danny Temkin, the founder and president of Temkin International, Inc.

Below: A fitness shake is kept fresh in Temkin stand up pouch bags.

Danny Temkin has been wrapped up in his business for more than three decades—and is likely more wrapped up than anyone else living in Utah Valley.

That is because the owner of Temkin International provides customers with superior flexible film packaging products ranging from clear polypropylene wrapped around fresh flowers to earth-friendly wrappers that cover fruits and vegetables. A consumer may not necessarily select a product because of the packaging but he or she purchases superior goods because they have been protected and preserved by Temkin International.

Temkin provides products to major national brands and distributor networks. With 470,000 square feet of production facilities, Temkin can process more than 20 million feet of material a day. A small sampling of its clients include Costco, Hallmark, Great Harvest Bread Company, Jelly Belly, Meadow Gold, Home Depot, Target, and Safeway.

The seeds of Danny's business took root in Los Angeles more than thirty-five years ago when, by his own admission, he was not doing very well financially. As he considered business options, Danny heard that cellophane had gone up in price three times that year, and retailers were unhappy. He thought polypropylene would not only be a reasonable alternative, it would also have some distinct advantages over cellophane. He decided to go into plastics.

Easy to customize, polypropylene can be colored and is printable without degrading the plastic. It also does not spoil or deteriorate in the presence of bacteria or mold and is lightweight and flexible.

Danny initially promoted polypropylene in the Los Angeles flower markets. He took product samples and was on hand in the wee hours of the morning when the markets opened. That meant Danny was on site at 2 a.m. when the Japanese vendors arrived, and he could be seen visiting American merchants when they arrived at 4 a.m. Outgoing and friendly, Danny is an extrovert's extrovert whose personality and sense of humor easily attracts potential clients.

It turned out to be an excellent business choice. It was not too long before Danny was building a prosperous career.

Danny spent fourteen years in California believing that the business world ended in Las Vegas with nothing in between until New York City. His perception changed, however, when he and his then wife came to Utah Valley to visit her grandparents.

"I fell in love with the place," he says. "My wife at the time was originally from Utah, and we decided to move to Springville, Utah, where I opened our first factory." In a piece of serendipity for Danny, California experienced a large, damaging earthquake in 1994, and he had removed his equipment just prior to the disaster and before his building was condemned. "I was so happy to have my equipment in Utah," he says. "It was saved because we left California. This personal move became a tremendous business opportunity."

Danny has always taken great pride in being able to surround himself with the kind of employees that will help make Temkin better and better. He believes he has a winning team, which is demonstrated by the loyalty of so many. Some have been with him for more than twenty-five years and even moved their families from California when he moved the company to Utah County.

Temkin International now operates manufacturing facilities in four strategic locations to provide exceptional products and excellent customer service. Its Utah headquarters grew so rapidly the business had to be housed in four

separate locations until Danny found a building large enough in Payson, Utah, for his operation; 500 of the company's employees work at that location. Two hundred other workers are employed at sites in Miami, Florida; Ontario, Canada; and Bogota, Colombia, and Danny welcomes additional, qualified employees into his labor force. His facility is largely self-contained with welders, electricians, and machinists as well as production and office workers. Much of his equipment is purchased, but if the plant needs a piece of equipment unavailable elsewhere, his team builds it. Danny also buys American goods whenever possible to augment his business.

Danny, a self-described workaholic, considers being in the office a good way to take a vacation, and keeps state-of-the-art equipment running around the clock to ensure a fast turnaround. Determined to exceed customer expectations, he insists that all products are inspected meticulously to guarantee quality.

Temkin International may have originated as a floral packaging enterprise, but it has grown to serve many major industries as a leader in the flexible film packaging world. In fact, floral now constitutes only about fifteen percent of the business. From flowers, Temkin has moved into food and confectionaries, fresh produce, stationary and crafts, pharmaceuticals, gift items, personal care, pet supplies, and horticulture. Temkin products are so abundant, it is almost a sure bet everyone encounters them. They might be the treat bags you buy from a party store, the flower sleeves wrapped around bouquets when you buy them, or the bright wrapping covering a holiday ham. The Temkin touch is evident everywhere on all types of flat bags, lip and tape bags, and zipper pouch bags.

Temkin also has its own in-house design department that can create that custom look for its customers. Everything is done in-house and even makes its own printing plates.

Danny, clearly the heart of Temkin International, has operated consistently with the promise of delivering remarkable customer service, superior products, and peace of mind while being friendly, yet determined.

A businessman whose education came from the "school of hard knocks," Danny says his best teacher was "Mr. Experience." His solid work ethic and his vow to exceed expectations has been recognized by the State of Utah and other industries. In 2000, Utah named him Entrepreneur of the Year in the field of Industrial and Consumer Product Manufacturing. In 2005 the Produce Marketing

✧

Above: Temkin International Headquarters in Payson, Utah.

Below: Love Letters in pink, one of the popular flower wraps.

❖

Left: Temkin employees match color on Temkin packaging.

Top, right: Temkin International warehouse does its entire production in house.

Right: Temkin pouch machine.

Association named Danny, the Floral Marketer of the Year. (Danny insists that as welcome as these recognitions are, he considers his four children his greatest achievement.)

Danny attributes his considerable success to several core beliefs. He sees merit in choosing a personal path and then sticking to it. "You need to believe that what you are doing is right and pursue it passionately," he explains. "Over the years I have seen many people who moved from their path and ended up in places they would never have chosen." With a focus on the health of the business, he also strongly believes a company must avoid using the business as a bank. Additionally, he advocates a solid business model that includes service, efficiency, innovation, loyalty, and creativity. He says that with in-sourcing, Temkin can provide customers with quality, value, performance speed, trust and partnerships. Those objectives support his corporation mission statement:

"To deliver peace of mind by providing the highest value packaging experience."

So what does Temkin do to ensure such enviable results? It starts with a commitment to support a healthy environment for the benefit of future generations in every step of operation. It begins with its selection of raw materials and earth-friendly packaging reinforced by solid product development and superior manufacturing processes.

- Recyclable Materials: Temkin's 100 percent recyclable films help the company meet packaging needs of today while preserving natural resources for tomorrow. Digital in-house ink mixing enables Temkin to recycle excess ink into viable color options, substantially reducing surpluses, storage costs, and waste.

- Earth-friendly Packaging: In addition to standard recyclable films, Temkin offers every major eco-film on the market, including EarthFirst® PLA made with Ingeo™,

NatureFlex ™, BioBOPP, Kraft paper, and Stone Wrap.

- Manufacturing Practices: All water used during production is treated on-site before disposal, removing all chemicals and metals so only pure, clean water is returned to the environment. The air they take in is also purified and returned to the environment cleaner than when it entered the facility. Because Temkin uses recyclable films, scrap material acquired during manufacturing is repurposed for future uses, and domestic manufacturing facilities help reduce carbon emissions by eliminating the need for overseas shipping.

As Danny's son, Noam Temkin, explains, "Temkin focuses on the impact of their products over the entire life cycle from design and manufacturing to consumer use and disposal."

To that end, Temkin uses controlled atmosphere packaging where oxygen flow is reduced to slow the respiration and aging process, and moisture is retained and excess CO_2 is allowed to escape.

Among the packaging is an FDA-approved standup zipper pouch that comes in a variety of sizes and features high-barrier lamination, a reseal-able zipper and self-supporting bottom gusset. Custom options include laser micro perforation, vent holes, hang holes, tear notches, alternative bottom seals and metallic film options.

Other packaging also offers multiple options as well and includes wicketed bags, gusseted bags, head bags, flat bags, plant and herb sleeves, and rigid containers. Temkin works to provide packing innovations, including nearly invisible packaging, ultra-clear grape bags, and large food service bags.

In addition to packaging that is almost infinitely adjustable, Temkin offers a creative in-house team of designers as well as top-of-the-industry printing presses that offer superior print quality for logos, UPC, designs, or additional information.

Danny praises the Payson community where he does business. "The Payson City police department, fire department and other business leaders have been extremely nice to us," he says. "They have been very friendly and helpful regarding our business." And because he feels he has been so blessed in his business, Danny is quick to be generous to his community, both local and national. He especially likes to donate to hard working organizations and communities. Temkin is charitable with many corporations, including the American Cancer Society, Utah Symphony/Opera, City of Hope, United Way, Cancer Recovery Foundation of America, Children's Miracle Network, Families for Effective Autism Treatment, Women in Crisis, Habilitat, JDFR (improving lives, curing type 1 diabetes), Ronald McDonald House, Make-A-Wish Foundation, Special Olympics, Festival of Trees and Larger Than Life.

To say Danny Temkin gets wrapped up in his business is absolutely correct. And while others may use the cliché "It's in the bag" to describe success in their business, Temkin can add, "It's not only in the bag… it is the bag."

✧

A sampling of the extensive Temkin inventory.

Young Living Essential Oils

By the time D. Gary Young developed his first herb farm and distillation operation more than twenty years ago, he had already learned about the amazing power of essential oils. The oils—extracted from the leaves, flowers, stems, roots, or barks of plants—can be very beneficial, but only when painstaking efforts are made to keep them pure and unadulterated.

"I knew that pure essential oils had the ability to produce spectacular results," he explains. "I also knew that chemically altered or impure oils on the market were often ineffective and sometimes even harmful."

Because Gary had grown up on a ranch farming all his life, he was naturally interested in how aromatic plants were different and how they were distilled. He instinctively knew that by growing, harvesting, and distilling the botanicals himself, he would be able to control the quality of the plants he distilled and the oils that were produced.

This was the beginning of his path in the essential oil world. He was excited to produce and offer pure oils that were superior to what he had seen offered in commercial markets. Through the establishment of Young Living Essential Oils, he was able to pursue his goals.

With a clear vision and undeviating purpose, Gary devoted himself to the two-plus decades of hard work, research, and discovery that allows Young Living to deliver pure, authentic, therapeutic-grade essential oils. He started by turning first Idaho and then Utah farmlands into acreages of growing lavender, peppermint, melissa, clary sage, and many other plants. As demand grew for pure essential oils, he designed and built the largest, most technologically advanced distilleries for the production of essential oils in North and South America.

Today, Young Living is at the forefront of the essential oils and wellness solutions industry. It is headquartered in Lehi, Utah, with offices in Australia, Europe, Canada, Mexico, Ecuador, Japan, Malaysia, Hong Kong, Singapore, and Croatia, as well as farms and distilleries around the world. The impressive Utah Valley-based company currently boasts over 1,800 employees worldwide in eleven markets. It operates eight farms and distilleries, oversees many partner and co-operative farms worldwide, and had more than one million active members as of early 2015.

Gary dedicated himself early on to sharing the precious gift of essential oils with others. He spent years traveling the world to study essential oils and the ancient tradition of oil distillation and was trained by the two great masters of distillation, Marcel Espieu, who was the president of the Lavender Growers Association in France for twenty years, and Henri Viaud, who was considered to be the "father of distillation" in the essential oil world of Europe.

As Gary's expertise grew to match his dedication, his unrivaled knowledge regarding the power of plants led to the creation of the world's largest line of essential oils and blends and is part of what has established Young Living as the world leader in essential oils.

As part of Young Living's commitment to oil purity and potency, Gary understood that careful monitoring of the entire production process was paramount. It was this unwavering commitment to produce only the highest quality essential oils that led him to establish Young Living's Seed to Seal® promise. Seed to Seal is a philosophy, a practice, and a guarantee that Young Living will produce only 100 percent pure, unadulterated oils that maintain their vital potency. It is with this promise that Young Living has set the industry standard for oil quality and authenticity.

Young Living's unique Seed to Seal process has been researched and perfected; and this exacting method includes five painstaking steps—Seed, Cultivate, Distill, Test, and Seal—that create the world's finest essential oils. From the time the seed is sourced until the oil is sealed in the bottle, Young Living applies rigorous quality controls possible to ensure that individuals receive essential oils exactly the way nature intended.

"Seed to Seal sets the standard for the industry," Gary explains. "The process of carefully producing an oil from seed to cultivating, distilling, testing, and sealing in the bottle yields oils as nature intended."

While Young Living Essential Oils maintains an international focus and a deep commitment to its sense of global stewardship, the company's origins were humble. Gary and his wife, Mary, built the business from the ground up; and they did it without loans or investors. During the week Gary ran the farm and on weekends traveled as a lecturer, while Mary focused on running the business. Mary's mother, LaRue, poured oils and put labels on by hand in the laboratory in the early days. She also ran errands, cleaned, and did many other projects. Today, Grandma LaRue, at age ninety-one, is still happy, enthusiastic, and enjoys "her" oils every day.

Gary started his essential oil business in Reno, Nevada, in 1989 and a year later moved his headquarters to Spokane, Washington. In 1993, he relocated to an 8,000 square foot building in Riverton, Utah, and incorporated the new Young Living Essential Oils in 1994.

Gary wanted to start developing a farm immediately, so he began looking for property. In early 1995, he finally found a 160 acre farm in Mona, Utah, which Gary and Mary were able to purchase by selling a small piece of land that was part of the Riverton building property. Then a year later, they leased another 1,600 acres that he eventually bought in 1998.

Young Living quickly outgrew the little 8,000 square foot building in Riverton, so they began searching for a bigger building. The cost was too great to stay in the Salt Lake

area, so they started looking south and eventually found the old Payson middle school that was slated to be torn down. However, they negotiated with the city and bought the 30,000 square foot building that seemed very big at the time.

However, within a couple of months, they were using the entire building. The old kitchen was converted into a lab, and the sports equipment room became the shipping room, which lasted for about a month. Next, they moved upstairs into the gym, and that demanded more equipment. Gary went to a big foreclosure auction and bought shelving, racks, dailies, cabinets, storage containers,

✧

Above: Sunset reflects off the Mona Reservoir bordering the lavender farm. Pictured is an old farmhouse that was on the property. It has been restored and repurposed for a year-round visitors center.

Below: Lavender seedlings, nurtured in the greenhouses on the farm until they are mature enough to be planted—by hand— in the fields.

Above: Two horse team is cutting oats grown on the farm to feed livestock.

Below: Gary and Mary Young with son Jacob around 2001. The home in the background is Gary's childhood home near Challis, Idaho.

and anything else that might be used. He even bought a circular slide to send packages down to the FedEx trucks; and for a little fun, some of the employees also went for a fast ride from the second floor to the first floor, laughing all the way.

Always hands-on with the farm and the business, Gary and Mary spent weeknights in sleeping bags in the upstairs of the Payson building and went home to Alpine, Utah, on weekends. It was a bit disconcerting when Mary heard noises in the old building at night and told Gary she thought it was haunted. Gary just laughed, but other employees who also worked in the building claimed to hear the same thing. Maybe it was just the voices of the children from the past playing games, but the building has since been sold and torn down, so one will never know where "those sounds" came from in the middle of the night.

From the Payson building, which soon became too small, the Youngs found a warehouse in Springville. Mary explained, "It seemed so big and overwhelming with its 100,000 square foot but to our amazement, we grew out of it, too, within two years."

At the same time, they began looking for a new headquarters, something that was a little more sophisticated than the old dilapidated Riverton building and the fated middle school of Payson. They finally decided on moving to a building in Thanksgiving Point in Lehi, Utah, that everyone felt would meet their needs, and so they moved from Payson. Everyone was excited because the new building was modern and had a great business look.

In the meantime, they rented buildings across the street while they looked for a new location for a warehouse. A large parcel of land was purchased a few months later in Spanish Fork. Plans were drawn and construction began. The lab and bottling stayed in Payson until the warehouse was finished, but there was a great celebration when they also moved into their new home.

But as time would have it, the new global headquarters began to bulge and spread; and as of early 2015, the corporate team had spread into five buildings.

There has been much talk over the past few years about building a new global headquarters. The architectural renderings have now been made, the plans have been drawn, and a new headquarters building is on the horizon that will bring the entire staff together.

Young Living has many goals on the horizon, which, not surprisingly, include expansion into additional international markets. But even with all the transformations and rapid growth, there have been two constants: founders Gary and Mary. And after more than twenty years of actively steering Young Living as an executive, Mary recently accepted Gary's request to become Young Living's new chief executive officer.

With Mary now at the head, Young Living has become the largest female owned and operated company in Utah.

An outgrowth of Young Living Essential Oils is the Young Living Foundation. Spreading the message of helping others worldwide to live a healthy, successful lifestyle led to the creation of this foundation, which has the purpose to educate, awaken, and inspire individuals to discover their God-given talents, to live a healthy lifestyle, and to give back to the world.

Young Living provides essential oils, essential oil-infused nutritional products such as Power Meal and Protein Complete, many other supplements and mineral products, as well as Thieves cleaning products, which offer solutions for the kitchen, laundry, and many other household needs, to underserved communities around the world. Products are sent to clinics, orphanages, and schools in Uganda, Kenya, Cambodia, Mexico, Guatemala, Somalia, Nigeria, and Haiti, in addition to the United States. The Young Living Academy, which provides preschool through high school education to almost 400 children in Chongon, Ecuador, was built and is supported by Young Living and its members.

Domestically, the company has been generous with hands-on corporate service projects that include helping abused children, providing assistance to homeless families, and participating in food drives. Young Living employees love being directly involved in serving others.

At its core Young Living Essential Oils retains a continual commitment to essential oil purity combined with a spirit of generosity. This has inspired millions of people everywhere to experience nature's gifts of wellness, harmony, and abundance as Young Living members carry the message to those looking for new opportunities for a lifelong transformation.

For orders and member services, call 1-800-371-3515, visit their website at www.YoungLiving.com or mail directly to Thanksgiving Point Business Park, 3125 Executive Parkway, Lehi, Utah 84043.

✧

Top, left: Peppermint is planted on the borders of the farm. In the background is Mt. Nebo and big cottonwood trees that date from late nineteenth century. The vintage truck is typical of the company's early day. Gary Young would attend farm equipment auctions, looking for a hidden gem. Even today some of those relics survive, including a water truck from the 1940s that is used to keep the dust down on event days.

Top, right: Gary Young is shown with clary sage, which is harvested and distilled at the Mona farm.

Above: After you harvest a plant for essential oils before putting it in the cookers you leave it out for a few hours—but you have to "turn" it, like stirring a simmering dish. Sometimes that will be done, as in this picture, by letting it lay in the field. Or it is cut and loaded into a truck in the same moment. The cut plants are dumped and spread out on the cement in front of the distillery. Often being "turned" by pitchfork.

REDX: Real Estate Data X-Change, Inc.

✧

Top: A night view of the REDX building.

Above: Mark Leck, the founder and CEO of REDX.

It seems as if all the great technology companies—Apple, Microsoft, Facebook—are spawned from an idea in someone's garage, basement or college dorm room. Real Estate Data X-Change (known as "REDX") is one such story right here in Utah Valley, starting in a BYU college apartment.

In March of 2003, a few friends got together with nothing more than a question of "How do we provide real estate agents with an 'expired' leads solution?" (Expired refers to a home seller whose contract has "expired" with one agent, and the owner may be looking for a new one). While the other founders focused on developing potential sales channels and future business operations, Mark Leck, REDX's CEO and co-founder, was responsible for creating the product and overcoming the technical and logistical hurdles associated with building this type of system.

Hundreds of hours were spent doing research and trying to overcome many of these obstacles, but one obstacle almost shut down the startup. Minutes before a meeting intended to disband the company, Leck received a miraculous phone call from a real estate agent with whom he had been doing research that helped redefine the strategy and restart the startup.

With a clear pathway forward, the trio set up shop by converting an outdated desktop computer to a Linux server, bumming a DSL line from a friend, and sub-leasing a fifty square foot closet as their first office space and started development. Just two months later, REDX launched its first lead generation product in August 2003 and sold its first subscription September 26, 2003. In the fall of 2003, Leck also engaged their first and largest strategic partner, which helped push REDX's nationwide expansion over the next several years.

"We were a scrappy start up. We had no money, little resources, just a determination to get to market with a solution that could help real estate agents be more successful," says Leck. This bootstrapped startup eventually became real estate's largest seller lead company, specializing in lead generation, homeowner and property data, and prospecting products and services for real estate professionals.

Four years later, in 2007, REDX launched its industry leading For-Sale-By-Owner (FSBO) service throughout the United States and Canada. In July of 2010, Leck bought-out the remaining cofounder of the company. Because of Leck's background as a software engineer, he envisioned the company as a technology company rather than a real estate company. This vision completely changed the company's course. The new leadership team, composed of Mark Leck, CEO, Curtis Fenn, CMO, and Patrick Bailey (who originally suggested the acronym "REDX" that the company is known as, and whose wife designed the original company logo) as the CFO.

"It is hard to overstate the impact Curtis and Patrick have had on the business." says Leck, "Curtis has been instrumental in diversifying REDX's sales strategy by building an industry leading sales and marketing team. Since he started in August 2006, new sales have increased on average by more than 407 percent."

This new team sparked a cultural revolution as well as an era of innovation, which has resulted in the launch of several new products, including their new SaaS (Software as a Service) platform Vortex®, and which guided and continues to guide them into the future.

As the industry adapted to the economic recession and the increase in short sale/foreclosure leads, REDX produced its pre-foreclosure service. Then, because of their commitment to data quality, in 2011, REDX pioneered an innovative new measurement of lead quality (known as Octane™) as well as a method of data quality analysis. The results confirmed REDX was still the industry leader for data quality and revealed new ways to make improvements that have allowed REDX to maintain its competitive advantage. Then in 2013, REDX launched the first version of their auto-dialer, Storm Dialer®, to help assist real estate professionals in their prospecting.

In addition to a renewed entrepreneurial spirit, one of the greatest features of REDX is its amazing culture. REDX has employed hundreds of people across Utah Valley and takes pride in bringing together a group of people who have a common vision and purpose, and the will to bring that vision to reality.

"We've built an amazing culture here," says Patrick. "We have some of the most talented people in the valley, and we are building solutions that are really making a difference in people's lives. We love that!"

The results from REDX speak for themselves, with more than a decade of experience under its belt, having worked with more than 40,000 real estate agents, and actively serving tens of thousands of agents throughout the U.S. and Canada, REDX's industry expertise and unique approach to data research empower its clients to produce at an average of three times the national average for real estate agents. REDX solutions enable customers to make connections, measure objectives, and maximize time to achieve greater success in business.

What started in 2003 in a college apartment with a simple question, has grown into an industry leading technology company with an amazing culture that is influencing the lives of their clients and employees for good.

✦

Left to right, the executive team of REDX is Patrick Bailey, CFO, Mark Leck, CEO, and Curtis Fenn, CMO.

FLOWSERVE

Valtek® was founded in 1966 in Provo, Utah, when Charlie Bates, Forest Anthony and Larry Haines recognized several critical needs and opportunities in the automatic control valve market that suppliers were not addressing. They developed the Valtek Mark One™ linear control valve based on customer needs, and this valve became the workhorse and premier product offering to the market. Due to its early success, the company outgrew its Provo facility in 1978 and moved to its present location in Springville, Utah.

In 1987 the Duriron Company acquired Valtek. Duriron already manufactured valves at its Cookeville, Tennessee, facility, and these two plants formed the valve division of Durco International, Inc. In 1997, Durco and BW/IP International, Inc., merged to form Flowserve Corporation, which now provides pumps, mechanical pump seals, and valves for the process industries. Flowserve, a large, international company with more than 18,000 employees in more than fifty-seven countries, has its headquarters in Dallas, Texas.

Flowserve's Valtek automatic control valves are used to control the flow of liquids and gases in a number of industries worldwide. Flowserve is known as a leading automatic control valve supplier in areas such as cryogenics, liquefied natural gas (LNG), gas-to-liquid (GTL) conversion, floating production storage and offloading (FPSO), molten salt control in solar power plants, petrochemical and chemical production, refining, mining, power generation (both conventional and nuclear), and aerospace.

The Valtek product line includes both linear and rotary valves, which are supplied in sizes ½ to 48 inches, pressure classes 150 through 4500, and in a wide variety of materials such as carbon steel, stainless steel, chrome-moly, titanium, Hastelloy, and zirconium. The Springville operation has evolved from a business that produced 100 percent of its own parts in the factory to being a globally-integrated operation. By combining outsourcing with improvements in manufacturing, we have doubled our sales volume while maintaining the same level of employees at the site. As the Center of Excellence for the Valtek product line, we have been an integral part of the growth of Flowserve's global organization and have become the largest product line in the Flowserve Flow Control Organization.

The Springville facility is a modern, high-volume manufacturing plant with CNC machines, assembly and testing capabilities. The plant has more than 320 employees. It includes 2788 m² (30,000 ft²) of office space and 8364 m² (90,000 ft²) of manufacturing and assembly space. In recent years, we have seen a pronounced trend toward larger valves with increased flow capacities and higher pressures. To address these new market requirements, we recently completed a 1858 m² (20,000 ft²) addition to the facility to assemble and test larger valves, some of which weigh over 22.7 metric tons (25 tons) and are 9+ meters (30 ft) tall.

✧

Below: Cryogenic valves are among the specialties at Flowserve.

Bottom: Flowserve Corporation is nestled in Springville, Utah, with a postcard picture view of the nearby Wasatch Mountains.

Flowserve's Springville operation has gone through many changes. The facility has met the challenges, and that is a testament to the people who work here. We have a stable workforce, and many of the employees have been here for many years. This team of people has consistently delivered on ever-increasing operational objectives.

Flowserve's diverse automatic control valve product portfolio is a combination of traditional control valves and new severe service trims and digital product offerings. The Mark One globe-style control valve and cylinder actuator with a positioner offers our customers accuracy and control not available through competitive suppliers that offer only diaphragm actuated valves.

One of the major differentiators for the Valtek products is the digital controls that were developed in Springville. These include StarPac, Logix and ValveSight. By fully integrating digital controls with the valve hardware, the customer is able to control the operation of the valves and receive online diagnostics and monitoring of the equipment. Many customers use Flowserve's equipment on off-shore oil production platforms due to their low weight compact design.

Customers rely on Flowserve to solve their difficult applications. Gas and steam applications are notorious for creating high levels of noise. Flowserve engineers and supplies a number of different noise controlling internal valve trim configurations to ensure compliance with work site noise requirements and prevent noise-induced vibration damage.

Other customers look to Flowserve to help control and minimize the high damage potential associated with high pressure drop liquid applications. A phenomena called cavitation is responsible for millions of dollars of equipment damage every year. By accurately predicting the magnitude and severity of cavitation in any given application, Flowserve is able to design and supply cavitation controlling control valve trim that allows our customers to safely operate their facilities under challenging process conditions.

While we have enjoyed the ability to grow the business by increasing our capacity in the low-cost and high-quality supply chain, we will always require a strong engineering and sales team and a capable and competent machine shop to serve the needs of a diverse set of customers for new projects and the maintenance and repair side of the business.

Flowserve continues to work with local schools to develop engineering and manufacturing talent, and enjoys strong ties with the community. Our location in Utah Valley, the quality of life enjoyed by our employees, and our strength as an organization makes Flowserve's Springville operation a great place to work.

✧

Above: Large valves at Flowserve.

Below: A selection of valves manufactured by Flowserve.

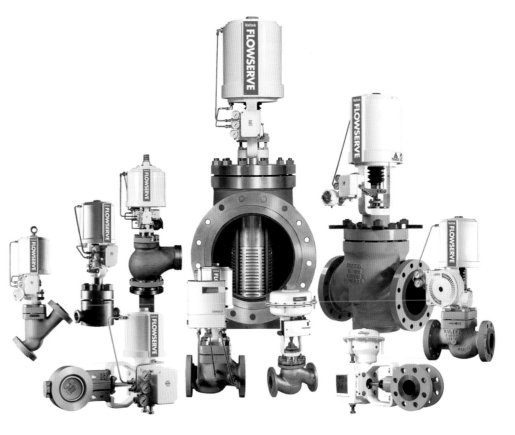

MityLite

Greg Wilson's 1980s vision of a lightweight, durable table that could transform hospitality, religious, and public assembly settings has become a reality, a global reality. MityLite, the company he founded, produces much sought-after, professionally designed, and highly durable furniture.

In the beginning the entrepreneur oversaw a ten person business that upholstered church pews, and it was through a church purchasing agent that the seeds of a much larger enterprise emerged. The agent invited Wilson in 1987 to create a durable, lightweight, folding banquet table. Wilson presented him with an ABS plastic folding table prototype, and to prove durability, Wilson jumped up and down on the table. He received a contract: the formidable task of manufacturing 1,000 tables.

"It was hard work with long hours, tight deadlines, and a whole lot of hope," he says. A company was born.

MityLite's ABS plastic table emerged as a staple for customers, establishing its market dominance. Recognizing great opportunities for complimentary products, MityLite began producing banquet seating, folding chairs, and dance floors, all of which have strong sales in several vertical markets, including hospitality, restaurant, worship, education and the private- and semi-private club industry. In 2007, MityLite was acquired from its public shareholders by private equity investors Sorenson Capital and Peterson Partners; in 2013, Prospect Capital Corporation acquired the operation from the former owners.

Based in Orem, Utah, the award-winning and well-resourced manufacturer's products include: ABS, aluminum, laminate, plywood, and linen-less folding tables; banquet, folding, and stacking chairs; portable dance floors; staging; and partitions. Through the early 2015 acquisition of Carroll Chair Company, MityLite made a strategic move into the restaurant and foodservice table and chair category as well, expanding its product line-up to include several high quality, metal-framed seating, table bases, and tabletops.

Durability is forged into everything MityLite designs, engineers, and represents. The company's talented product and customer teams stand ready to exceed its customers' furnishing expectations to deliver a superior product and purchasing experience. It is vital to realize that MityLite gives its customers, both large and small, a dedicated account representative who ensures a superior, single-source purchasing experience. MityLite's "customer first" philosophy combines with the best-in-the-industry warranties on products designed for long-term performance.

During its nearly thirty year history, MityLite has risen to many challenges. One of the most extensive involves the SLS Hotel & Casino®, a three year $415 million renovation on the site of the legendary Sahara & Casino at the north end of the Las Vegas strip. The SLS Hotel presents a modern aesthetic with its appealing combination of luxury, style, service and creativity.

Every detail thoughtfully reflects SLS' signature luxurious and iconic style, and extending this vision and direction across 30,000 feet of dedicated meeting and event space is a major design undertaking. On behalf of SLS Hotel, Avenue Interior Design worked to create visually stunning meeting venues and sophisticated settings for signature SLS events. An overriding desire for their design was a banquet chair that

did not look like a banquet chair, and one that was not heavy or cumbersome.

MityLite was invited to present its banquet seating lines for purchase consideration. What happened next wholly contributed to a curated décor decision; the ideal chair was discussed with the design team, drawn on a slip of paper, refined by MityLite, and a sample presented. MityLite's Royale Series was born and now adds to SLS' contemporary palette. With plush seating comfort to match its fresh style, the chair's streamlined aluminum frame met the design team's lightweight specifications. MityLite also provided glammed versions of its Reveal Duo Linenless and Madera Laminate folding tables both delivered with Carrera marble tabletop finishes and textured silver leg frames.

The company's diligent attention to detail has not gone unnoticed. Frost & Sullivan's Manufacturing Leadership Council recognized MityLite in 2014 for shaping the future of global manufacturing, specifically for its supply chain leadership. MityLite President and CEO John Dudash says, "As a persistent and determined organization, MityLite completed a supply chain transformation yielding remarkable results that are keeping and bringing new jobs to the U.S. The award recognizes the contributions of our dedicated employees and the direct impact of their efforts on MityLite's success and longevity."

In 2012, MityLite received the Manufacturing Leadership 100 award for Operational Excellence from *Manufacturing Executive* magazine, as well a Utah Genius Award, which acknowledged the company's exceptional innovation and inclusion among the top twenty Utah patent registrants

for 2011. The Utah Manufacturer's Association designated MityLite the "2011 Manufacturer of the Year" as well.

Through its 245 employee efforts, MityLite has "re-shored" several products from Asian vendors. Through a SKU rationalization and a kaizen-driven cell layout in the manufacturer's leg shop, all table legs were re-shored from a Chinese vendor. Also, through employee-driven process innovations, MityLite continues to win bids for its chair products against competitors. This competitive spirit is improving MityLite's ability to capture market share and win more overall business.

A recent analysis of the economic benefit of MityLite's Utah operations showed that by keeping manufacturing jobs and vendors in Utah and the USA, the company is directly contributing more than $10 million to the local economy, an additional $9.7 million to other Utah vendors, and $8.5 million to other vendors in the USA. By focusing on operational excellence and improvement, and expecting the same from its vendors, MityLite and its supply base will continue to strengthen the local and national economies. As always, MityLite's track record for success extends to every table and chair product made, even to more value-conscious lines.

✧

Below: SLS Hotel.

Bottom: The MityLite comprehensive product line.

KENCRAFT, INC.

It all began with an egg—a hollow sugar egg trimmed with icing and featuring a peep-hole at one end with a beautiful panorama nestled inside. These Easter treats originated from a small kitchen workshop in the home of Kenneth and Marlene Matheson.

This cottage industry called Kencraft® (Ken for Kenneth and craft for his wife's skills) did exceptionally well, and they were kept busy at home from 1969 to 1974 making their charming Victorian vintage confections. The first dioramas featured scenes from wood, but as their skills improved they were fashioned from royal icing. All that changed, however, when a nationally-recognized chocolate company salesman discovered them when Kencraft exhibited the eggs and some sugar Christmas ornaments at a national tradeshow in Chicago.

"We were encouraged to attend a national show and got the last booth," Kenneth says. "We sold quite a few, and as we were getting ready to leave, we got lucky. A top salesman took what we had left, and within a week he placed an order for 5,000 more. Three weeks later our orders exceeded 15,000. We knew we had to get a little more serious."

The resulting growth in their business meant the Mathesons eventually needed to move from their small home-based operation to a plant, which they located in picturesque Alpine, Utah. Business thrived, despite being hit twice by lightning while the plant was open and making candy, and while being haunted by a resident ghost they named Willard who was known for messing around with lights and moving items.

Forty years and three expansions later, Kencraft outgrew that facility and now is housed in a former big box retail store at 708 South Utah Valley Drive in American Fork. (The Mathesons sold the company after twenty-five years.)

Much more than a creative egg confectionary, Kencraft also produces innovative hard candy treats, and icing flowers and decorations distributed throughout the United States and exported in limited supplies. All Kencraft products are made by hand using time-honored methods and are sold in stores ranging from the smallest boutique candy shop to the largest club stores. The company uses only the finest ingredients from throughout the United States and processes its products using mountain spring water from the nearby American Fork Canyon.

It has a flourishing online business and also offers a factory outlet and candy store at its American Fork facility where videos show the candy-making process and customers are greeted by the sweet smell of its candy operation. It remains a popular place for teachers to bring their students for field trips and is particularly popular during holiday seasons.

❖

Left: Chris Jeff, machine operator, is working on rolls of candy.

Right: The final stage of making candy Twist Pops® is still a handmade operation. Here completing the process are left to right, Elaine Horne, Letty Velasquez, Collette Emshoff and Tyson Blanco.

Walk in at Christmas time, and you will see a variety of seasonal items such as clear green and red lollipops with three-dimensional Santas, trees, penguins, gingerbread men, and ornaments as well as an armload of candy canes in multiple flavors. Halloween candies include bats, cats, eyeballs, monsters, pumpkins, and more, while Easter features its famous large and small sugar eggs and bunny lollipops.

The hard candy specialties showcase their creators' abundant imaginations. There are alphabet lollipops with every letter available decorating suckers with interesting background textures, animal print imagipops®, baby boy and baby girl candies, candy sticks, dozens of different college logo lollipops, crushed candy chip sprinkles, daisy pops, and much, much more.

Special occasion candies—graduations, baby showers, birthdays, and weddings, for instance—have brought wedding and party planners to Kencraft for more than thirty years. A particular highlight for Kencraft was being licensed to produce candies emblazoned with the Olympic mascot images when Salt Lake City hosted the 2002 Winter Olympics.

Other popular candies, such as chocolate confections and nut brittles are also found at the Kencraft candy store, the Peppermint Place®.

Kencraft was one of Utah County's earliest winners of the Employer's Council Award for family-friendly local employers, and has won numerous awards for Manufacturer of the Year at the city, county, state and national level. It garners additional attention whenever it is featured on national television on shows such as *Unwrapped* and *Kid in a Candy Store* for the Food Network.

Kencraft has always been an active member of the Utah Valley community. It makes candy donations to local schools, bands and performing arts groups and Kencraft has won awards for its participation with the March of Dimes Walk America (finishing in the top ten teams), Toys 4 Tots, Special Olympics and the Utah National Guard.

"We have built Kencraft by using the artistic talents of Utah County residents throughout our history," says Kencraft CEO Justin Boyle, "The strength of the company

is its workforce. We have employed nearly 6,000 workers in our forty-five year history, and we envision remaining a Utah County corporate citizen in the years to come. We are pleased to enrich family events with our locally handmade sweet treats."

For more information call (801) 756-6916, fax (801) 756-7791 or visit us on the Internet at www.kencraftcandy.com.

✧

Above: Left to right, Socorro Zarate and Paola Hernandez are decorating Kencraft's popular sugar eggs while Jill Johns observes.

Below: Sugar eggs (where it all began) as well as other confections in the Kencraft spring line.

LITTLE GIANT
LADDER SYSTEMS

✧

Above: Hal Wing, founder of Little Giant Ladder Systems.

Below: The Little Giant Ladder System®, known as the strongest, safest, most versatile ladder anywhere, is professional grade and can be set up in twenty-four different positions.

Since 1972, Hal Wing and his sons, Art and Doug, along with their world-class team, have worked to prevent injuries and save lives with Little Giant's innovative climbing equipment. The company's foundation is built on the guiding principle that every rung, every rivet, and every weld matters because every person who uses a Little Giant ladder matters. This principle is the guiding force that drives Little Giant to innovate and improve climbing equipment today. This family business began in Springville, Utah, and has become the global leader in ladder safety and innovation as it conducts business in more than fifty countries around the world.

Although Little Giant Ladder Systems are now found worldwide, it was not an easy road. Hal's family and friends at Little Giant remember one story from the first year when he spent months on the road selling his new ladders toe-to-toe at state fairs and home and garden shows. One particular event close to home in Utah was not going well. Hal was having a hard time getting people to listen to his demonstration. The next morning, Hal, a great lover of German culture, donned his

lederhosen, climbed to the top of his ladder, and started yodeling. A crowd immediately gathered to stare at the yodeling "Ladder Man." Hal climbed down from his perch and started his demonstration. By the end of the show, he had sold all the ladders he had on hand, and his company was off and running.

Even from their humble beginning, however, Hal and his team had a vision that Little Giant would spread throughout the world. Over time, Art, now president and chairman of the board, created partnerships and satellite offices on six of the world's continents. Art explains, "The power of the Little Giant brand transcends borders and cultures. Worldwide, we find that people want a better experience with the ladders they use and with the people who represent them."

Little Giant Ladder Systems has climbed north to Vancouver, British Columbia, Canada; south to Mexico City, Mexico, and on down to Sao Paulo, Brazil. Their global office is located in Shanghai, China and has expanded to satellites in Osaka, Japan, Singapore, and Seoul, Korea. Little Giant Ladder Systems has spread across Europe

from Cardiff, Wales, United Kingdom to India, Russia, and Australia. Since its humble beginnings, Little Giant's footprint continues to expand worldwide.

Little Giant's growth is driven not only by the number of ladders it builds, but also by the individuals who use them—the hard-working men and women who are the backbone of industry and progress. These are dedicated working people with families, hopes and dreams; they are the motivation behind Little Giant's mission: preventing injuries and saving lives."

Every day nearly 2,000 people are injured while using a ladder. Nearly 100 of them suffer a long-term or even permanent disability. And every day, a person dies from a ladder accident, never returning home to family and friends. These numbers are staggering when you think of each individual's life, and especially the people who love them and are left behind.

Ryan Moss, CEO, explains, "If Little Giant Ladder Systems can help one more person get home safely each day, then we will have done our job. They are what gets us out of bed each morning. They are our motivation to push the envelope of innovation and product development."

Little Giant Ladder Systems is the safety and innovation leader in climbing systems and professional access equipment, partnering with safety professionals all over the country to develop real solutions to the most prolific safety problems. In only the past five years, the company has filed for more than fifty patents on safety improvements in climbing equipment design.

Little Giant's commitment to leading the world beyond Grandpa's ladder has helped organizations such as Comcast, Disney, NASA, DirecTV, Tyco, ExxonMobil, and many others to achieve new standards in ladder safety.

Little Giant and the Wing Family Benevolent Fund demonstrates their commitment to their community and to worthy causes that assist individuals. They are active participants in many charities, especially the American Indian Services, the Honoring Heroes Foundation, and the Mentors International.

Little Giant's employees, or as they like to call them, their extended family, are the leading factors in the company's success. As the plaque on the front of the building reads, "If you concentrate on building the business and not the man, you will not achieve. If you concentrate on building the man, you will achieve both." With this guiding principle, the Little Giant family has created a culture of caring, hard work, fun, and purpose.

✧

Above: Little Giant Ladder Systems, with its headquarters at 1198 North Spring Creek Place in Springville, Utah, is a worldwide leader in ladder safety in the United States and more than fifty countries.

Below: The cage system provides a safe way to maneuver stairs with a Little Giant Ladder.

Little Giant
Ladder Systems

CLIMB ON

POWER INNOVATIONS INTERNATIONAL, INC.

✧

M-SOC Line of Integrated Solutions:
Homeland Security, Military,
First Response.

Power Innovations' products are deployed to critical and rugged application customers globally, but the company may be one of Utah Valley's best kept secrets. Founded by Robert Mount in 1997, Power Innovations is a technology company pioneering multiple energy and integration solutions. The company was purchased in 2014 by Lite-On Technology (TWSE:2301) but retains its local presence, with Mount still at the helm as president/CEO.

In forming Power Innovations, Mount changed the power industry's typical one-size-fits-all approach by forming a customer-oriented, solution-based company. From its fully integrated solutions to its high demand power quality and backup, generation, storage, and management products, Power Innovations responds to customer needs. This approach has attracted high-profile customers (Boeing, L-3 Communications, Lockheed Martin, Transocean, Hydril, Baker Hughes, C-Innovation, Canadian Air Transport Security Authority, Canadian Coast Guard, Bay Area Rapid Transit, to name a few), who require power and integration solutions that are customized to meet their specific needs. Power Innovations fills that niche, with its customers regularly returning with new projects.

In response to the needs of its Homeland Security, Aviation Simulation, and Marine Oilfield customers, Power Innovations currently implements its technologies and integrated solutions, as well as those of other companies, into new and existing vehicles, ships, aircraft, trailers, and containers. Developed in response to customers needing to generate power in mobile applications, the Auto-regulated Motion Power System™ (AMPS™), which is not dependent on engine RPM, generates perfect quality power from a boat or vehicle engine.

Power Innovations' customers in the know are anxiously awaiting the release of the company's new line of modular options. Full modularity of all product lines will make available additional customization and integration options, as well as expandability for growing needs.

Locally and nationally, Power Innovations' integrated solutions are used by emergency first responders, search and rescue operations, and military and law enforcement personnel. One of Power Innovations' M-SOCs was featured on KSL-TV before being used for auxiliary power and surveillance at the 2014 Super Bowl.

The company's technologies are well known in the eastern parts of the United States hit hard by Hurricane Sandy and other natural disasters. Power Innovations' PowerHawks® (which carry up to 70 kW of onboard power), Mobile-Special Operations Centers (M-SOCs), and generator trailers now help keep local and national communities safe and prepared for disasters.

Canadian Coast Guard search and rescue lifeboats once had electrical power only when they were running at full throttle. Today, the Power Innovations Auto-regulated Motion Power System™ (AMPS™) also generates RPM independent power while the boats are at idle. Crew (and those rescued) have the consistent benefits of heating, air conditioning, and communication.

Pilots of both civilian and military aircraft are now taught to fly without ever leaving the ground. For flight simulation, perfect quality power is essential to simulate true flying conditions or to rehearse mission flights. Power Innovations has been in the background of flight simulation since starting to sell product in 2002. The company's power

quality and backup systems, as well as its integrated container options, are assisting in training pilots and service personnel in the war-torn desert areas of the world, the countries of our global allies, and here at home.

Airport luggage scanners operate flawlessly—even in power outages—with Power Innovations' solutions in the background ensuring scanners have perfect power. The company's equipment can sometimes be seen near luggage scanners, although it is more typical for this large equipment to be invisibly protecting behind the scenes.

Power Innovations' technology is widely recognized in the oil and gas industry for both large trucks navigating almost impassible terrain and oil rigs on the world's oceans. On the best equipped rigs, Power Innovations turns rig generator power into the perfect power needed to back blowout preventers and other equipment essential to crew and environmental safety, as well as the flawless operation of highly sophisticated equipment. For dockside, onshore containers protect the environment by providing frequency conversion, which allows drilling ships to utilize shore power instead of generators,

regardless of the global power standard built into the ship.

The "big guys" already know Power Innovations; but the company's more recent product lines were developed for small businesses, homeowners, and sports enthusiasts. Some of the products for the "little guys" protect expensive electronic equipment during normal operation and keep it running in a simple power outage. Other products generate power to be used for emergencies—or in remote locations. After use, power can be renewed for repeat use via solar or other charging methods.

Power Innovations provides its full-scale equipment, integration solutions, and custom products globally. The company's product lines range from complex mobile and power generation solutions to its original lines of basic power quality equipment. Power Innovations takes pride in being a part of the Utah business community.

✧

Above: Innovative Custom Systems and Technology Integration.

Below: Westfield Police Department at Super Bowl XLVIII.

DHI Computing
Service, Inc.

✧

Top: DHI Corporate headquarters located in Provo, Utah.

Above: A family business from the beginning, DHI leaders have included Bliss Crandall, center, and his sons, left to right, Ken and Lynn, c. 1967.

With more than 50,000 technology-related jobs in Utah Valley, the region is earning its reputation as "Silicon Slopes." While most of the upsurge has occurred since the early 1970s, the grandfather of these technology companies has just entered its seventh decade as a multinational, technology-leading force.

DHI Computing Service, Inc. (DHI)—an information-processing service organization so profitable that it has never had a layoff—has its roots at Utah State University (USU). It was there the late Bliss H. Crandall (1913-2001) and Lyman H. Rich developed the first punch-card system in 1950 for processing Dairy Herd Improvement Association records.

The method was successful—so successful, in fact, that USU requested they move the enterprise off-campus. This now family-run business was officially founded as DHI Computing Service, Inc., in 1954, and originally operated out of the basement of the Crandall home in Logan, Utah.

For the first few years, Bliss worked other full-time jobs to support his new venture (including dean of admissions at BYU), requiring the collective efforts of his wife, Mildred, and their three children to sustain and grow the fledgling company. Bliss' two sons, Lynn and Ken, have since played an integral role in the development of DHI; and under Lynn's leadership as CEO, the company

has branched into the financial and healthcare industries as well. Today, DHI has more than 300 employees with its main offices in Provo, Utah, and sales, service, and training branches in California, Washington, and Ohio.

Like his father, Lynn has always believed that information must be carefully measured to be appropriately managed. Their commitment to this guiding principle has turned the family's basement punch-card venture into a business that deals with all facets of data processing, including software programming, telecommunications, equipment utilization, systems, computer operations, and customer support.

The company is composed of several divisions serving different industries:
- DHI-Provo (dairy),
- FPS GOLD (banking),
- GOLDPoint Systems (consumer finance),
- PCIS (healthcare), and
- an Internal Services Department that supports these divisions and DHI as a whole.

DHI's original line of business, the dairy, was created by people who understood herd management because of their hands-on experience in the industry. Thanks to the ongoing collaborative efforts of several renowned dairymen across the country, DHI has become a premier developer of herd and feed management software with a long history of innovation. DHI now tabulates records for 1.76 million cows monthly and manages the rations of more than 21.76 million animals.

In 1964, DHI entered the financial industry after being approached by Deseret Federal Savings and Loan Association to develop a

mechanized system to handle their growing needs. Lynn rallied a couple of his programmers, and after only a few months, introduced the new system to the banking industry. Since then, FPS GOLD has grown to service more than seventy clients with corporate offices in more than thirty states and now supports approximately 14 million banking transactions per month. FPS GOLD's presence in the banking industry naturally led to the development of GOLDPoint Systems, which provides service to 900 branches of financial institutions across the United States with a network of 79,000 dealers. In 2014 alone, GOLDPoint Systems processed 13 million loan applications and funded billions of dollars in new loans.

Also in 1964, DHI entered the medical data processing field by designing and developing one of the first applications for patient billing and collections for a thirty-five physician medical clinic in Salt Lake City. Today, PCIS has developed and supports a single-source solution that includes an integrated practice management, electronic health record, and patient web portal software package. This software is used by both large multi-specialty medical groups and smaller medical facilities across the country.

DHI's ability to service these diversified markets has largely been the result of the company's continual commitment to research and development. As CEO, Lynn has always advocated a strong financial philosophy that includes reinvesting twenty-eight percent of profits annually back into the company to sustain future growth. Provo's Mayor John R. Curtis, who spoke at the company's sixty year celebration in 2014, said it was highly unusual to have a company that has endured and succeeded so long. "How valuable it is to have owners…who are interested in the company more than they are in the dollar," he said. "Those who could have taken advantage of this company have instead plowed those dollars back into the company and invested in this company."

Over the years, DHI's views of diversification have helped the company weather economic downturns. When one industry has been stung by negative conditions, other divisions have picked up the slack to allow DHI to maintain excellent financial stability. It is this financial stability, along with the company's commitment to providing innovative products and services to their clients, that has allowed DHI Computing Service, Inc., to be a leader in the data-processing industry for more than sixty years.

✧

Above: When DHI celebrated sixty years of business without a layoff in 2014, many people in the audience had been with the company more than forty years.

Below: DHI server room where millions of transactions are processed per day, c. 2014.

QUALTRICS

✧

Top: Tucked away in the mouth of Provo Canyon, Qualtrics' 100,000 square foot Provo office space is one of the most beautiful in the entire state.

Above: Started as a family operation in a basement, Qualtrics has become the leading insights platform.

More than a dozen years ago, Brigham Young University marketing research professor Scott M. Smith wanted to create an online analytics research and data collection tool sophisticated enough for a PhD, but simple enough for an intern.

He launched Qualtrics as a father-son business in the basement of his Provo home in 2002 with his sons, Ryan and Jared, and Ryan's college friend, Stuart Orgill.

Smith believed that he and his small team could create user-friendly, online research software to meet the insight needs of small and large businesses—and that is exactly what they did.

Profitable since its first year, Qualtrics has become a billion dollar enterprise with an international profile boosted by such publications as *Forbes* and the *Wall Street Journal*.

Such success is no accident. Smith understood from his marketing expertise that

businesses want to know what their customers are thinking to help them implement effective business decisions. While the insights were important in 2002 when Qualtrics launched, they became even more essential after the economic downturn in 2008 convinced companies of the importance of making data-driven business decisions.

"We spent the first five years running the company out of the Smiths' basement," says Stuart Orgill, Qualtrics co-founder. "If we needed to transfer a call, we just knocked on the wall next to us and handed over the phone. It might sound humorous, but our basement operation was doing business with major clients such as Ameriprise and Royal Caribbean. We were generating more than a million dollars of business each year," Orgill continues. "It even got to the point where the neighbors were getting annoyed. Just imagine twenty cars pulling up to the front of your home each morning—it looked like a wedding reception was taking place."

Not surprising, given Smith's marketing research background, Qualtrics began as a research solution for academics. For its first three years, the company worked solely in academia, assisting professors and students working on sophisticated research problems. Learning to support students' rigorous thesis and doctoral positions ultimately helped Qualtrics' employees sharpen their software development skills.

With academia as a niche, every major university in the United States and more than 1,600 colleges and universities worldwide now use Qualtrics software. Additionally, Qualtrics soon realized a major benefit of

building a student following in that graduates tended to gravitate toward Qualtrics as the research solution of choice once they entered the professional world. Students turned professionals understood that Qualtrics offered the capabilities needed to easily collect, analyze, and act on data-driven decisions.

Today, the company boasts nearly 7,000 diverse customers, among them JetBlue, Gogo, Kellogg's, Crate and Barrel, The Weather Channel, Neiman Marcus, MasterCard, Land's End, eHarmony, E*TRADE, and Citrix.

Success for Qualtrics is due, in part, to its savvy growth strategy and scrappy can-do attitude. From the beginning, Smith imposed a rule that the company could not rely on outside funding.

"Scott is a brilliant serial entrepreneur and innovator," Orgill says. "He is great at keeping expenses in control and helping young people maximize their potential."

Under Smith's guidance, the company did not consider investment funding for nearly a decade, at which time, Qualtrics was already highly profitable and bringing in $50 million in annual revenue. The savvy, driven team successfully established several years of revenue, profits, and happy customers. It was only over time, after the owners had moved into the 100,000 square foot office in Provo, and as its client base continued to grow, that Qualtrics considered offers from venture capitalists.

"Seeing the vision of where the company could go and after careful consideration, we determined the need to scale the business at an accelerated rate," Orgill says. "At that point, we saw the value of tapping into the talents of such companies as Accel Partners and Sequoia Capital."

That is when, in 2012, Qualtrics accepted initial Series A funding of $70 million from Sequoia Capital and Accel Partners, putting Qualtrics in the national spotlight. The more recent Series B round of $150 million, led by Insight Venture Partners, has further established the company as a major player in the insights market.

"At one point, Qualtrics was also offered $500 million dollars to sell, which means the founders could have easily retired for life. But it's rare that are you given the opportunity to do something truly great," Orgill says. "My plan back in 2002 was to stay in Utah for just a little while to help my friend and then move to California to do some consulting work, get an MBA, and then eventually do something entrepreneurial," Orgill continues. "But I came to realize that this opportunity was simply too unique. I could have looked the rest of my life for an experience similar to the one I was having at Qualtrics, and I probably wouldn't have found one this good. Still to this day, Qualtrics energizes me and our more than 650 employees."

✧

Above: Practicing transparency in all they do, this is just one of the many all glass office spaces for employees to work and meet in.

Below: With over 600 employees working onsite, Qualtrics makes sure its employees have plenty of kitchen space to hang out and refuel.

MOXTEK

✧

Moxtek headquarters in Orem, Utah, houses an enterprise where engineering innovation is a lifestyle.

Moxtek is a leading supplier of advanced nano-optical and x-ray components used in display electronics, imaging, and analytical instrumentation. For more than twenty-five years, Moxtek has improved the quality of life through expert partnerships and consistent breakthroughs in science and technology. Since 1986, Moxtek x-ray and optical components have been sent from Orem, Utah, all over the world. This year they completed the newest building on their nine building campus housing in excess of 200 employees.

Moxtek has partnered with many prestigious private and government research institutions as well as small and large businesses. Included in their remarkable history of technological advancements, Moxtek revolutionized portable and handheld XRF instrumentation with the new generation of the miniaturized Bullet™ x-ray source, which replaced radioactive isotopes in many applications. They are compact, lightweight and operate with low power consumption, which is ideal for portable application. Their handheld XRF instrumentation continued to push the limits of performance in projection, imaging, and optics, completely revolutionizing the technology along the way. Today their products are used in a variety of instruments including handheld and benchtop XRF and XRD applications.

In 1986, Moxtek began its first research collaboration, resulting in an exciting initial breakthrough—their ultra-thin polymer x-ray window. In 1991, Moxtek released the DuraBeryllium x-ray window platform. Chemplex Industries, Inc. and Moxtek

worked to develop a homogeneous sample that would fluoresce low-energy x-rays for making repeatable x-ray transmission measurements through thin films. Alongside one of the world's top space agencies, Moxtek's team of experts collaborated with some of the top minds in the world, and the result was a custom version of their x-ray window that fit into a state-of-the-art planetary explorer. In 2004, Moxtek's x-ray window landed on Mars as part of the *Mars Rover*.

Another of Moxtek's partners, 4D Technology, specializes in designs and manufactures laser interferometers, surface roughness profilers, and interferometry accessories for accurate measurement of optics, optical systems and precision machined surfaces. In Moxtek's efforts to better their polarizer and their product, they worked with 4D to obtain feedback on the performance of their sensor arrays and on the interaction of our polarizer with the array. This feedback was necessary in creating a part that could perform short exposure measurements accurately, while functioning in a cold space environment on the James Webb Space Telescope.

Moxtek has invested many man-years of research into producing high performance polarizer options to complement many emerging technologies. In 2002, Moxtek introduced the nano-tech based ProFlux® Polarizer. The ProFlux Polarizer was awarded the 2002 Silver Award by the Society for Information Display (SID).

The need for high performing UV polarizers has been growing dramatically both in size and

breadth of application. Security applications are increasingly demanding. Under polarized light, an image or security ID is printed onto currencies and securities to reduce forgeries and onto pharmaceutical containers to reduce counterfeiting. In the medical and forensic fields, Polarized UV light assists in the detection of specific tissues and their condition. In astronomy ultraviolet imaging of objects in space gives an enhanced view and can detect differences not seen in visible light images.

Other partners include Nanofab, University of Utah; University of Illinois, EAS, Eastern Applied Research; Space Dynamics Laboratory, Utah State University Research Foundation; Quad Group, Inc.; and EAG, Evans Analytical Group.

Moxtek is also partnered locally with Foothill Elementary School in Orem in their STEM program. Moxtek's technical employees volunteer their time to prepare lessons and demonstrations for elementary students to help them enlarge their scientific understanding.

Above and below: To push the limits of performance in optics and x-ray technology, cleanrooms for scientists and researchers are imperative. Such facilities have helped Moxtek become a leading supplier of advanced nano-optical and x-ray components for display electronics, imaging, and analytical instrumentation.

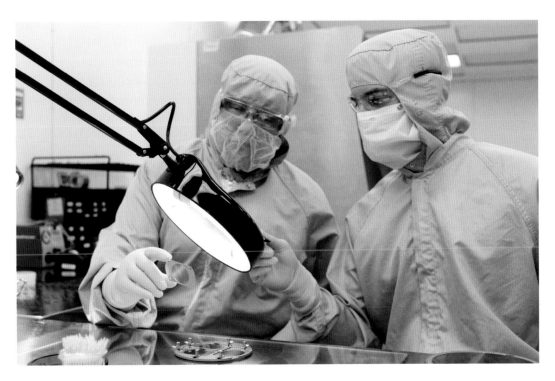

VIVINT

Todd Pedersen is a textbook American success story, yet in his early career years not everyone saw his potential. Despite his best efforts, recruiters turned down young Pedersen for a summer job selling pest control services in California, thinking he did not have what it took to earn their workers' typical $10,000 summer salary.

He accepted a job from a rival company and not only pulled in $82,000, but also expanded his direct-to-home sales team to eighty people by the end of the year.

At the same time, Pedersen watched two employees leave to pursue home security sales. Although their business flopped and they returned to reclaim their former jobs, Pedersen saw enough promise in the industry to venture into door-to-door home security systems.

Under the banner of APX Alarm, Inc., he sold about 900 systems that summer, recruited a team of talented employees and learned some tough lessons about the value of customer service. Pedersen realized if APX did not take control of building customer service support, he was not going to be able to continue. In short order, customer service became a Pedersen strength.

"It's an interesting ride when you build a business," he said. "There are amazing challenges every day. The bottom line comes down to personal interaction with customers and employees and whether you are delivering."

From Pedersen's earliest days as a businessman it became apparent that earning money has always been among his talents, but it is not the force that drives him. If it were, he could have accepted a more than $1 million offer to sell his startup altogether in 1993.

He declined that offer.

Savvy and determined, the can-do entrepreneur assembled a highly educated, first-rate team of executives and expanded his business from pest control and alarm security to launch Vivint, a highly successful residential security and home automation business. Vivint helps customers create simple, affordable smart homes with smart locks, lights, cameras, thermostats and more.

The Blackstone Group, a premier global investment and advisory firm, acquired Vivint in 2012 for $2 billion, the largest tech buyout in Utah history, and retained co-founder Pedersen as CEO. This gave Vivint additional resources to continue expanding and developing new services.

"I could see the potential for something much greater than we had," he said. "And even though we hit $2 billion a couple of years ago, I still think Vivint is just getting started."

❖

Right: Todd Pedersen, Vivint CEO and founder.

Below: The Vivint SkyControl panel.

Vivint is all about smart home solutions that capitalize on emerging technologies in the arenas of home security, home automation, energy management, wireless Internet and residential solar.

Vivint provides services to nearly 1 million customers throughout the United States, Canada and New Zealand. The company has more than 7,000 employees and was the second largest job creator in the U.S. in 2013, according to *Inc.* Magazine. The company was also named to the *Forbes'* list of "America's Most Promising Companies" in 2013 and to the *Forbes'* list of "America's Best Employers" in 2015.

The company is on a rapid trajectory for growth, competing in the smart home technology market estimated to reach $100 billion in 2018. In 2014, Vivint spun off its solar business with a successful IPO valued at $1.8 billion. Vivint Solar is now the second largest residential solar company in the U.S.

In 2015, Pedersen was featured on the season finale of the award-winning CBS series, *Undercover Boss.* Wearing a wig glued to his head and colored contacts, he got to check out the inner workings of his company incognito. Guised as a video storeowner from Bend, Oregon, Pedersen worked with employees in various jobs across the company, which involved walking along a slippery roof in Utah, taking customer calls in the Minnesota monitoring station, installing a Vivint system in a Chicago home, and working in a Vivint Solar warehouse.

Of his experience, Pedersen said he enjoyed it so much that he almost did not want it to end. In the early days of the company, he knew every job and enjoyed interacting with every employee. Thousands of employees later, he remains a highly accessible and personable CEO.

While Pedersen could have cashed out after the Blackstone acquisition, once again he chose to continue running the business.

"I love the people I work with every day," he said. "So leaving just because I made a lot of money did not make sense. Money has never been the driver. If so, I would be in Italy right now."

For more information visit www.vivint.com.

✧

Above: The Vivint Innovation Center in Lehi, Utah.

Below: Vivint remote control of a smart home.

LIBERTY SAFE AND SECURITY PRODUCTS, INC.

❖

Liberty's state-of-the-art robotic manufacturing at work.

Liberty Safe and Security Products, Inc., may have modest roots, but there is nothing modest about the largest gun, fire, and home safe manufacturer in the world. And certainly nothing is modest about its two million satisfied customers.

What began in 1988 with a couple of business partners producing five or six gun safes a day from three storage sheds, the security business has grown into an expansive enterprise with a 300,000 square foot production and distribution facility in Payson, Utah, that employs 350 workers who produce between 350 and 750 safes daily.

From the beginning the owners have used the latest state-of-the-art procedures and recruited highly skilled and trained employees who are comfortable and capable in a high tech world. Equally important, however, is that Liberty Safe is an American company, and the overwhelming majority of its parts and services come from the United States. (The company recently invested in a $10 million high end production line to bring all of their entry-level safes back to the U.S.)

Twenty-five years ago, people typically kept their guns in wood cabinets that usually featured a glass door with a simple lock that would only deter a toddler. Liberty saw the need for security with built-in measures against fire, theft and the danger of easy gun access. The company launched with the idea of promoting a high-quality safe to store and keep guns. Hunters and shooters remain a core audience—but the business quickly expanded to help all homeowners protect what they value most.

Liberty Safes are designed for multiple purposes in a variety of styles, colors and finishes; plus options, such as a monitoring device that detects motion and sends you a text message, Biometric finger swipe technology, interior lighting and accessory door panels.

At one end are small two-foot high and two-foot wide home and office safes to hold valuable documents and other treasures. At the other are large capacity safes that can hold up to seventy-two guns. In reality, there are as many uses as there are owners who want their valuables more secure, whether it is a valuable painting, camera equipment, computer hard drives, ammunition, baseball cards, laptop computers, jewelry, sentimental memorabilia or even gold and silver bullion stored as a hedge against the dollar.

Designed especially to guard against fire and theft, Liberty Safe and Security is built on three prongs:

- Quality,
- Service, and
- Reliability.

And they have a proven reputation that reinforces these objectives. One of their safes, for example, survived San Diego wild fires and 2,000 degree temperatures. Another flew 200 feet during an F4 tornado in Tennessee and landed upright and intact. In both instances the owners' valuables survived, and the owners received a new safe as part of the company's lifetime guarantee.

There is nothing like a real life situation to show the value of a steel-cased safe, but Liberty Safe also tests products aggressively on site.

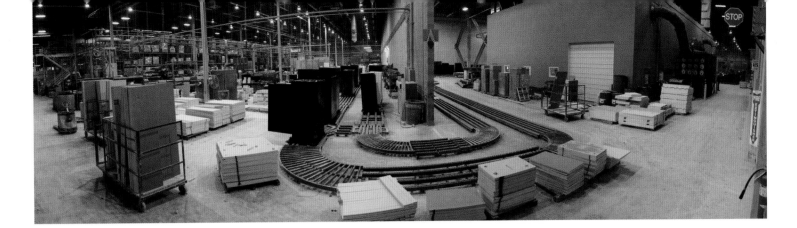

They have dropped a competitor's safe from a 200 foot free fall onto a Liberty Safe and, while the exterior may have sustained a dent or a slight rip, it remained intact with a secured door. They have even dropped one of their safes onto a competitor and had that safe ripped to shreds from the impact. Employees have also tested with demolition derby cars that bang into each other, or tried unsuccessfully to blow up their safes with dynamite.

One reason they are so effective is their investment in quality and process. It has the manufacturing and engineering technology to take one piece of steel and fold it to make the main safe body. That means one weld. Most safes have three seams, and each seam further weakens the steel.

Liberty Safe has been willing to make investments in tooling and equipment to allow the company to build a superior box in an economical time frame that competes favorably with import products. Over the last three years, Liberty Safe has invested $30 million to increase their capabilities.

They have a safe, for instance, that has such thick steel and fire-rated sheet rock that it can withstand the heat of a raging inferno for two-and-a-half hours, and even their more economical safes can survive for thirty minutes.

If you have a home safe, the odds are good that Liberty Safe manufactured it. It may have another brand name like Cabela's, John Deere and Freedom Security, for example, but it was built by Liberty Safe.

Heading the team of engineers, quality controllers, machinist, welders, grinders and other employees is Kim Waddoups, president and CEO, who leads

with the belief that everyone has valuables they want to protect, so we have tried to build a safe to meet every need. And he is so convinced in the superiority of their safes, that Liberty offers a lifetime warranty unmatched in the home safe industry. If an owner's steel safe has ever experienced an attempted break-in or a fire, Liberty will repair or replace the safe for free, and the warranty is even transferrable.

And while their safes range from about $399 to $7,000, the company markets something that money cannot buy. With a quality product and a superior guarantee, Liberty is truly providing peace of mind.

For additional information on Liberty Safe, please visit www.libertysafe.com.

✧

Top: Liberty's 300,000 square feet factory can produce up to 750 safes a day.

Above: A beautiful batch of burgundy Freedom Security safes manufactured at Liberty Safe is moving through the production line.

Below: Liberty employs 350 American workers who take great pride in their work.

Precision Assembly, Inc.

Any new business idea must answer two basic questions: "What problem am I trying to solve?" and "How can I solve it better than anyone else?" Mark Seastrand, a seasoned businessman, and Steven VanBibber, a manufacturing engineer with experience in high reliability electronics manufacturing, recognized the need for a local electronics manufacturing service that specialized in low to medium volumes that also could meet the highest quality requirements of manufacturing not typically found in small manufacturing operations. In 1996, Seastrand and VanBibber founded Precision Assembly and began a journey that would take them down paths neither could have imagined.

Precision Assembly is an Orem-based electronics manufacturing service (EMS) company, providing electronic circuit board assembly services to regional companies that choose to outsource the manufacturing of their electronic products. Precision Assembly's customers fit in a broad range of industries, including medical, industrial, instrumentation, and educational technology markets. It appreciates that each customer has distinct needs and is dedicated to meeting each client's unique assembly requirements. The manufacturing systems, processes, and service levels they developed have won them several awards and the long term loyalty of their employees, customers, and vendors.

In 1998, Seastrand departed Precision Assembly to pursue a career in publishing management, selling his half of the company to VanBibber and leaving him with a business built on a firm foundation and poised for growth. The engineer-turned-businessman knew early on that the future of the business was dependent upon surrounding himself with the right people, the right customers, and the right vendors. The core of the story of Precision Assembly is the people.

VanBibber quickly learned that although sophisticated equipment and processes are used in electronics manufacturing, it starts and ends with the people. Precision Assembly customers have quickly realized they could rely on the people who assemble the product, who respond to their inquiries, who define the critical processes and who support the manufacturing team. Those who oversee the quality systems define the way the organization does business as they manage the flow of the various components that are assembled to create custom electronics. The company motto of "Our Service….Your Success" became the focus that delivered the real value to the customer.

In 2001, Precision Assembly was recognized by the Utah Valley Entrepreneurial Forum as the ninth fastest growing Utah-based organization fewer than five years old. Additionally, in that same year, Precision Assembly was recognized by the Mountain West Venture Group as fifth on their list of Utah's top 100 companies. Mountain West Venture Group (now known as

✧

Above: Left to right, Steven VanBibber and Mark Seastrand with a circuit board manufactured at their plant.

PHOTOGRAPH COURTESY OF THE OREM *DAILY HERALD*, JULY 1997.

Mountain West Capital Network) is Utah's first and largest business networking organization devoted to supporting entrepreneurial success. Annually they honor Utah's 100 fastest growing companies for their efforts to create a sustainable niche, consistent growth, staying power, and the ability to thrive in an often brutal business environment. Precision Assembly remained on this list for three consecutive years. 2015 marks the nineteenth year of business for Precision Assembly, demonstrating that the awards of 2001 were an accurate assessment of Precision Assembly's niche and staying power.

More and more local companies want local manufacturing and greater control over their supply chain. On-shoring is a real movement as manufacturing is returning to this country. The desire to control one's critical intellectual property, the ease of change coordination, and the lower risks associated with a local vendor are market conditions that will continue to drive the growth of Precision Assembly. The electronics content of today's designs continues to escalate, and all those electronics need a manufacturing resource. Along the Wasatch Front, Precision Assembly is the sought after leader for electronics assembly.

Precision Assembly has always been true to its focus on people. Loyalty among its employees has provided great stability over the nineteen years of its existence. Seventeen employees have been with the company more than ten years. Thirty-four percent of the employees have been with the company more than nine years. Even with some significant growth over the past two years, the average tenure of its eighty-nine employees is six years.

Customer loyalty also plays a big part in the long term success of Precision Assembly. In 2014, three of its top six revenue customers have been partners with Precision Assembly for more than sixteen years. Its customer base stretches from North Carolina to Seattle but remains strongly concentrated along the Wasatch Front.

The journey begun in 1996 still continues due, in large measure, to the family environment established and maintained by VanBibber and his management team. VanBibber's story of Precision Assembly is one of a solid

beginning under the leadership of Seastrand followed by many years of on-the-job training as a business manager. In his nineteen years with Precision, seventeen of those as sole owner, VanBibber's only lament is that he wished he had taken his accounting class in college more seriously, and that he had augmented some of his engineering classes with courses in human psychology. The success of his team proves that hard work, a focus on people, and a drive to deliver high quality products does solve a problem and does it better than anyone else.

NU SKIN ENTERPRISES

✧

Above: Nu Skin Enterprises began on a kitchen table and has become a global company in more than four dozen countries.

Right: Nu Skin founders Blake Roney, Sandie Tillotson and Steve Lund.

Below: Monochromatic, clean lines of the interior building of Nu Skin Enterprises.

A little more than three decades ago, three friends sat around a kitchen table in Provo, Utah, to create a business that would make a difference and improve the lives of their customers. They were dissatisfied with the skin care products on the market and were confident they could come up with a better alternative.

They were right, and they called their new venture Nu Skin Enterprises.

Blake Roney, Sandie Tillotson and Steve Lund formulated a line of products that supported their philosophy of "all of the good, none of the bad"—meaning they contained only ingredients known to be beneficial without a lot of fillers.

They sensed success when the first product order quickly sold out. Popular from the start, people loved the products so much that many even brought their own bottles and lined up to have the unique formulas spooned into their jars.

More than the products, however, were the business opportunities. Nu Skin's mission is to be a force for good throughout the world by empowering people to improve lives with rewarding business opportunities, innovative products, and an enriching, uplifting culture.

The company established a global view from the beginning. True to that vision, the company operates in more than fifty markets worldwide. Its roots, however, remain deep in Utah Valley. It maintains its corporate headquarters from an impressive high rise in the center of Provo, and 1,500 of its more than 3,000 employees work in Utah County.

"One of Nu Skin's strengths over the years has been the ability for focus on specific aspects of the company that differentiate it from competitors," says founder Lund, chairman of the board. "What the company founders initially lacked in start-up business skills, they more than made up with their passion to provide products and an opportunity that had the potential to greatly benefit people's lives."

Supporting this vision was a razor-sharp focus on clear goals about what it would take to make this new venture successful.

Lund remembers that the original business plan was a work in progress from the first hour. "We didn't have a fully developed business plan when we started the business," he says. "The business started with cool products—products for which there was a demand. That was the first part of the business plan."

Next, the young entrepreneurs focused on how to sell these products. They put together a rewarding compensation plan that would attract a motivated sales force.

The third question they had to answer was how to create an actual business plan to introduce the product line and business model into the market. "Once A and B were answered—the products and the way to market them—the horse was out of the gate, and we had to backfill the business plan," Lund remembers.

One important lesson the founders learned was that their business strategy really came down to understanding and providing solutions to real problems. They focused on each problem that arose and found ways to overcome them.

The company's "all of the good" philosophy is also reflected in its approach to social responsibility. Nu Skin Enterprises created the Nu Skin Force for Good Foundation, a nonprofit organization whose mission is to improve the lives of children by offering hope for a life free from disease, illiteracy and poverty.

Its employees around the globe are encouraged to participate in service projects as much as possible. Corporate employees and company distributors make monetary contributions to the Nu Skin Force for Good Foundation and work together on many projects year-round, including gathering and wrapping presents for needy families, serving as mentors to young school children and donating food to homeless shelters.

During June, Nu Skin organizes a day of service where employees can participate in an organized project. The most recent endeavor included assembling 10,000 comfort kits for hospitalized children. These included books, DVDs, fleece quilts, small toys and get well cards. For the exceptional service Nu Skin gives every year, the Utah Governor declared June 4, 2015 the State's Force for Good Day. Val Hale, executive director of the Governor's Office of Economic Development, read the declaration, which was signed by Nu Skin founders Tillotson and Lund as well as Nu Skin's current CEO and President Truman Hunt.

The company that subscribes to being a force for good has been honored many other places as well for their business performance, management team and product innovation. A sampling includes DSA's Ethos award for outstanding corporate social responsibility; a Top 10 Charity Enterprises designation for humanitarian efforts in China; the Golden Dragon Award for business, product quality and contribution for the Vietnamese economy; best employer awards in Taiwan and Thailand; and the number one ranking in TotalBeauty.com's sixteen best Anti-Aging Serums. Among others, Utah has named Nu Skin one of its fasted growing and highest revenue companies.

For additional information on Nu Skin, visit www.nuskin.com.

✧

Above: Interior look of Nu Skin Enterprises' headquarters.

Below and bottom: The Nu Skin reach extends into more than fifty countries, including the Republic of Malawi.

FISHBOWL INVENTORY

✧

Above: David K. Williams, CEO, Fishbowl.

Top, right: The home of Fishbowl Inventory in Orem, Utah.

Below: The team at Fishbowl Inventory.

It would be easy to simply list the accomplishments of Fishbowl, but doing so would ignore the almost magical corporate culture found in a company ranked the number one provider of manufacturing and warehouse management software for QuickBooks and asset tracking solutions for enterprises.

The magic begins with believing that its workers should be called Fishbowlers because the term employees is too impersonal. It comes from an environment with gray three-dimensional walls that give the wavy appearance of water. It is augmented by a deep blue "think tank" room complete with fish-filled fish tank.

Walk into the entry and see a ping pong table, peek into the break room and find foosball, basketball, golf games and a corner card table for playing hearts. Interview for a job, and if you are seriously considered, you will be invited to play a game—after all, observing how a prospective worker interacts with others is as vital as getting the job done.

The northeast Orem company has become known for friendly, smiling Fishbowlers who are happy, in large part, because they are company owners. Everyone that applies, following a year of probation, is eligible for stock in Fishbowl.

CEO David Williams empowers his Fishbowlers by putting people first among his priorities. "I believe in people, not just their output," he says. He works in tandem with President Mary Michelle Scott.

Under their leadership, Fishbowl has achieved extraordinary growth and is poised

to continue as one of Utah's most prominent businesses. They encourage their Fishbowlers to take risks and try new things. It is this unique leadership skill that transformed a small, struggling software company into an industry leader.

"When leaders trust their employees and give them creative freedom to try new things, they consistently achieve positive results in the long run," Williams emphasizes.

Fishbowl developed as a team and built a successful company, and more important, a place where people could enjoy working in collaboration. "That's what we do," Williams insists. "We collaborate. We won't dictate. It's important to us that the companies we work with retain ownership of their journey to success."

Fishbowl's custom solutions are designed for those looking to create long-term, sustainable, positive transformation within their organization. Training begins with creating shifts in approach and perspective and continues by developing a culture that ensures maximum buy-in that leads to winning results.

By implementing principles from Fishbowl's book, *7 Non-Negotiables of Winning; Respect, Belief, Trust, Loyalty, Commitment, Courage, and Gratitude*, companies will see growth in hard results as they improve their soft traits. "You will become more motivated to increase and improve your soft traits to deliver more hard results!" says Williams. "This is not training or consulting as usual. It's life changing. Let's work together to make positive changes in your organization!"

Fishbowl offers a customized training program. They can come to your organization and work side-by-side with you and your team. Activities including storytelling and roleplaying to inspire and empower new behaviors, perspectives and attitudes.

Fishbowl is among a handful of employee-owned companies in Utah and is committed to support humanitarian efforts through the Courage Above Mountains (CAM) Foundation, named for David's son Cameron. CAM provides business incubation space and digital learning programs for small businesses in Utah, as well as offer learning, health, and enrichment services to underserved individuals in the U.S. and abroad.

Fishbowl's dozens of awards over the past seven years reflect its impressive growth. In 2014, Fishbowl received four revenue growth awards: Inc. 500/5000, MountainWest Capital Network Utah 100, Deloitte's Technology Fast 500, and Utah Business Fast 500. Other awards include Top 100 Champions in Small Business Influencer Award, Community Partner Award from Utah Valley Chamber of Commerce, a SAMY awards for John David King, vice president of sales for sales success, and the Humanitarian Service Award for Williams.

Williams was honored as one of vSpring Capital's Top 100 Venture Capital Entrepreneurs in 2011, and with Scott in 2012 and 2014. He was also awarded the Excellence in Leadership award from Utah Valley University.

The award honors a national leader who is recognized within his or her chosen profession, and whose body of professional work makes him or appropriate mentor and example for students in the Woodbury School of Business.

Williams serves as president of the Woodbury School of Business National Advisory Council at Utah Valley University. In this role, he mentors business students, offers career advice, and prepares young entrepreneurs to succeed in business. Prior to joining Fishbowl, in the past David served as CEO of Franklin Quest Canada, and later as managing director of First Things First, a division of Covey Leadership.

The leadership team shares its unique vision on *Forbes*, *Harvard Business Review*, and several other leadership publications regularly.

Scott, Fishbowl's president since 2011, received an honorary PhD in 2014 from the Washington Institute for Graduate Studies for her humanitarian work has helped several of Utah's most prominent high-tech firms progress from incubation to national and global leadership status. She played a key role in Fishbowl's successful company buyback, helped the company achieve an overall growth rate of seventy percent, and was named one of Utah's 30 Women to Watch.

Fishbowl was recognized in 2015 as one of the Utah Best in State in the category of business services.

Top, left and right: Fishbowlers hard at work cleaning out Cascade Springs.

Below: Finding a solution on the Fishbowl wall.

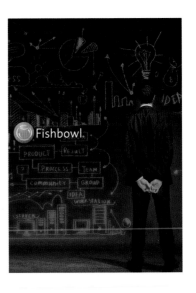

ANCESTRY.COM

Throughout time people have been interested in their family history, but the daunting task of embarking on a genealogical search kept many from learning about their past.

All that began to change with the launch of Utah-based Ancestry in 1983. What had been time-consuming and often difficult research—visiting or writing individual letters to county record offices, parishes, newspapers, and people around the globe—started to become more accessible to anyone interested in their family history. With innovations in technology, digging into family history can now be done on a computer or smartphone. At the same time, television shows like *Who Do You Think You Are?* have helped to spark an interest in family history in a larger audience.

Today, Ancestry is the largest online family history service in the world, with a mission to help everyone discover, preserve and share their family history. Ancestry's service is built on an extensive and unique collection of billions of historical records that has been digitized, indexed and put online since 1996. Ancestry has developed efficient and proprietary systems for digitizing handwritten historical documents, and has established relationships with national, state and local government archives, historical societies, religious institutions and private collectors of historical content around the world. These digital records and documents, combined with proprietary online search technologies and tools, enable members to build their family trees, research their family history and make meaningful discoveries about the lives of their ancestors.

Members are also able to add their own content to their family trees. They have uploaded and attached to their trees hundreds of millions of photographs, scanned documents and written stories. This growing pool of user-generated content adds color and context to the family histories assembled from the digitized historical documents found on Ancestry.

Ancestry has also launched AncestryDNA, using the latest DNA science and technology to tell users about their ethnic background and match them with cousins they may never knew they had. With the advances in DNA, it is now as easy as providing a saliva sample and mailing it in.

Additionally, Ancestry offers a suite of online family history brands including Fold3 that provides access to U.S. military records, including the stories, photos, and personal documents of the men and women who served; Newspapers.com, which offers a historically rich collection of U.S. newspapers dating from the late 1700s into the early 2000s; Find A Grave, a free resource for finding the final resting places of famous folks, friends and family members with photos of grave sites and memorials from all fifty states; Archives.com, which represents a simple way for anyone to begin to discover their heritage; and Family Tree Maker, the top-selling family history software that makes it easy to create beautiful family trees and charts.

AncestryProGenealogists is the official research arm of Ancestry. Their highly-skilled and well-trained researchers serve thousands of professional, government, media and individual clients worldwide. They also provide the research on celebrities' family history for all of the episodes of the television series *Who Do You Think You Are?*

With more than 1,000 employees based in Utah and 1,400 employees around the world, Ancestry is committed to supporting their local communities. Their charitable giving is rooted in their belief in family, and they generously support organizations that strengthen families in need, improve education for young people, and preserve family history. Their giving includes financial contributions, product donations, and employee volunteer efforts. Among the organizations they support are Barrettstown Children's Charity in Ireland, Dimensia UK, Ronald McDonald House, SF-Marin Food Bank, Primary Children's Hospital in Utah, Habitat for Humanity, and the Red Cross.

Ancestry has been named a "Best Company to Work For" in Utah for several years by *Utah Business Magazine*. They are particularly proud of this honor, as it is based on feedback directly from their employees in Utah. Ancestry has also been named to "Best Places to Work" lists in the San Francisco Bay Area and Dublin, Ireland.

One of Ancestry's satisfied customers is Kathy Schlendorf of Orem, Utah, who began to search for her ancestors in 1972 by attempting to obtain birth, marriage, and death certificates with her family's surname. All she knew was that her father's family came from northern Germany. After several failed attempts to obtain information on her own, she used a $2,000 inheritance and hired a professional researcher who uncovered the names of some of her great-grandparents and great-great-grandparents and where her ancestors had lived. Unable to afford more research, she tucked the precious results in a box under her bed. Forty years later, she discovered and subscribed to Ancestry, and within a few hours she had verified the facts from the original research and expanded on them substantially.

"I now have more than 700 family names and dozens of sources that support my research," she says. "I don't have just one family tree. I have a family forest. I owe it all to Ancestry, and I am not alone."

Above: Ancestry employees take a break to have some fun together.

Below: Ancestry recently launched a redesigned site with cool new features.

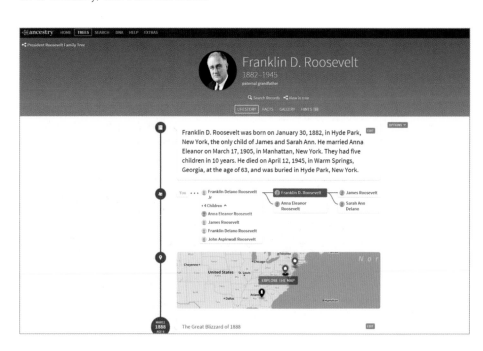

FORT KNOX, INC.

Fort Knox Vaults prides itself on exceeding expectations. For eight decades Fort Knox, the fortress-like vault, lined with granite walls and protected by a blast-proof door weighing twenty-two tons, has set the standard for security in the United States.

Fort Knox, Inc., the safe and vault manufacturer located at 993 North Industrial Park Road in Orem, its owners and nearly 100 employees are sufficiently confident in the quality of their products that their very name suggests.

Tom James was an outdoors enthusiast and felt a responsibility to secure his firearms. He realized that this responsibility extended to all gun owners and that there was not a product available that he was comfortable securing his firearms in. Tom and a few of his friends got together and constructed a few safes for themselves. As others saw the product, demand grew and an industry was born. Fort Knox used a two-prong approach that included selling directly to consumers nationwide as well as to gun stores. Tom would travel the country doing trade shows with trucks and trailers delivering safes to customers and stores, and the business did well.

T. J. James, Tom's son purchased the company in 1991, and since then it has expanded to include more than 150 dealers found across the country. Fort Knox still participates in trade shows as well as in several factory shows and sells direct from its showroom in Orem, Utah.

The team at Fort Knox markets their safes and vaults to gun and homeowners throughout the country. Fort Knox customers understand that valuables, guns, and important documents should be locked up and they trust the quality craftsmanship and security that Fort Knox offers in their product line up. In addition to their superior quality and security, Fort Knox is proud that all of their products are made in the United States. They understand that offering jobs and keeping work and jobs in the USA is vital to a strong and healthy national economy.

Customization is a key selling point. They customize everything from design, size, the number of compartments, amount of steel and color found in the product. Fort Knox once sold a dark blue safe and a light silver safe displayed side by side. They painted murals from the Civil War on them and did blue for the North and silver for the South. The owners were Civil War collectors. Because of this ability to produce a product that meets consumer's needs, many Fort Knox customers eventually purchase more than one safe. The first purchase is typically for

✧

Fort Knox Vaults come in a variety of sizes, colors and styles, according to customer preference.

firearms, but once the new owner gets it home, the perspective of security changes a bit. Suddenly the owner wants to put a coin collection in the safe or he or she wants to put valuable papers inside it, then perhaps it would be ideal for scrapbooks, photographs or irreplaceable mementos.

In the past few years, Fort Knox has seen a significant increase in sales of safes and vaults that are purchased for collectibles rather than firearms; the customers might like a secure place for grandma's diamonds, for instance. And although diamonds can be replaced; grandma's diamonds cannot. You cannot put a price tag on sentiment or history.

When it comes to quality the team at Fort Knox is known for exceeding expectations. For over thirty years Fort Knox has perfected the art of creating premium safes and vaults. The team has worked hard to earn the reputation "America's best" through innovation, dedication to quality, and personalized customer service. Fort Knox strives to provide:

- Unequaled security
- Superior fire protection
- The most comprehensive lifetime warranty in the industry
- All made 100 percent in the USA

The extensive product line is handcrafted to exceed expectations of consumers as well as those of independent testing facilities. Fort Knox surpasses industry standards set by Underwriters Laboratory, the largest nonprofit consumer protection organization. The buyer gets peace of mind knowing that Fort Knox has passed rigorous testing.

Fort Knox uses premium materials combined with precision craftsmanship to create each Fort Knox safe or vault, and they take pride in developing products with the most innovative engineering, design and manufacturing process. Fort Knox offers many unique and exclusive features in their products; these include a Reinforced fire door, rack and pinion gearing and star corner bolts. Additionally, Fort Knox offers superior fire protection.

The purchase of a safe is one of the most important decisions consumers will make in a lifetime because of what is placed inside.

Fort Knox invites you to take the Fort Knox challenge by making an honest comparison of quality, value, and warranty.

Fort Knox is proud that it offers an extensive lifetime warranty, which not only covers burglary, burglary attempt, fire, flood and incidental damage; it also covers lock and paint, two items most often excluded by other manufacturers.

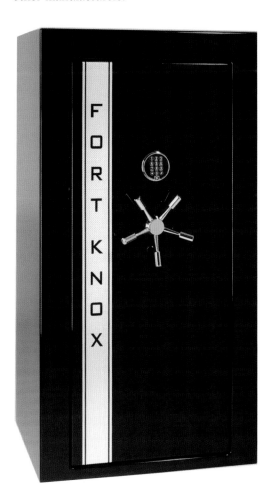

While they sell many safes and vaults across the country, many of them are sold to friends and neighbors. They want be able to look anyone in the eye who has purchased one of their products and know they have sold them the best possible product. Their aim is to exceed expectations.

Tom started the company because he wanted to offer a product that would meet his high standard of security, a place where he could put his valuables and know they are safe. Today thousands of Fort Knox Customers enjoy that same high standard of security and peace of mind because they own a Fort Knox Safe or Vault!

ROCKETSHIP

From the outside there is little to suggest that within the walls of the historic Provo seminary building explosions of creativity are a common occurrence. Step inside, however, and you will find a workspace filled with just about everything: wearable devices, camp stoves, kitchen utensils, radiation detectors—you name it.

✧

Above: Rocketship, an industrial design shop that creates products worldwide.

Welcome to Rocketship—Utah's recognized leader in product design and development. Since its inception more than a decade ago, Rocketship has emphasized user-centered, strategy-driven design solutions to create new product experiences for some of the Utah's most admired companies.

"We design products that will resonate with our customer," says the firm's founder, Michael Horito. "It is about having a deep understanding of customers, trends, technology, and business. It takes a different kind of firm to interweave all of these. We generate creative solutions that embody our client's technology, giving it a usable, manufacturable form, while balancing the costs and constraints."

Infused with a passion for good design, Rocketship has created more than 350 new product experiences for clients around the world in diverse categories: outdoor recreation, health and wellness, consumer electronics, medical equipment, housewares, and more. By leveraging strengths and experiences across multiple disciplines, their highly collaborative team brings a fresh perspective to client challenges.

"Design occurs at the intersection of technology and people," Horito says. "It is not always about designing the object. More often it is about creating the connections between ideas, technologies, brands, and users. Once these are defined, the design of the product starts to fall into place. It is an iterative process that often requires exploration and discovery."

With expertise in areas ranging from target user research and trend watching to design forecasting and manufacturing processes, Rocketship brings the highest level of creative talent to every project, providing unmatched attention to detail. Working closely with their clients, they offer an all-encompassing approach to design and development, and a commitment to creating meaningful products and concepts that enhance brand identity and loyalty. And the firm's approachable attitude keeps clients coming back.

"At its essence, what we do is communicate," says Horito. "We communicate the value of the product to the consumer, the function to the user, and the design to the manufacturer." By facilitating understanding between all parties involved, Rocketship is able create a smooth flow of information. "Our biggest challenge is educating our clients on what design really is and how it benefits their bottom line. When they understand this, they realize that design is not something you add to the end of the process—it is an integral component throughout."

Additional information is available on the Internet at at www.rocketshipdesign.com.

Sue, an economically struggling middle-aged woman, secured an interview with a local travel agency, and as she fielded questions from a weary interviewer trying to usher her from the room, finally said, "I have not had a chance to show my certifications."

Puzzled, the interviewer asked Sue what she meant, and she pulled out several industry certifications, including a certificate signed by the CEO of Microsoft® that affirmed her skills in Microsoft Excel. When asked to create an Excel spreadsheet with pivot tables, she quickly accomplished the task. Instead of leaving the interview empty-handed, she left with a position.

Sue certified her office skills through Certiport, a home-grown Utah Valley company dedicated to helping people achieve certifications and increase their marketability. Certiport is the sole provider globally for Microsoft Office certification as well as for other globally recognized IT companies.

"Our business dedicates itself to helping people excel through certification," says Vice President of Marketing, Craig Bushman. "On a resume, someone may indicate proficiency with Microsoft Office, for example, but what does that mean? Not much. There is nothing in that statement that guarantees the person has the required skills. But with a Microsoft© or Adobe® certificate, the designation has cache and credibility."

Since launching in 1997, Certiport has delivered more than 20 million exams and averages three million exams per year. It has gone from a local to a global company serving three key markets: academic, corporate, and workforce development. Certiport is present in 140 countries and provides certification exams in twenty-seven languages. Additionally, it has 12,000 academic testing centers located directly within schools. All testing is proctored, and Certiport's full pathway of materials helps students learn, practice, and certify.

Notable growth and success led, Pearson VUE to acquire Certiport in 2012. (Pearson VUE delivers millions of high-stakes tests a year across the globe for clients in the licensure, certification, academic admissions, regulatory, and government testing service markets.)

"Certiport still maintains its own brand, particularly in education," Bushman says. "Our sweet spot is K-12, but we also have a significant presence in community colleges and higher places of learning. We want individuals to have the tools for success in education and their careers."

As part of that goal, Certiport sponsors national and international competitions for Microsoft and Adobe. These competitions have helped winners experience tremendous success. One examples is a teenage student from Great Britain. She won the Microsoft Excel World Championship and received a $200,000 job offer as a result of her victory. Another example is an extremely shy young man. He had been bullied and wanted to be the first in his family to graduate from high

school. He won the U.S. championship for Microsoft Word and is experiencing tremendous success in his life. Another used her certification to accept a design job with NASA.

"It is extremely satisfying to see people open doors they thought were closed to them," adds Bushman. "I love when they get certified, because they then get noticed."

CLOSE TO MY HEART

It was love at first sight, actually love at first touch. The first time Jeanette Lynton held a rubber stamp, she knew it was the key to her future and something she wanted to do for the rest of her life.

Lynton, the founder and CEO of Close to My Heart, heads a successful direct sales scrapbooking and stamping business. For more than thirty years, Lynton has provided the resources for individuals who wish to enhance their artistic talents and pursue a business. Close To My Heart now extends throughout the United States and into Canada, Australia, and New Zealand, offering beautiful and intuitive products to crafters of all stripes.

Her love of stamps fueled Lynton's venture from the beginning. She demonstrated and sold stamp sets at craft fairs while her children played under the table.

"People could feel my energy and sense my sincerity," she says. "And they wanted a taste of that joy, that creativity, and that possibility for themselves."

As interest in the business grew, many expressed an interest in selling the products, asking if she would expand her direct sales model.

"I welcomed the opportunity—and them—with open arms," she says. Lynton cut and pasted the catalog for that initial foray at the kitchen table. She worked with a local copy center to get it printed, engineered a compensation plan, and, with a small but enthusiastic group of demonstrators, began her business.

After experiencing major setbacks, including the dissolution of her first marriage and the loss of her early business, Lynton was determined to prove to the world that she mattered, and that what she did mattered. She initially sought a position to be home with her children, be creative, interact with other women, and earn a living. Not finding one, she started over with a new business venture—Dozens of Terrific Stamps, more commonly known as D.O.T.S. It was not long before she once again found others who shared her passion. Over the years D.O.T.S. expanded its product offerings and became Close To My Heart.

Now recognized as an industry leader, Lynton's company is a premiere resource for self-expression with albums, papers, stamps, markers, stamp pads, design software, and more, all designed to help individuals discover their creativity, celebrate relationships, and preserve and share the moments that matter most. Lynton has brought many consultants with her on her thirty year journey of product passion, community building and creativity. And as the company name suggests, her business remains close to her heart.

✦

Right: Close To My Heart Founder and CEO, Jeanette Lynton.

Below: Close To My Heart Headquarters based in Pleasant Grove, Utah.

The year was 1932, during the worst economic crisis of modern times. Businesses were failing at a breakneck pace. Despite this, Henry Schein, determined to achieve his dream of opening his own drugstore, borrowed $500 to open a modest store in Woodside, Queens, New York.

Henry shifted to a larger service model after hearing local doctors complain about high prices and inconsistent service from their medical supply sources. He and his wife, Esther, decided if they distributed professional supplies from their store, they could do a better job and charge less. By following the model of pioneering mail-order giant Sears & Roebuck, they applied that formula to their customers and transformed their business as well as the healthcare professionals they served.

The Scheins exceeded their own expectations; more than eight decades later the simple roots of that first enterprise have grown considerably. Henry Schein, Inc., is now a Fortune 500® Company and a member of the NASDAQ 100® Index. As the world's largest provider of healthcare products and services to office-based dental, medical and animal health practitioners, it is featured on the *FORTUNE's* World's Most Admired Company List, ranking first in the Wholesalers: Health Care industry category. It also appears on *Ethisphere's* list of World's Most Ethical Companies.

Those roots have extended to American Fork, Utah, where the company has opened a 100,000 square foot building for its Practice Solutions headquarters as well as a state-of-the-art training facility on digital dentistry. It includes a Center of Excellence that contains high-quality digital dental equipment to showcase innovations to dentists and provide dental professionals a facility to offer free, high-quality oral care to the community's underserved population. American Fork is also home to Henry Schein Dentrix after the company acquired Dentrix Dental Systems in 1997. Today, Henry Schein leads the industry with 33,000 dental practices currently using its market-leading software system, Dentrix, and state-of-the art web-based solutions, designed by Henry Schein Dentrix engineers.

While company headquarters are in Melville, New York, on Long Island, its reach extends beyond the United States into twenty-eight countries, employing more than 17,000 Team Schein Members. In 2013 the company's sales reached $9.6 billion.

HENRY SCHEIN, INC.

From the beginning Henry Schein, Inc. has established a culture focusing on the well-being and success of employees and clients, which has been sustained by Henry Schein Cares, the company's global corporate social responsibility program. Henry Schein Cares stands on four pillars:

- Engaging Team Schein members to reach their potential;
- Ensuring accountability by extending ethical business practices to all levels;
- Promoting environmental sustainability; and
- Expanding access to healthcare for underserved and at-risk communities around the world.

Henry Schein champions the vision of "doing well by doing good." It recognizes that health providers require the guidance of trusted advisers to help them operate more efficiently and to select the correct supplies, software, equipment, pharmaceuticals, and vaccines. They also recognize the need to help clinicians build their practices so they can focus on improving their patients' health.

BOOSTABILITY

Boostability founders Travis Thorpe, Jared Turner and Rick Horsley knew they had a good idea in 2009 when they decided to help small businesses by creating a set of tools their clients could use for effective and affordable search engine optimization (SEO).

✧

Above: The lobby of Boostability corporate headquarters.

Below: Boostability corporate headquarters at Thanksgiving Park in Lehi.

At that time the marketplace for SEO services included only large-scale operations and big business. SEO companies had avoided marketing to small businesses, because they were unable to provide a profitable scalable service on a small business budget.

This challenge intrigued Boostability founders, who started their company in January 2009 with the goal of creating affordable, effective DIY SEO tools for the small business marketplace—something no SEO company had been able to do.

They believed that by using their tools, the visibility of their clients' websites or web pages would appear higher in the search results page, thus being seen and used by more visitors.

It was a good idea, but at one point profits were so low, they ran out of payroll and asked a few key employees to get contracted somewhere else because they could not pay.

After unsuccessfully trying to convince customers it was easy to use their tools, they realized their clients would rather pay Boostability to do the work for them and their good idea became a great one. Boostability turned itself into a full-service enterprise using the same technology. They partnered with organizations that service small and local businesses and who wanted to provide quality SEO to their clients.

Within five years the company had grown from zero to more than $34 million. It received the UVEF award two years in a row for fastest-growing company in Utah County, and is featured on *Inc.com*'s 2014 list for fastest-growing companies nationwide.

"One of the first glimpses of how successful this could be came when we saw the results we were getting for our clients, their rankings in the search engines were improving and they were seeing more traffic to their websites," says Thorpe, CEO. "Our technology platform enabled efficiency and scalability, allowing us to take large worldwide partners. We've grown to over 17,000 active customers today."

Boostability has more than 500 employees as well as a crowd-sourcing platform of thousands of at-home writers. Its corporate headquarters in Lehi have expanded to include sites in Lindon and Orem. Plans are under way to expand into the United Kingdom, Europe and eventually Latin America.

"We provide value for our customers," Thorpe says, "and we deliver a valuable online presence for our clients, which can grow their business and give them jobs. It comes down to just people and we've been able to help a lot of people. We want to continue doing this."

Building a Greater Utah Valley

Utah Valley's real estate developers, construction companies, heavy industries, and manufacturers provide the economic foundation of the region

ANDERSON CRG

Anderson CRG and Jonathan C. Anderson, its principal broker, have received a Costar Power Broker Award in back to back years for 2013 and 2014 for the State of Utah. The Power Broker Awards recognize the top ten performers in each category. Anderson CRG's Power Broker awards include, Top Leasing Firms, Top Retail Leasing Brokers and Top Industrial Leasing Brokers.

✧

Above: Jonathan C. Anderson.

While all the other companies who received this prestigious award were much larger in terms of people, some having as many as 180 agents, Anderson made the list

as a one-man practitioner who closes between 50 and 60 deals a year. The company had its office in Riverwoods Business Park in Provo for a number of years and recently moved its headquarters to nearby Orem, Utah.

As one of the most prominent commercial real estate brokers in the area, one could make a convincing case that Anderson has had more impact on the long-term market in Utah County than any other broker. The owner and principal broker of Anderson CRG offers his clients more than thirty-five years of experience in a broad range of commercial and corporate real estate. At any one time, he is actively working on fifty to 100 projects. Anderson's enviable record includes completing transactions as a principal, buyer, seller, and broker totaling more than $1 billion and more than 10 million square feet in office, retail, industrial, and multifamily properties as well as hundreds of acres of developable land.

His breadth of experience prepared him uniquely to serve clients in all aspects of commercial real estate. In his ten years with Equitec Properties Company, Anderson led a team of professionals acquiring commercial investment properties throughout the South and lower Midwest. There was no bigger stage than that in commercial real estate and Anderson thrived in the environment, acquiring a steady crop of strong-performing commercial investment properties for the company.

During his eight years as director of Corporate Real Estate of Amdahl, a Fujitsu-owned Fortune 500 company, he directed real estate worldwide, overseeing all lease and purchase negotiations as well as disposition strategies, project design, and construction groups for the company's 160 locations.

Although the Utah County market was smaller than most he had worked in, Anderson could see that Utah Valley was poised to explode as a leading business and technology center, and he wanted to be part of the growth. "I know what I can do," he says, "and I was confident I could find success here."

Anderson co-founded Commerce CRG in Utah County, which over the next thirteen years grew to become the largest commercial real estate brokerage firm in Utah County, with the largest market share, peaking at

twenty-seven agents. He sold that company in late 2011 and formed Anderson CRG, where he is owner and principal broker.

"Many of the agents I trained are now my competitors, but that's all good," he says. "We work together well in cooperating roles, which in this business is key."

The sheer numbers of properties and acquisitions through the decades are positive proof of his success, but he also has the endorsement of community leaders and clients.

Dixon Holmes, deputy mayor of the mayor's office of economic development, applauds both his talents and his work ethic. "I have worked with Jon in a variety of settings and found him very knowledgeable and professional," he says. "As a commercial real estate broker, Jon knows how to meet the needs of his clients and provide them with the most accurate and up-to-date information. Jon works hard to put deals together and close them. I know that if I need local or regional market information, I can go to Jon for the latest data."

Rona Ralph, president, Utah Valley Chamber of Commerce and former publisher of the *Daily Herald* says, "I trusted Jon with the sale of our commercial building because I knew him to be professional, knowledgeable, resourceful, and a person of integrity. I have found the same in my associations with him on the board of directors of the Utah Valley Chamber of Commerce and as a friend for years."

A private investor, Steven Thayne adds, "Jon's experience and knowledge has been invaluable to me for many years. Through many years of working with Jon, I've developed deep trust in him. For any commercial real estate needs Jon is the professional I call."

Chris Matthews, chief credit officer of Cache Private Capital Diversified Fund has worked with Jon on multiple transactions, saying, "Jon Anderson is extremely knowledgeable…with more than three decades of experience in the industry, he has extensive and deep relationships, which give him the ability to provide immediate insights on properties and developments in his market areas. I give him my highest recommendation."

Most importantly, Anderson loves using his decades of experience in a business where he can provide one-on-one, personalized service to his clients. "I love what I do and can see myself continuing to serve those buying, selling or leasing commercial real estate properties in Utah County until I'm ninety-five," he says.

✧

UTAH CENTRAL ASSOCIATION OF REALTORS®

When it comes to buying a home or finding a building for business, it is gratifying to know that a seasoned professional association exists to provide leading-edge programs, products, and services to their clients.

It is also satisfying to realize that this same association carefully trains its members and real estate professionals to become leading advocates for real estate and property rights in Utah County as well as twelve other counties.

✧

Utah Central Association of Realtors® Headquarters, 1031 West Center Street, Orem, Utah.

That organization, the Utah Central Association of Realtors®—newly renamed after merging with several other Utah area Realtor® associations—has roots that extend nearly a century into the past. Then and now it has been the local echo of the state and national goal of providing the Voice of Real Estate.

Outside the industry many people are likely unaware that the terms *real estate agent* and *Realtor®* are not the same thing. A Realtor® is held to a higher standard of ethics. As a nonprofit, the Utah Central Association of Realtors® is not only dedicated to helping its Realtors® meet this standard of ethics, but to be proficient and cooperative as they help protect property rights and enhance the Realtor® image.

"We pride ourselves on our professionalism and on our efforts to enhance and improve the quality of life in the community," says Taylor Oldroyd, CEO.

The roots of the national Realtor® organization began in 1908 when 120 founding members gathered in Chicago to create the first iteration of the National Association of Realtors®, which was then named the National Association of Real Estate Exchanges. The Utah State Realty Association, a child organization of the National Association of Real Estate Exchanges, was formed in Salt Lake City on April 8, 1920, with D. Carlos Kimball as president.

The Utah County Real Estate Association, which falls under the umbrella of the national and state associations, was first formed in 1916, but it was not until 1921 that the association was officially admitted to the national association. It then became the Provo Real Estate Board and gained T. H. Heal as president.

The association has had a rich history of dedicated leaders, among which is Gary Herbert, current governor of Utah, who led the board in 1985.

Recently, the Utah County Association of Realtors® and the Uintah Basin, Carbon/Emery, Grand/San Juan, and Central Utah Boards have merged to become the Utah Central Association of Realtors®. It is anticipated that a new level of real estate professionalism will expand to a greater part of the state. According to Oldroyd, the merger is critical both to improve real estate professionalism in the state and to comply with the National Association of Realtors'® standards. As he explains: "Expect us,

- To provide Code of Ethics training for all Realtors®;
- To promote advocacy and to ensure good public policy and pro-business regulations;
- To be involved in quality community engagement activities each year;
- To be unified and supportive of the National Association of Realtors® goals and mission;
- To improve our technology communications; and
- To be fully financially solvent and to ensure we will be around for the next 100 years."

Beyond its dedication to its members, the Utah Central Association of Realtors® solidly involves itself in community life. It participates in a Utah Valley University Scholarship Fund that helps business management students with

a real estate focus. It works with the Red Cross, Habitat for Humanity, and UARHOF (a housing opportunity fund), among others.

Additionally, the Utah Central Association of Realtors® believes in being involved in many pursuits that benefit the overall community along with Realtors®, such as a yearly Housing Summit, to which members of the public, government leaders, and Realtors® are all invited so they can better stay informed on the housing market and the issues the community faces.

"We also own and host the Utah Valley Home Expo, which we put on yearly for the community with the help of Bennett Events." Oldroyd adds.

A sampling of the past four years includes:
- The Utah County Innovator Roundup, an event which found, brought together, and supported local entrepreneurs.
- The Walkable Neighborhoods Conference, an event designed to discuss walkability and the many benefits it offers to the health of individuals, the environment, finances, and the overall community. The conference focused on achieving these outcomes through sustainable development, transit-oriented development, and form-based coding and zoning.
- The Water Forum, geared toward examining Utah's risk for water-related issues and protecting and conserving this vital resource.
- Stop the Stench, a forum held in Pleasant Grove that informed the community of the Timpanogos Special Service District and what could be done to mitigate the stench from composting waste.
- Front Runner Welcome, an event for the public welcoming the front runner transportation system and all the business and smart growth it affords.
- "I Wish This Was," an event in Provo that focused on identifying the growth the community would like to see in Provo by asking businesses and residents what they want to see in vacant spaces downtown.

For more information about the Utah Central Association of Realtors® visit www.ucaor.com or call 801-226-3777.

✧

Realtors® in Utah County are dedicated to helping families achieve the American dream of homeownership.

CURECRETE DISTRIBUTION, INC.

✧

Above: Jerald W. "Jerry" Jones has become the worldwide leader in concrete densification.

Below: Ashford Formula enhances concrete appearance and durability.

In the world of concrete, Jerald W. "Jerry" Jones embodies the American success story. He took a process that revolutionized the durability of concrete, spent more than forty years educating others about its merits, and broke through barriers of skepticism to become the worldwide leader in concrete densification. In addition to manufacturing world renowned densification products, Curecrete Distribution, Inc., also has products for concrete diamond polishing, surface preparation, repairs, and maintenance.

So, why densify concrete? Because, making concrete durable and long-lasting requires a far better solution than topical coatings. Under a microscope, concrete resembles a large, porous sponge. This creates problems in the concrete as it absorbs contaminants, allowing staining and deterioration, especially under heavy surface use. Although coating the surface gives a nice appearance and makes it easy to clean, it does not strengthen the concrete. Coatings will not last; they need reapplication every two to three years as the surface loses it aesthetic appearance and becomes susceptible to contaminants and wear.

Densification, on the other hand, is best accomplished using Curecrete's Ashford Formula, first developed in the late 1940s. Penetrating and reacting with concrete, it creates hard crystals that fill the concrete's pores. Once densified, the surface never has to be retreated. The resultant surface develops a marble like sheen that is forty percent harder, free of concrete dusting, easy to clean, and able to bead water on the surface. Four and a half billion square feet of concrete treated with Ashford Formula (enough concrete to construct a side walk circling the equator more than eleven times), combined with the countless floors still in service after decades of continuous use, attest to the true and lasting value of the Ashford Formula. This is what really substantiates Curecrete's claim to superiority and innovation in densification.

"Jerry single-handedly built an industry; how many times do you get to see that?" asks Scott Liggett, CEO. "Everyone in the concrete densification industry knows of Jerry Jones. He proved that with hard work and ingenuity you really can create your own destiny. He is a true inspiration and many try to emulate his example."

The Ashford Formula was invented by a German chemist and applied on a small scale prior to 1978, when Jones purchased the formula and moved Curecrete to Springville, Utah. Prior to that Jones applied the formula to floors as an independent applicator. Once he owned the formula, Jones' strategy was to educate architects, engineers and owners about the benefits of densifying concrete, "In the beginning my approach had to be low-profile, because I wanted to address some challenges."

The first challenge was credibility. At first, few people accepted densification. Jones had to convince potential users that densification was superior to coatings. "Professional reputations were on the line. Architects and engineers hesitated to consider a process and product they weren't familiar with," he explains. He did a lot of educating. For example, the product was used on BYU's Marriott Center, but only after a year of communications.

The second was competition. "We weren't out there telling everyone we were the best," recalls Jones. "The large chemical companies would have picked up on that. It wasn't until the mid '80s when Walmart, Costco, Lowes, Home Depot and other 'big box' companies put Ashford Formula exclusively in their specifications, resulting in the massive loss of coating sales, that the larger chemical companies took notice."

Jones acknowledges that other companies today produce products that make similar claims as Curecrete's. "Although they use some of the same chemical ingredients, the results are not the same as the Ashford Formula." Ashford Formula's proprietary catalytic densifying reaction is what sets it apart as the most effective densifier in the world, making Ashford Formula as uniquely different today as it was six decades ago. Its unfailing delivery of consistent superior results is the reason for the product's longevity and decades of customer satisfaction.

Significant in a world that demands environmental responsibility, the Ashford Formula is truly green. It produces incomparable results without expense to the environment. Its water-based formula contains no volatile organic compounds (VOCs) and is free of hazardous characteristics.

Jones has always understood that the product's superiority alone would not bring success. It had to be coupled with hard work and determination. In the early years, Jones compared himself to a hat rack with different hats on it: salesman, manufacturer, truck driver, and applicator. "I did about everything to get a project from start to finish," he says. "You had to unless you were well capitalized with a substantial investment. We were truly an out-of-the-garage business at first."

Jones treated many projects in the Intermountain West, including the original and second Salt Palaces, South Town Convention Center, Energy Solutions Arena, E-Center, and many others. As the business expanded, he grew domestically by setting up sales representatives throughout the United States. Jones then expanded internationally and currently has distributors in more than fifty foreign countries.

In 1999 the application of densification expanded into retail and other markets looking for green floors with a more sophisticated appearance. Curecrete met this demand by combining densification technology and diamond polishing to produce the RetroPlate System. Like its predecessor, Ashford Formula, the introduction of the RetroPlate System has pioneered another worldwide industry that produces floors with unrivaled durability and artistic beauty.

Today, Curecrete Distribution, Inc. shows no signs of slowing down. Its second-to-none products, combined with Curecrete's remarkable people, assure that Curecrete will continue to lead the densification industry for decades to come.

✧

Above: RetroPlate provides durability as well as endless aesthetic possibilities.

Below: An Ashford Formula treated floor at a Costco Distribution Center.

ACE RENTS, INC.

Cecil Hortman and his wife, Marge, set out from South Dakota in 1955. Their plans were to escape the harsh winters of Oneida and open a bowling alley in California.

✧

Above: Marge and Cecil Hortman.

Below: ACE Rents, Inc., has four rental stores in Utah Valley, and one of its earliest opened in Orem, Utah. The original location was surrounded by farms in the 1950s.

Somewhere along the way, they met Sam Greenberg*, owner of Sam's U-Drive, a rental store in Van Nuys, California. Sam made the rental business look like an attractive and lucrative endeavor and planted the seed.

Cecil had fallen in love with Utah and its beauty on his trip to California. Being a business-minded man and a hunting enthusiast, he saw an opportunity to rent to the outdoorsman. He and Marge began renting rifles for deer season, ice skates and snowshoes in the winter, and wheelbarrows and tillers for the summer.

The first Ace Rents yard was located in Provo next to a nursery because Cecil thought a rental yard at that location would attract gardeners. He was right.

Before long, the Hortmans developed a sense of what the community needed— hospital beds, forklifts, cement mixers, you name it. If they did not own it, they acquired it according to the needs of the public. At one time, even Marge's washer and dryer and their children's beds were part of the rental inventory!

By 1956 they had outgrown the Provo location and moved to Orem. One mechanic was added to the workforce, making it three employees. When their kids were not in school, you would find them working beside their parents, learning responsibility, work ethic and the ins and outs of the rental business.

Cecil and Marge were early members of the ARA (American Rental Association) and were one of a handful of rental companies in the nation. The ARA was established in 1955 and there were only twenty-one members. When Cecil joined the association, there were seventy-six. There are more than 9,400 members worldwide today.

The needs of Orem changed with the scenery. They opened the store when the region was essentially orchards and farms. With the development of Geneva Steel came a sudden growth in the construction of homes, shopping, businesses, factories, theatres, freeways, roads and churches, each demanding state-of-the-art equipment and access to tools that were too expensive to own.

Once again, acquiring equipment to supply the needs of the building community, Ace Rents, Inc., took its place in meeting the demands of the growing city.

In the late 1960s, Cecil hired the future owners of Ace Rents: his son Barry Hortman and son-in-law, Sidney Paskett. Cecil's health began to deteriorate and his dependency on Sid and Barry grew. In 1979, Cecil and

Marge sold the business to their children and their spouses.

Three more locations were added. They opened the Lindon yard in 1980, Provo in 1991, and Spanish Fork store in 1998. With this growth their rental inventory increased substantially requiring the addition of their independent parts department.

Skilled mechanics and technicians became an integral part of the business to keep up with the ever-changing technology. Continued education and training became mandatory to acquire dealer status and certification with such suppliers as Honda, Wacker-Neuson, Multiquip, Bosch, Sumner, Genie, and Doosan, to name a few.

The key figures of Ace Rents figured out early that all the equipment in the world is nothing without service. This quality became the endeavor behind every rental. While some local rental stores became a part of a larger chain, Ace Rents was determined to remain slow and steady and not outgrow its values—in other words, not get too big to offer everyone the exceptional service they had come to expect.

Still maintaining a family business, Ace Rents changed hands in 2000 when daughter Miki and her husband, Sidney Paskett, purchased the business. Their passion for the rental business was a major reason for their success. That same kind of passion is found in their children, grandchildren, and long-term employees. Some of them have been at Ace Rents for more than thirty years.

Improvement and growth is an ongoing quest. In regards to future stores and expansion, Cecil's great-grandson, Nick Last, says his dream is "to go above and beyond."

Ace Rents continues to adapt in the twenty-first century with the help of great grandson, Nathan Last, who is guiding them through web design and computer technology. One of Miki's favorite sayings is "It's not a problem. It's a challenge and an opportunity."

Today, the Ace Rents family owns and operates their four stores with the experience of four generations. Alongside Sid and Miki , their daughter Chaunté, son-in-law Craig Last, and grandson Nick Last continue the tradition, focused on retaining the value, integrity and service that Marge and Cecil established and perfected nearly sixty years ago.

*Affectionately known as the "Granddaddy of rental" by the ARA.

✧

Since the beginning, Ace Rents, Inc. has been a family-operated business and today includes three generations: left to right, Nick, Chaunté and Craig Last, and Miki and Sidney Paskett.

KENNY SENG CONSTRUCTION, INC.

✧

Above: Kenny Seng Construction working in a mountain site called Koholowo.

Below: A Kenny Seng Construction side dump being loaded.

Anyone who drives past what is left of Geneva Steel on the west side of Utah Valley will not see much beyond an old furnace pot for molten metal near the end of Center Street and Geneva Road in Orem.

This pot brings back old memories.

In the late 1970s and early 1980s, Geneva Steel was perceived as the heart of Utah County. Geneva had been the Industrial Revolution in the valley for several decades, and whenever Geneva Steel suffered, everything else went into a tailspin. As a major employer in the region, many people believed if Geneva went under, Utah Valley would cease to exist. Well, Geneva eventually did close, but the valley has thrived. The property on which Geneva stood is the home of a large-scale real estate development, and Chairman and CEO Kenny Seng, who founded Kenny Seng Construction, Inc., in June of 1985 with his wife Lena acknowledges Geneva's essential part of Utah Valley's evolution. He hopes Utah Valley residents appreciate its legacy as much he does.

"It was important in its day and is the grandfather of the technological revolution this valley is experiencing," he says. "We have a rich history."

He expects that same richness in his own company, which he operates with a sense of pride, patience, and perseverance. Those three words form the basis of his business philosophy. "We believe that our work must reflect pride in the total product we make, patience in obtaining that product and dealing with others, and perseverance in keeping our service the best available, at a reasonable price," he says.

Kenny's commercial construction business specializes in earthwork, structural and site concrete, utility line installation, custom crushing, and demolition. As the regional population exploded in the wake of a hearty business environment in the late 1990s, he decided it would be smart to focus on an apparent need for more schools. He has been involved in building many of the current schools that educate the youth in the Alpine, Provo and Nebo School Districts.

"I find it very satisfying to look at our work and know what's underneath, realizing that what we have done is structurally sound, solid and long-lasting," he explains.

Kenny Seng Construction, Inc., is a profitable and respected company and Kenny and Lena are celebrating three decades as business owners this summer. Their road to success, however, had its bumpy moments, which often reflected the state of the economy.

Kenny had worked about seven years for a construction company that laid him off when they encountered financial difficulties. The owners tried to survive by downsizing.

Kenny had already considered starting his own business but had not figured out the details of creating his own enterprise. He had a challenging year, working for four different construction companies while he obtained a contractor's license and became designated as a sole proprietor. He learned different elements about the construction business from each organization.

He still considers it fortunate that the last company for whom he worked allowed him to operate equipment at night on the construction of a large diameter pipeline through North Utah County. This provided income for his family and an opportunity to secure some small contracts that he could complete during the day. He did that for the next eighteen months, and then went into survival mode on his own!

By this time, Kenny had enough jobs he no longer had time to work for anyone else, and Kenny Seng Construction was born. With a backhoe, a dump truck and a few employees, Kenny grew his business. He now employs a specialized crew of 125 workers, has extensive equipment with GPS systems and multiple trucks, brings in revenues that exceed $30 million and has a wide customer base with some of Utah's leading general contractors. By design most of the work is focused on educational projects.

He has plenty of reasons to celebrate his company's thirty year growth, which he will do, in part, by moving his Orem office and Provo shop to a central location later this year. Kenny Seng Construction, Inc.'s future home is 800 South 3110 West in Provo, Utah.

Grateful for the success he and his family have experienced, he appreciates the opportunity to be generous and give back to other causes in Utah Valley.

And wherever he travels, Kenny can see his work and realizes that much of what his business has accomplished is at the heart of Utah Valley.

For additional information, please visit Kenny Seng Construction, Inc. on the Internet at www.kennyseng.com.

✧

Above: A freshly completed floor pour adjacent to walls previously constructed by Kenny Seng Construction on a school.

Bottom, left: Kenny Seng Construction specializes in building and site concrete, including this mezzanine deck.

Bottom, right: Working on a wall corner.

GENEVA PIPE AND PRECAST

For nearly sixty years, Geneva Pipe and Precast has provided high quality precast concrete products at competitive prices, and its growth reflects the considerable development of Utah Valley. Its founding vision was to build a locally owned and operated concrete manufacturer to provide infrastructure in Utah County.

From the day Joe Burnham founded the company in 1956, he recognized the talents and skills of young entrepreneur Aldo (Bush) Bussio who worked closely with Burnham in the planning and supply of materials in construction of the original facility. Burnham's belief in Bush eventually formed a valuable partnership that lasted until Burnham's retirement in 1977. Bush became sole owner and proved to be a respected and capable businessman as he responded to the community's needs.

Their focus was and continues to be quality products, a strong customer focus, and a profitable relationship with employees. What has changed is Geneva's scope and size. The Geneva Pipe Company was originally located on thirteen acres in Orem. A small facility with only one machine producing pipes from 4 to 36 inches in diameter and only 4 feet in length. The land still belongs to Geneva Pipe but is now the site of corporate offices and the facilities have expanded. Six decades later, the vision was clearly correct.

As demand developed Geneva Pipe added additional equipment. The first two equipment additions in 1962 were a Manhole machine and a Packerhead Pipe machine. These enabled the company to make specialty manhole bases that became important to customers as the area's sewer and storm drains developed into complex systems. The Packerhead Pipe machine filled the market need for 8 foot lengths of 12 inch up to 48 inch diameter pipe.

In 1976 a state-of-the-art Rimas Triomat machine upgraded the quality of the 4 foot length pipe in diameters of 6 inches up to 18 inches. Geneva Pipe installed a Module Simplex pipe machine in 1983, which increased capacity for 12 foot length pipe with diameters of 48 inches up to 96 inches. Then in 1993 a Betodan box culvert table offered a nearly endless capacity of rectangular and square drainage systems. A Transmatic Pipe machine completed the Orem operation in 1995, producing double station high quality 8 foot pipes from 12 through 48 inches. Geneva continues to add equipment and automation to develop efficiencies and keep up with new requirements and customer needs.

Today, Geneva Pipe and Precast is a full-service concrete infrastructure manufacturer and supplier specializing in all underground precast concrete products. The company offers a full line of Concrete Pipe, Manholes for sewer and storm drain systems, box culverts, electrical vaults and communication vaults. Also, there are endless specialty items on various projects that customers need engineered and manufactured.

The company's philosophy of modernization drove the complete refurbishment of the Orem facility in 1997. In 2001 the St. George facility was purchased and refurbished. In late 2006, Geneva Pipe expanded again to meet the needs of the growing Utah market with a new state-of-the-art robotic facility in Salt Lake City. Additionally, a metal fabrication facility has been added in Orem, which allows Geneva Pipe to fabricate a great deal of the equipment needed for all its facilities.

Consistency in vision and mission has been possible through long-term leadership. Geneva Pipe has had only four presidents in six decades: Burnham, Aldo Bussio, Vince Bussio, and current president and CEO

❖

Above: For nearly sixty years Geneva Pipe has been providing high quality precast concrete products.

Below: Geneva Pipe and Precast manufactures many of Utah Valley's underground sewer and storm pipes.

Kurt Johnson. From the beginning Geneva has been a leader in the industry. Bush was elected chairman of the Board of the American Concrete Pipe Association in 1990, which was awarded to him again in 2005 with the Richard E. Barnes Lifetime Achievement Award. The trend of leadership continued when Vince was elected chairman of the Board of the American Concrete Pipe Association in 2012.

Long-time quality of life supporters in Utah Valley, Geneva Pipe and Precast employees have been involved in Habitat for Humanity, Boy Scouts of America, Unified Fire Authority as well as supporting numerous charitable nonprofit organizations.

For a company to last decade after decade requires more than an ordinary business, it has to offer something exceptional. One element is described by President Johnson, who says, "When customers purchase concrete to build an infrastructure, they expect a product that will be long-lasting quality they can trust."

For nearly sixty years, Geneva Pipe has been dedicated to providing our customers with sustainable precast products that will be the foundation for many years to come.

Geneva Pipe and Precast takes their company mission statement seriously:

Geneva Pipe and Precast will be the name our customers associate with when they think of precast concrete products. We will supply consistent quality products, when our customers want them, at a competitive price. We will establish a rewarding and profitable environment with our associates, working together as a team.

As a local Utah business, we strive to maintain and improve the quality of our products; we maintain close relationships with our customers and employees. Geneva Pipe is producing more than concrete, we are producing the infrastructure for the future of Utah.

✧

Top: Members of the Geneva Pipe crew at work.

Above: Geneva Pipe employees with a sample of their impressive underground precast concrete.

FRANSON CIVIL
ENGINEERS,
INC.

✧

*Above: Among the Utah projects completed
by Franson Civil Engineers was the
Piute Dam rehabilitation.*

*Below: West side combined canals in Utah is
a FCE project that replaced over forty-six
miles of canals with one pressurized
irrigation delivery system.*

Since Utah is one of the driest states in the country, Franson Civil Engineers, Inc., of American Fork recognizes that water is the lifeblood of Utah—and indeed, the West—and dedicates itself to ensuring the wise use of this precious resource.

For twenty-five years, FCE, formerly known as Franson Noble & Associates, Inc., has maintained a clear focus on conserving water while simultaneously dealing successfully with sensitive public and environmental issues.

For the engineers and employees who work there, this is much more than a job. It is a commitment to contributing to the quality of life in a state they love. Many have spent their entire careers working with essential water resource development issues. (Founder Jay Franson even found time to be the Highland City mayor from January 2006-January 2010.)

FCE has specialized experience, for example, in water resource planning, water rights, groundwater source development, environmental resources and compliance, project funding, design and construction management, operations, AutoCAD services and support, geographic information systems, hydropower and more.

In its first year, FCE decided it was going to be the foremost leader in water development and management, and foster a work ethic of professionals that encouraged excellence, integrity, industry, dedication, and loyalty. That has not changed.

What has changed is its size and scope. The firm opened its doors in early 1989 with two employees. In the early 1990s, engineers would spread out their projects on the reception area floor of the veterinary clinic building where they had space. "We could practically hear each other's thoughts," Franson says. FCE now has twenty-five employees and its own suite at 1276 South 820 East in American Fork.

Water projects have ranged from relatively simple to exceptionally complex. Their work on the Piute Dam Rehabilitation Project, for instance, was named the 2005 National Rehabilitation Project of the Year by the American Society of Dam Safety Officials. Lack of detailed design and as-built drawings added to the complexity of the analyses and FCE designed creative solutions that brought the dam into compliance with current dam safety standards while saving the client millions of dollars. Other prestigious awards came from ACEC of Utah for designing and constructing a one-of-a-kind combined irrigation project for the Uintah Water Conservancy District, the Ouray Park and Uintah River Irrigation Companies and Bureau of Indian Affairs, known as the West Side Combined Canals Salinity Project, which received the Engineering Excellence Grand Award in Water Resources for 2009; their Wide Hollow Dam Rehabilitation work received the Engineering Excellence Grand Award in Water Resources in 2012.

FCE attributes their success to respectful collaboration, excellent service for clients plus creativity that enables them to deliver projects in a cost effective and efficient manner.

HADCO CONSTRUCTION

If Hadco Construction workers ever claim they can move mountains, it would not be much of an exaggeration. Among its heavy highway construction projects has been a $30 million, four-mile section of freeway spanning about fifty miles.

Hadco had to move a million yards of dirt—a mountain's worth—in three months, which they accomplished with 3-D modeling and GPS-guided special equipment.

The twenty-five year old company, based in Lehi, Utah, has moved figurative mountains as well since its initial founding as an agricultural irrigation business in 1989. Today, Hadco Construction provides development support to home and commercial builders as well as road construction services locally, regionally, and statewide.

To keep its more than 300 person work force employed year-round and adapt to changing economic conditions, Hadco has reinvented itself several times. By diversifying its services, it has emerged as a top Utah excavation company—not bad for one of the last independent, locally-owned enterprises not purchased by national enterprises.

"The business has a healthy residential division and maintains a long relationship with top builders such as Ivory, Perry, and Richmond Homes," says owner John D. Hadfield. It also ranks as the largest residential excavation firm in the state. Yet when the recession hit several years ago, homebuilding dipped substantially, and Hadco regrouped and expanded other services.

"Even during this challenging economic period, we didn't have layoffs," Hadfield says. "In fact, we haven't had a layoff in years, and our stable work environment in this industry makes us unusual that way."

Its development division specializes in site development, general contracting, site utilities, earthwork, excavation, and grading. Its concrete division poured 650 foundations this year, and focuses on flatwork, footings, and foundations. Additionally, Hadco has fifty semi-trucks to support its corporation, and in 2013 hauled nearly 46,000 loads and more than 1.85-million tons of aggregates.

With six pit locations, TM Crushing, also part of Hadco, has the extensive experience and equipment to provide quality aggregate materials used in road and building projects throughout Utah.

Hadfield finds satisfaction that his company can be a single source for site development. The company oversees infrastructure work that includes road creation, paving subdivisions, and lot development by digging basements, installing sewer lines, concrete, flatwork foundation and miscellaneous water work.

Hadfield attributes much of Hadco's success to a philosophy that underscores hard work, accountability, dependability integrity, lasting relationship and a commitment to service, quality, and safety. He especially wants potential clients to know what existing clients already know: that Hadco will do whatever is necessary to get the job done and get it done well.

"We've been a major employer for a long time, and we plan to continue serving Utah Valley well into the future," he says.

LDSAGENTS.COM

When Bob Lavender founded LDSAgents.com in 1999, his purpose was to reduce the stress of moving by connecting homebuyers and sellers with real estate agents who share their cultural interests. Many thousands of clients later, creating a real estate "comfort zone" remains the focus.

LDSAgents.com connects home buyers and sellers with real estate agents who share their values. "We now seem to be part of the LDS cultural fabric."

As Lavender explains, "I am a convert to The Church of Jesus Christ of Latter-day Saints and, over time, I figured out the obvious: The Mormon culture has its own 'language,' values, and even its own home buying criteria, from proximity to temples, to food storage space, to finding active Young Men's and Women's programs. I also saw that church members are generous with their time and resources and knew that such convictions would be appreciated in the real estate market."

Before creating LDSAgents.com, Lavender graduated from BYU, served for six years as a United States Air Force pilot and for many more years as a commercial pilot. Yet, he explains, he "was always more interested

in the 'relationship business' and bringing people together." In fact, LDSAgents.com was up and running long before Lavender retired from flying; thus, satisfying both "the need for 'relationship building' and the 'need for speed,'" he jokes.

Fortunately, the LDS culture/real estate idea clicked right away. "And, now, dozens of companies have followed LDSAgents.com in appealing to LDS interests." (Amusingly, at one point a "Kosher Real Estate dot com" popped up, showing that "culture" indeed, has appeal!) Today, LDSAgents.com has thousands of agents including several hundred non-LDS agents who have been highly recommended.

LDSAgents.com began advertising in 1999, but it was its multiyear association with BYU-TV that afforded it worldwide recognition. It is seen in such venues as KSL-TV, *LDS Living* Magazine, and *Deseret News*. Lavender adds: "Likewise we find that many clients are referred to us by their bishops, Relief Society presidents, and other ecclesiastical acquaintances. We now seem to be part of the LDS cultural fabric."

He emphasizes that, "Quality of Service has been essential to our success. Our "secret" to excellent 'word of mouth' advertising is that we: 1. React quickly to client needs; 2. Keep client information private; 3. Track agent performance; and, 4. Follow up closely on each transaction until it's complete."

For Lavender, this is not work, it is fun. "The business is demanding, but you cannot help but enjoy hearing about a primary president/ real estate agent who helps a family buy a house, then immediately calls the wife to teach in Primary. Such stories are common for us!" For more, see "Sweet Testimonials" on the LDSAgents.com home page.

WHEN A JOB TRANSFER MEANS SAYING GOODBYE TO YOUR HOME, THE CHALLENGES OF REBUILDING A LIFE ELSEWHERE ARE CONSIDERABLY EASIER WHEN YOU USE A REAL ESTATE COMPANY THAT NOT ONLY HELPS PUT A ROOF OVER YOUR HEAD BUT ALSO HELPS ACCLIMATIZE YOU TO YOUR NEW HOMETOWN.

That is a passion of Prudential Utah Elite Real Estate, the largest Prudential real estate company in Utah. Among its considerable strengths, Prudential is the go-to company for smooth relocations. Prudential specializes in handling clients who come from out-of-state or are being transferred elsewhere in the United States and internationally. This may mean everything from selling a home, creating a network of fellow transferees, or finding a rental for international clients. Local buyers and sellers are in high quality hands when looking for a Real Estate professional.

Prudential Utah Elite Real Estate is recognized as the best real estate company in Utah for five distinct reasons:

1. They Sell Homes–In fact, they sell a third of all the homes sold in Utah County. Prudential Utah Elite Real Estate agents know how to make sure that homes are staged to sell and how to get them sold. Being so deeply emerged in the market makes them uniquely capable to represent buyers and sellers in the market.

2. Technological Innovation–Prudential Utah Elite Real Estate is a technology innovator. They believe that emerging technology over the last few years has advanced to a point where every agent is able to leverage the best online and offline marketing tools. In that light, Prudential Utah Elite Real Estate provides partnerships with some of the industry's best online marketing and lead management solutions to make these systems accessible to every agent. They want to provide exceptional service to our clients with current data.

3. Top Producers in Real Estate in Utah— Prudential Utah Elite Real Estate have the top producing agents in Utah. Yet Prudential Utah Elite Real Estate maintains an atmosphere of learning and progress for all. They have the distinction of having high quality, professional and seasoned agents.

4. Real Estate Sales Training–Prudential Utah Elite Real Estate holds weekly meetings and provides access to videos, webinars, and other materials that make their agents the most up-to-date agents in the market. This gives Prudential's clients the inside track into best practices in real estate, top marketing strategies, and the newest game-changers in the market. Through their on-going training, you will find that Prudential Utah Elite Real Estate is the brokerage that is the premier standard of quality and service.

5. National Brand Name and Recognition– The real estate industry has been changing rapidly. Prudential Utah Elite Real Estate has the ability to earn immediate trust and recognition with any potential client and carries one of the most well-known names in real estate: Prudential.

The bottom line with any company is its success. By knowing how to ensure homes are staged to sell and by being deeply involved in the market and the transaction, Prudential Utah Elite Real Estate is uniquely set up to represent buyers and sellers in the market. And a significant bottom line is that Prudential sells homes—as we indicated, one in three of the homes sold anywhere in Utah County.

So with sales success, innovative technology, the top real estate producers in Utah, ongoing real estate training and national brand name and recognition, it is no surprise that Prudential Utah Elite Real Estate can confidently claim it is the best real estate company in Utah.

For additional information on Prudential Utah Elite Real Estate, contact one of their convenient locations.

Prudential | Utah Elite Real Estate

Orem Office	American Fork Office	Alpine Office	Spanish Fork Office
(801) 224-9011	(801) 763-1001	(801) 756-0088	(801) 798-7000

prudentialutah.com

SPONSORS

✧

Since 2014 these quaking aspens photographed in Provo Canyon—as well as the aspens found in all of Utah's twenty-nine counties— have been designated by the Utah State Legislature as the state tree.

ABOUT THE PHOTOGRAPHER

CHRISTOPHER ADAMS

Chris Adams has been a professional photographer since 1996. He has studied nature photography as well as portraiture, architectural work, and commercial photography. He is a past member of the Intermountain Professional Photographers association, as well as earning awards from the BYU Monte L. Bean Museum of Natural History, and has served multiple years as chief photography judge for the American Fork Arts Festival Photo Contest. His favorite medium is using his old 1960s Graflex 4X5 field camera shooting on Velvia transparency film. Chris enjoys spending time outdoors with his wife of thirty-three years. He and his wife are the parents of three children and currently have four grandchildren.

ABOUT THE AUTHOR

STEVEN THOMAS DENSLEY

He was born in the Cottonwood Maternity Home in the Salt Lake Valley and lived for a time in Riverton, Herriman, Blanding, Murray, and Sandy, Utah before graduating from Jordan High School. He was All-State, All-American in football and basketball before attending Brigham Young University on an athletic scholarship. He served an LDS Mission to the Eastern Atlantic States in Washington D.C., and returned to BYU where he graduated in 1970. He married Colleen Taylor, the current principal of Wasatch Elementary School and named principal of the year in 2013 in Provo and moved to Chicago where he worked in marketing with the Crown Zellerbach Corporation. He worked with the Electronic Development Corp. in Washington D.C., and was the general manager with Western Placement Consultants in Salt Lake City before becoming president and CEO of Kodiak Inc. in Orem, Utah.

Steve ran for U.S. Congress and for lieutenant governor of the State of Utah while serving as president of chamber of commerce. The chamber became the Utah Valley Chamber in 2009 and remains as such today. He served three terms as president of the Utah State Chamber of Commerce and served on the state board for over twenty years. He has written a column for the *Daily Herald* for the past twenty-two years where he remains as a weekly correspondent and has hosted his own television cable program on Channel 17 for the past five years. He is nationally published in *Chicken Soup for the Soul* and has hosted five different radio programs with the Citadel Group and others.

During Steve's time as chamber president he served on over sixty different boards of various organizations. These included president of both the Provo and the Orem Rotary Clubs and boards. He served on the Sundance Film Festival board for eighteen years, the Zion's Bank Advisory Board for eighteen years, United Way, Utah Valley University's National Woodbury School of Business Board, Pacific States Pipe Board, executive board for the BSA National Parks Council, Provo Arts Council, BYU Management Society, Utah Valley Convention and Visitors Board, Timpanogos Regional Medical Center Board, Blue Cross of Utah Board, Utah County Academy of Science Board and dozens of others.

Steve was the second longest sitting chamber president and CEO in the history of the State of Utah when he retired in August of 2012.

He attended the Institute of Organizational and Advanced Management at SMU, University of Oklahoma, Stanford, UCLA, San Jose State, and University of Colorado, Colorado College and for the past five years has attended Loyola Marymount University in Los Angeles where he served on the board of regents for the U.S. Chamber of Commerce.

He was given the Brigham Young University's Distinguished Alumni Award, The Mayors Medal of Honor, and *Utah Business* Magazine's Utah Pioneering Award, The Boy Scouts of America's highest award as a Silver Beaver and in 2013 he was recently given the Outstanding Alumni Award from Jordan High School in Sandy.

Steve and Colleen have six children in six states and seventeen grandchildren.

ABOUT THE PROFILE WRITER

"Cosmo is the only man in my life I can guarantee won't roar at me. Cardboard is like that."
–Charlene

CHARLENE RENBERG WINTERS

Charlene Renberg Winters has been a prize-winning writer since her student days at Brigham Young University where she earned a degree in communications and two decades later a graduate degree in theater and film theory, history and criticism. She is the alumni editor and an outreach administrator at BYU and has also been a news manager and science editor for the university. She worked as a newspaper arts editor, features editor, food editor and associate city editor as well as a restaurant critic and film and theater reviewer in Provo, Utah. For nearly two decades she wrote a humor column, *Kitchen Classics* and later, *A Winters' Tale*, for Provo's *Daily Herald*. She has her own freelance business, *It's Your Story*, and has a mild passion for all things BYU, including its mascot, Cosmo, an animated and athletic cougar.